THE *GLOSSA ORDINARIA* ON ROMANS

D1453473

COMMENTARY SERIES

GENERAL EDITOR

E. Ann Matter, *University of Pennsylvania*

ADVISORY BOARD

John C. Cavandini, *University of Notre Dame*
Robert A. Harris, *Jewish Theological Seminary*
Patricia Hollahan, *Western Michigan University*
James J. O'Donnell, *Georgetown University*
Lesley J. Smith, *Oxford University*
Grover A. Zinn, *Oberlin College*

A list of the books in the series appears at the end of this book.

The Commentary Series is designed for classroom use. Its goal is to make available to teachers and students useful examples of the vast tradition of medieval commentary on sacred Scripture. The series will include English translations of works written in a number of medieval languages and from various centuries and religious traditions. The series focuses on treatises which have relevance to many fields of Medieval Studies, including theories of allegory and literature, history of art, music and spirituality, and political thought. Notes are meant to provide sources and to gloss difficult passages rather than to give exhaustive scholarly commentary on the treatise. The editions include short introductions which set the context and suggest the importance of each work.

Medieval Institute Publications is a program of
The Medieval Institute, College of Arts and Sciences

 WESTERN MICHIGAN UNIVERSITY

THE
GLOSSA ORDINARIA
ON ROMANS

TRANSLATED WITH AN INTRODUCTION
AND NOTES BY

Michael Scott Woodward

TEAMS · Commentary Series

MEDIEVAL INSTITUTE PUBLICATIONS
Western Michigan University
Kalamazoo

Copyright © 2011 by the Board of Trustees of Western Michigan University
This book is printed on acid-free paper.

Library of Congress Cataloging-in-Publication Data

Glossa ordinaria. Epistola Pauli ad Romanos. English.
The Glossa ordinaria on Romans / translated with an introduction and
notes by Michael Woodward.
p. cm. -- (TEAMS commentary series)
ISBN 978-1-58044-109-4 (paperbound : alk. paper)
1. Bible. N.T. Romans--Commentaries. I. Woodward, Michael S. II.
Title.
BS2665.53.G6613 2011
227'.107--dc22
2010036637

Manufactured in the United States of America

P 5 4 3 2 1

CONTENTS

ABBREVIATIONS

CCCM   Corpus christianorum continuatio mediaevalis. Turnhout: Brepols, 1966–.

CSEL   Corpus scriptorum ecclesiasticorum latinorum. Vienna: Hoelder-Pichler-Tempsky, 1866–.

PG   Patrologiae cursus completus, series Graeca. Edited by J. P. Migne.

PL   Patrologiae cursus completus, series Latina. Edited by J. P. Migne.

SG   Corpus christianorum, series graeca. Turnhout: Brepols, 1977–.

SL   Corpus christianorum, series latina. Turnhout: Brepols, 1953–.

Introduction

The *Glossa ordinaria* (the Gloss) is the standard biblical commentary of the later medieval and early modern periods. It contains the Vulgate Bible with verse-by-verse gloss or commentary situated between the lines of Bible text (interlinear gloss) and in the margins (marginal gloss). The glosses are taken from the church fathers, mostly Western, up through Bede, passed along in the compilations of the Carolingians (ninth century), and then edited and brought into their final form by scholars in France during the first half of the twelfth century. The cathedral schools at Laon and Auxerre and the monastic school of St. Victor near Paris are the places chiefly associated with work on the Gloss. By the second half of the twelfth century, this comprehensive Bible commentary had taken its place as an authoritative resource in all theological schools. Its use continued in the Renaissance and Reformation, when both humanists and reformers consulted the Gloss extensively. In the dozen printed editions of the Gloss, it usually appears in six large volumes along with the *Postilla* of Nicholas of Lyra, which can be viewed as an extension and correction of the Gloss. In fact the first printed edition of the Gloss (Strasbourg: Rusch, 1480/81) is the only edition where it appears alone and in its entirety.[1]

Recent scholars have attributed the Gloss on the Pauline Epistles to Anselm of Laon.[2] I would suggest that it is an abridgment of Peter Lombard's *Collectanea in omnes divi Pauli apostoli epistolas* (PL 191: 1297–1696) and produced at the school of St. Victor around 1140. Lombard's commentary on Romans and the Psalms was known as the *Magna glossatura* (MG), while the Gloss on these books was called the *Parva glossatura*. The popularity of the MG rivaled that of the Gloss in the twelfth and thirteenth centuries. Others have remarked on the similarity between the Gloss and the MG, but argued that Lombard borrowed from the Gloss in his own commentary, the first edition of which is dated to around 1140.[3] A close comparison of the Gloss and MG on Romans shows that the borrowing is the other way around. The extensive parallels (over 80 percent of the Gloss, both marginal and interlinear, is found in the MG) can only be accounted for by systematic abridgment rather than expansion.

A brief example will help to show how the abridgment was done, and how untenable is the view of Lombard's borrowing from the Gloss. First from Lombard's MG on Romans 1:1, with the parallel material in the Gloss underlined (marginal with single underlining, interlinear with double underlining):

> Gratiam vero commendans, non simpliciter ait Apostolus, sed et ponit, vocatus, quasi non a se veniens tanquam sibimet honorem sumeret, sed a Deo vocatus est Apostolus, id est ad apostolatum; et aeterna electione, quae est secundum propositum, et temporali missione qua a Christo missus est, ex qua et apostoli vocati sunt. Nam, sicut Graece angeli, Latine nuntii vocantur, ita Graece apostoli, Latine missi vel legati appellantur. Vel, vocatus Apostolus, id est dictus ab hominibus excellentia et privilegio nominis, sicut excellenter, cum dicitur Urbs, intelligitur Roma.
>
> [And commending grace, he does not say simply "an apostle" but "called an apostle," as though he were not claiming this honor for himself, but was called an apostle, i.e. called to the apostolate, by God. He was called through an eternal election that is according to God's will, and through a temporal mission to which he was sent by Christ. The apostles were called such on account of this mission. For just as "angels" in Greek are called "nuncios" in Latin, so "apostles" in Greek are called missi and legates in Latin. Or when he says "called an apostle" he means addressed by people with the excellence and privilege of this title, as when Rome, because of its superiority, is called "the city."]

Here is the Gloss:

> [Marginal gloss:] Vocatus. Non a se sed a Deo. Vel vocatus ab hominibus dictus privilegio nominis. [Interlinear gloss:] Vocatus. Eterna electione et temporali missione. Apostolus. Missus legatus vel nuncius. [Called. Not by himself but by God; or called such by people and addressed with the privilege of the title. Called. By eternal election and in temporal mission. Apostle. Sent as a legate or nuncio.]

(See the appendix, for a comparison of all Romans 1:1.) Now if Lombard were borrowing from the Gloss, he would have to be taking these pithy marginal and interlinear glosses and interweaving them into a larger whole. And he would be doing this over and over again throughout his commentary, following the same sequence of authorities as the Gloss. Such an endeavor would be strange and unprecedented. It makes much more sense to understand the glossator as abridging Lombard for the sake of space, sometimes resulting in cryptic phrases.

Thus, Lombard can be considered the author of the Gloss on the Pauline Epistles, although the abridgment was likely the work of others. I have suggested a Victorine provenance because Peter Lombard is thought to have been at St. Victor's in the late 1130s and then spent the remainder of his life in nearby Paris, where he died as bishop in 1161. In the endnotes to my translation, it would be pointless to cite the hundreds of uses of Lombard's MG. Therefore I only cite the MG in my endnotes (as Peter Lombard, *In Epistolam ad Romanos*) when no other source can be traced.

The Gloss on Romans incorporates many patristic sources, often without naming the author. Exact quotations are rare; rather the Gloss reproduces the sources as they were filtered through florilegia and the tradition of biblical studies, which edited, rearranged, and modified them. Augustine is the foremost authority, cited by name sixty-one times in the text, while I have identified forty more "quotations" from him. The glossator had at his disposal a wide range of Augustine's writings and quoted from thirty-four separate works. Ambrosiaster's influential commentary on the Pauline Epistles (late fourth century), which went under the name of St. Ambrose, is cited twenty-eight times. Other patristic authorities include Ambrose, Jerome, Gregory the Great, Fulgentius of Ruspe, Prosper of Aquitaine, Vincent of Lérins, Cassiodorus, Isidore of Seville, and Bede. Greek fathers seldom appear: Origen, from the Rufinus translation of his commentary on the Pauline Epistles, is cited six times; Hesychius of Jerusalem and John of Damascus are cited once each on their own and then again through the mediation of Ambrosiaster and Fulgentius respectively. Of the Carolingian sources, Haimo of Auxerre stands out above the rest, cited by name sixteen times. And most of the quotations from Haimo are his own interpretations, rather than quotations from patristic authorities. Without naming them, the Gloss avails itself of Rabanus Maurus and Sedulius Scottus, other ninth century commentators, for gleaning earlier sources. Any use of *moderni* remains unacknowledged in the Gloss. Besides the ever-present Peter Lombard, the two that appear most often are, strangely enough, Peter Abelard and William of Saint-Thierry, who were theological rivals.

The Gloss on Romans seeks to explain the plain, literal sense of the text by using textual and historical methods. While allegorical interpretations are common in the *Glossa ordinaria*, they are scarce in the Gloss on Romans because of the didactic nature of the Pauline epistles. A lengthy spiritual interpretation occurs only in the introduction (p. 5), which uses the parable of the Good Samaritan to speak of all salvation history and the place of Paul's writings in particular.[4] Within the commentary proper there are etymologies that seem fanciful to us, but the Gloss views them as elucidating the literal, grammatical sense. Theological reflections and discursions are prevalent (e.g., the rational proof of the Trinity in the marginal gloss on Rom. 11:33), as well as moral or practical application, even when a passage is not specifically one of moral instruction. Such are due, no doubt, to the purpose of the glossator and to the type of works from which glosses were taken: sermons, letters, and treatises that address theological and moral issues. Three historical layers are always at work in the Gloss: the time and circumstances of the biblical authors (the middle of the first century AD for Paul, and earlier for Old Testament authors whom Paul cites), of each particular gloss, and of the glossator. A clear example of this multilevel meaning is where the Gloss follows Augustine in applying Paul's litany of rebukes in the second chapter of Romans to ecclesiastical leaders of his own day (see marginal and interlinear glosses to Rom. 2:3).

The Epistle to the Romans has played a central role in the history of doctrine. It is the longest of Paul's epistles and the only one he wrote to a church he had not personally established. Therefore it presents Paul's initial preaching and foundational message, which had been honed by over a decade of establishing churches. The Gloss's preface suggests that Romans is placed first because of its rudimentary nature: "Some wonder why the Epistle to the Romans is placed first when it is clear that it was not written first. . . . Some would have it understood that all the epistles are so arranged that Romans is placed first, even though it was sent later, so that more perfect things are reached in steps through all the epistles in order." At the same time, Roman Christians formed the most educated and cosmopolitan congregation, where the relations between Greek and Jewish converts had become very strained. The struggle for leadership threatened to split the congregation, with each camp proud of its own heritage and accomplishments and disparaging those of its rival. Paul's main purpose, then, was to humble everyone, showing their utter dependence on God's mercy, and thus to bring concord to the church at Rome.

The introduction summarizes the conflict:

> In this Epistle to the Romans the apostle writes to address a controversy
> among them. And this was the controversy: the Jews were saying that
> they were of the race of Abraham, that they had received the Law and
> the Prophets, and that they had never worshiped idols, but only the one
> true God. They were calling the Gentiles unclean dogs. On the other
> hand, the Gentiles were saying that they had become obedient when
> they first heard the Gospel, ascribing this to their own good intelligence
> and nature. And they were saying that the Jews were not only disobedi-
> ent to Christ, but had even condemned him to a most horrible death.
> Thus there was pride on both sides and no humility. The apostle placed
> himself between them in the center, refuting both sides in order to bring
> them to humility, that they might attribute everything to the grace of
> God.

Attributing all to grace will bring harmony to the church of Rome. Paul's
emphasis on grace, the introduction continues, can be accounted for by
his own background as one who persecuted the Church: "[Paul] wisely
and forcefully fights for God's grace and argues against the arrogant and
proud who presume on their own works. No doubt divine grace stood
out more evidently and clearly in him because, having vehemently persecuted the Church of God, he was worthy of severe punishment, but
found grace instead of malediction; in place of condemnation he received
mercy. And this lifts high our own hope."

The Gloss subordinates the theme of an initial instruction in the
faith—God's grace as the justification for sinners—to the central purpose of reconciling Jew and Gentile in Christ. As stated in the prologue:

> [Paul] confirms that neither of them had merited salvation by their
> own righteousness, but that both peoples had sinned knowingly and
> grievously: the Jews dishonored God by disobeying the law, and the
> Gentiles, although recognizing the creator from creation and knowing
> that they should worship God, changed his glory into manufactured
> images. He also demonstrates with a most convincing argument that
> both are equal in obtaining grace, showing in particular that both Jews
> and Gentiles were to be called to faith in Christ as was prophesied in
> the Law itself. Wherefore, humbling each in turn, he encourages them
> toward peace and concord.

Such a view has recently been called the "New Perspective on Paul,"
which downplays the opposition between law and gospel.[5] While this

view may be new to proponents of the New Perspective, it actually shares much in common with the perspective found in the Gloss.

Another interesting feature of the introductory material of the Gloss is that it is drawn from heretical sources that were preserved pseudonymously. There are four preliminary writings: a preface, attributed to Jerome but very likely by Pelagius; a prologue by Pelagius; an introduction along the same lines; and an argument that is Marcionite and possibly by Marcion himself (see endnotes to the text, nos. 1–3, 6). The Pelagians and Marcionites took opposite sides on the question of the relationship of law and gospel: Pelagius held to a strong continuity of law and gospel, with the law being essential to Christian life and salvation; Marcion rejected any continuity and any role of the law in Christianity. The Gloss's short argument indicates its Marcion origin when it sees the problems at Rome stemming from "false prophets" who taught the Old Testament rather than the "evangelical faith": "They were approached by false prophets and, under the name of our Lord Jesus Christ, had been introduced to the Law and the Prophets. The apostle calls them back to the true and evangelical faith."

Pelagianism can be seen in the lengthier preface, prologue, and introduction when the Gospel is seen as a continuation of the Law, giving moral lessons and commandments. The preface begins by asking, "Why would the apostle wish to send these letters to individual churches after the Gospels, which are a supplement to the Law, have fully provided us with examples and commandments for living?" And the answer: to provide moral instruction and application, analogous to the Prophets who applied the Law: "that he might cut back immediate and prevalent sins and anticipate impending problems. This follows the pattern of the prophets: after the publication of the Law of Moses, which contains all the commandments of God, the prophets suppressed by their teaching the constantly recurring sins of the people. This they transmitted to us in their writings as a lesson in right living." There is a strong affinity between the Old and New Testaments: "There are fourteen Pauline Epistles, ten to churches and four to individuals. By this number the apostle wished to show that he was in harmony with Gospel and the Law, for the ten refers to the Decalogue of the Law and the four to the Gospels." And Paul is even seen as a New Moses: "Paul leads out the people taken from the devil and the slavery of idolatry with the same number of epistles as commandments Moses used to establish the people freed from Pharaoh." Pelagius's commentary on the Pauline Epistles was preserved as the work of Jerome, and circulated widely in the Middle Ages through a revision by Cassiodorus. Such "Pelagianism" in the introductory material contrasts with the predominant use of Pelagius's great adversary Augustine in the Gloss proper. In reality both views are represented throughout the Gloss, which at times shows the strain of attempted harmonization. The tension is evident, for example, on the question of faith and works, where various positions are taken.

None of the polemic of later times, of course, is present in the Gloss, and the quest for harmonization of conflicting authorities, the hallmark of scholasticism, has not yet arrived in full force. Thus the Gloss is content to let incompatible interpretations lie side by side. For example, after declaring the impotency of circumcision and the ceremonial law, the Gloss boldly affirms, sounding quite ecumenical, the efficacy of sacrifices and circumcision: "What the water of baptism does for us, faith alone accomplished for children and the power of sacrifice for adults among the ancients, and the mystery of circumcision for those who are of Abraham's lineage" (marginal gloss to Rom. 4:11).

In a much disputed chapter of Romans, the Gloss seems not to be able to make up its mind whether Paul is speaking of himself or in the voice of humanity under the law:

> It is clear that the apostle is not speaking of himself, but in the person of humanity in general. . . . The apostle is not speaking unsuitably of himself according to the flesh as long he lives in this world and depends on the motions of the flesh . . . it is not completely clear whether the words are better understood of Paul himself or in the person of universal humanity. (Marginal glosses to Rom. 7:9, 14, 25)

The Gloss on Romans is a collection of sources from many periods and places, which accounts for such inconsistencies. And this is what gives the Gloss much of its charm: the innocent and unselfconscious way it has of jumping from source to source. The twelfth century was an age of gathering sources and commentaries, in theology (Lombard's *Sentences*), canon law (Gratian's *Decretum*), and biblical studies (the *Glossa ordinaria*). Education began to flourish into what would become universities, where the master's role was to elucidate traditional, authoritative texts. And chief among these was the Bible, not standing alone but with the accompanying Gloss. Lombard's stature and influence rise even further if, as I argue, he can be considered the author of the Gloss on the Pauline Epistles.

I follow the pattern of earlier translations of the Gloss in this series: directly after the biblical verse appear the corresponding marginal glosses, followed by the shorter interlinear glosses. Cited words from each verse appear in bold and italics in the glosses.

APPENDIX

COMPARISON OF LOMBARD AND GLOSS ON ROMANS 1:1

Lombard (PL 191, col. 1302D-1304B)	Gloss On Romans (Rusch, vol. 4, p. 273) [interlinear gloss]
...ut ait Beda super Actus apostolorum, anno passionis et resurrectionis Christi ad fidem venisse perhibetur; tertio vero decimo anno post Christi passionem apostolatum gentium cum Barnaba, et Pauli vocabulum accepisse. Prius enim vocabatur Saulus a Saule persecutore, quia sicut ille David, ita hic Ecclesiam Dei est persecutus. Quarto autem decimo anno, juxta condictum apostolorum, ad magisterium gentium est profectus. Huic autem sententiae de nomine Pauli, consentit Augustinus sic dicens: Non ob aliud hoc nomen, quantum mihi videtur, Paulus sibi elegit, nisi ut ostenderet se parvum tanquam minimum apostolorum: ipse primo Saulus, postea Paulus dictus est: nec quasi jactantia aliqua nomen sibi mutavit Apostolus, sed ex Saulo factus est Paulus, id est ex superbo modicus, id est humilis; paulum enim modicum est. [Ambrosius] Immutatum ergo se esse significans, ex Saulo quod interpretatur inquietudo vel tentatio, Paulum se dicit, id est quietum. Qui enim prius tentationes aliis inferebat, post eas passus est. [Victor episcopus Cap.] Porro ex more sanctorum apostolorum id fecisse perhibetur, qui in virtutibus proficientes mutato nomine sunt vocati, ut essent etiam ipso nomine novi, ut Cephas, et filii tonitrui, et hujusmodi. Unde et sancta Ecclesia jam in consuetudinem duxit, ut quos in cathedra beati Petri apostoli sublimat, nomina eis mutet. Vel, sicut Hieronymus ait: Paulus a primo spolio quod sanctae Ecclesiae contulit, scilicet a Paulo Sergio proconsule, quem apud Cyprum convertit, hoc nomen sibi imposuit, ut sicut Parthicus, qui Parthos superavit, et Germanicus, qui Germaniam vicit, est dictus, sic ab eo principe quem prius subjugavit Paulus sit appellatus. [Origenes] Sed, quia nulla talis in Scripturis divinis consuetudo deprehenditur magis placet quod in	Paulus. Beda super Actus apostolicos Paulum anno passionis et resurrectionis Christi ad fidem venisse dicit: Tercio vero decimo anno post Christi passionem apostolatum gentium cum Barnaba et Pauli vocabulum accepisse. Prius enim Saulus a Saule persecutore vocabatur, quia sicut ille David hic ecclesiam persecutus est. Quarto decimo autem anno iuxta condictum apostolorum ad magisterium gentium est profectus. Augustinus. Non ob aliud hoc sibi nomen elegit, nisi ut se parvum ostenderet tanquam minimum apostolorum. Non iactantia aliqua, sed ex Saulo factus est Paulus, id est ex superbo modicus. Paulus enim modicus et quietus, Saulus inquietudo et tentatio interpretatur. [Hebraice, quietus graece, modicus latine Ambrosius. Porro ex more sanctorum apostolorum illud fecisse perhibetur, qui virtutibus proficientes mutato nomine sunt vocati ut et ipso nominee essent novi ut Cephas et filii tonitrui. Hieronimus. Paulus a primo spolio quod ecclesiae contulit, scilicet a Sergio Paulo proconsule quem apud Ciprum convertit hoc sibi nomen assumpsit.

nostra consuetudine frequenter reperitur. Invenimus enim in Scripturis, alios binis, alios ternis usos esse nominibus, et hoc utique in utroque, ut Salomon qui Ecclesiastes et Idida vocatus est; et Matthaeus qui et Levi dictus est, et alia plura in hunc modum. Secundum ergo hanc consuetudinem videtur nobis et Paulus duplici vocitatus vocabulo, sicut scriptum est in Actibus apostolorum: Saulus qui et Paulus (Act. XIII). Ubi evidenter ostendit Scriptura non ei tunc primum Pauli nomen impositum, sed veteris appellationis id fuisse assignat. A Hieronymo autem in libro Hebraicorum nominum Paulus mirabilis sive electus interpretari dicitur, quem et Dominus ipse vas electionis vocavit (Act. IX), et tam vita quod doctrina mirabilem fecit.	Origenes. In scripturas alios binomios alios trinomios invenimus. Sicut Salomon qui Ecclesiastes et Ydida, Matheus qui et Levi. Secundum hanc ergo consuetudinem videtur nobis et Paulus duplici vocitatus vocabulo, sicut in Actibus ubi scribitur, Saulus qui et Paulus evidenter ostenditur. Hieronimus. Paulus mirabilis sive electus, quem et Dominus ipse vas electionis vocavit et tam vita quam doctrina mirabilem fecit. *[see below] Servus. Ex servo et humili fecit Deus apostolum et sublimem ita et vos humiles sitis. Qui enim se humiliat exaltabitur.
Servus Jesu Christi. Ecce conditio. [Origenes] Sed quaerendum est cur servus dicatur, qui alibi scripsit: Non enim acceptis spiritum servitutis, etc. (Rom. VIII). Et iterum alibi: Itaque iam non est servus sed liber (Gal. IV). Et Dominus apostolis ait: Jam non dicam vos servos, sed amicos (Joan. XV). [Haim.] Ad quod dicendum est quod duo sunt genera servitutis: Est enim servitus timoris, et pene servilis; et est servitus amoris et filiationis et humilitatis, qua, instar filii, qui servit, non vult offendere patrem. Si ergo id secundum humilitatis et amoris servitutem dictum putemus, non errabimus [Origenes] Non enim per hoc laeditur veritas libertatis in Paulo, quia omni libertate nobilior est servitus Christi. Dicendo ergo servus, nomen humilitatis ponit, ut ad eam provocet superbos quibus scribebat. Et ne misera servitus videatur, non simpliciter ait servus, sed addit, Jesu, id est Salvatoris, cui merito omnes servire debent: ei etenim servire regnare est. Jesus vero Hebraice, sother [σωτήρ] Graece, Latine salvator dicitur. [Haim.] Quod nomen ab angelo fuit impositum Dei Filio, eo quod salvum faciat populum suum a peccatis eorum (Matth. I). Addit, Christi, id est regis et sacerdotis. Christus enim Graece, messias	Haimo, Origenes. Servus amore filiationis et humilitatis non timoris. Non enim acceptis spiritum servitutis, etc. Item itaque iam non est servus sed liber. Et iterum iam non dicam vos servos sed amicos. [Nomen humilitatis ut ad eam provocet [Salvatoris cui merito omnes servi cui servire regnare [regis et sacerdotis

Hebraice, Latine dicitur unctus, et in Veteri Testamento reges et sacerdotes ungebantur. Christus autem unctus est, non oleo visibili, sed invisibili, id est oleo gratiae spiritualis. Unde in Psalmo: Unxit te Deus, Deus tuus, oleo laetitiae (Psal. XLIV). Hoc nomen aliis olim fuit adjectum, sed Jesu factum est proprium. Et est hoc sacramenti nomen. [Augustinus, Haim.] Servum autem Jesu Christi se profitens Apostolus, a lege factorum se exutum ostendit, et utrumque nomen ponendo, id est Jesu Christi, unam Dei et hominis contra haereticos personam esse testatur, ne alium quidem Jesum, alium vero Christum suspicaremur fuisse, sed unum et eumdem sciremus esse.	Ihesu Christi. Ambrosius. Christus graecae, messias hebraice, latine unctus, Christus quidem unctus. Rex et sacerdos invisibili oleo plenitudine gratiae spiritualis, unde Unxit te Deus Deus tuus, etc. Augustinus, Haimo. Utrumque ponendo unam Dei et hominis personam esse testatur. Alterum pro Iudaeis, alterum pro gentibus ponit. Christus enim hoc nomine Iudaeis est cognitum, quo nomine Dei Filium designatum vident et audiunt in lege promissum. Quibus et si alium praedicatet non crederent. Gentibus vero quia in aliquo non legerant praemittit salvatorem, id est Hiesum. Christus. Quamvis non sit proprium sed nomen sacramenti sicut propheta et sacerdos, Iudaeis tamen cognitum recte proponitur. Et si pluribus indita haec nomina, tamen sola figura, hic enim solus verus rex et sacerdos.
Vocatus apostolus. Ecce dignitas ad quam promotus est, ecce de humili factus est altus. Ac si illis superbis quibus scribebat diceret: *Ex servo et humili fecit me Deus apostolum et sublimem, ita et vos humiles sitis ut exaltemini: Qui enim se humiliat exaltabitur (Luc. III.)	Apostolus. Ecce de humili altus. *[see above]
Gratiam vero commendans, non simpliciter ait Apostolus, sed et ponit, vocatus, quasi non a se veniens tanquam sibimet honorem sumeret, sed a Deo vocatus est Apostolus, id est ad apostolatum; et aeterna electione, quae est secundum propositum, et temporali missione qua a Christo missus est, ex qua et apostoli vocati sunt. Nam, sicut Graece angeli, Latine nuntii vocantur, ita Graece apostoli, Latine missi vel legati appellantur. Vel, vocatus	Vocatus. Non a se sed a Deo. [Eterna electione et temporali missione] [Missus legatus vel nuncius]

Apostolus, id est dictus ab hominibus excellentia et privilegio nominis, sicut excellenter, cum dicitur Urbs, intelligitur Roma.

Segregatus in Evangelium Dei. Ecce officium. [Ambrosius] Quasi dicat: Paulus dico, segregatus, id est a doctrina Scribarum et Pharisaeorum et ab utero Synagogae ubi locum doctoris habebat, utpote Pharisaeus separatus in Evangelio Dei, praedicandum. Et dicitur hoc contra Iudaeos a quorum lege dissimulavit, ut Christum praedicaret, qui quod lex non potuit credentes justificaret. Vel segregatus, [Haim.] id est a grege separatus, scilicet ab aliis apostolis, non mente, sed corpore. Unde Spiritus sanctus in Actibus apostolorum ait: Segregate mihi Barnabam et Paulum in opus ad quod assumpsi eos (Act. XIII), ut scilicet praedicent nomen meum in gentibus. Unde et hic addidit, in Evangelium, scilicet praedicandum in gentibus. [Ambrosius, Haim.] Destinatus est Apostolus gentibus totius orbis praedicator, at reliqui, singulis provinciis facti sunt legati ac praedicatores. Est autem Evangelium, bona annuntiatio, εν enim Graece, Latine bonum, αγγελος nuntius, inde Evangelium, bonum nuntium, vel bona annuntiatio. Ea vero est de his quae ad fidem Catholicam et bonos mores pertinent. Evangelium dico, Dei, quasi non ab homine inventum, sed divina inspiratione revelatum.

Vel vocatus ab hominibus dictus privilegio nominis.

Segregatus a doctrina scribarum et Pharisaeorum. Hoc contra Iudaeos.   [Ab utero sinagoge in qua quasi mortuus fuit
[Praedicandum
[Ecce officium

Vel ab aliis apostolis corpore et non mente, unde: Segregate mihi Barnabam et Paulum in opus ad quod assumpsi eos.

Evangelium. Haimo. Bona annunciato est quae ad salutem.

Ea vero est de his quae ad fidem et mores. Dei. Non ab homine inventum.

¶Paulus. Beda sup actus apostolicos paulum anno passionis 7 re-
surrectionis christi ad fidem venisse dicit: Tercio vero decimo anno post
christi passione apostolatu gentiu cu barnaba 7 pauli vocabulu accepisse
prius eniz saulus a saule psecutore vocabat quia sicut ille dauid hic eccle-
siam psecutus e. Quartodecimo aut anno iuxta pdictu apostolor ad ma-
gisterium gentiu est pfectus.

¶Aug. Non ob aliud hoc sibi nome elegit: nisi vt se puum ostederet tan
cp minimum apostolor. Non iactantia aliqua sed ex saulo factus e paulus i ex supbo modi-
cus. paulus enim mo-
dicus 7 quiet. Sau-
lus inquietudo 7 ten-
tatio interpretat.

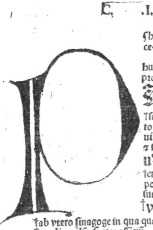

C. I.

hebraice quiet gre-
ce modic latine
nomen
humilitatis vt ad ea
pronocet

¶Ambro. Porro
ex more sanctor apo-
stolor illud fecisse p-
hibet qui virtutibus
pficientes mutato no-
mine sunt vocati vt 7
ipso nomine essent no-
ui vt cephas 7 filij to-
nitrui.

Aul ser
t saluatoris cui meri-
to omes serui cui ser-
uire regnare regis
7 sacerdotis
u libesu xpi
eterna electone 7 te-
porali missioe mis-
sus legat vel nuci
vocatus apo-

¶Diero. Paulus
a primo spolio qd ec-
clesie ptulit scz a ser-
gio paulo procosule
que apud ciprum co-
uertit hoc sibi nomen
assumpsit.

fab vtero sinagoge in qua quasi mortuus fuit
predicau du ecce officiu.
stolus segregatus in euangeliuz
tcomendatio euagelii a quattuor ppletionem
deus pater gratis vt re vtile 7 necessaria
qui ex deo no ex se magni
Sa tpe sab autore sa testib co
dei qd ante pmiserat p pphe-
tno modo verbis sne darcie obliuioni sactis
tas suos in scripturis sanctis de

¶Drige. In scriptu-
ris alios binomios q-
lios trinomios iueni-
mus. Sicut salomon
qui ecclesiastes 7 ydi-
da. Matheus qui et
leui. Secundu hanc
ergo cosuetudinez vi-
der nobis 7 paul du-

plici vocitatus vocabulo sicut in actibus vbi scribit. Saulus qui 7 pau-

Fig. 1. Romans 1:1. (Photo: *Biblia Latina cum Glossa ordinaria, Facsimile Reprint of the Editio Princeps* [Turnhout, Belgium: Brepols Publishers, 1992], 4:273.)

PREFACE OF ST. JEROME TO ALL THE EPISTLES OF ST. PAUL

First it is asked: Why would the apostle wish to send these letters to individual churches after the Gospels, which are a supplement to the Law, have fully provided us with examples and commandments for living? The reason seems clear: that he might respond to the beginnings of a newborn church with its new conditions; that he might cut back immediate and prevalent sins and anticipate impending problems. This follows the pattern of the prophets: after the publication of the Law of Moses, which contains all the commandments of God, the prophets suppressed by their teaching the constantly recurring sins of the people. This they transmitted to us in their writings as a lesson in right living.[1]

Next it is asked: Why did he write no more than ten letters to the churches, including the Epistle to the Hebrews and four addressed to particular disciples?

He made his epistles equal in number to the earlier commandments of the Decalogue to show that the New Testament agrees with the Old Testament and does not contradict the Law of Moses. Paul leads out the people taken from the devil and the slavery of idolatry with the same number of epistles as commandments Moses used to establish the people freed from Pharaoh. Similarly scholars have taught that the two stone tablets symbolize the two Testaments.

Now some argue that the Epistle to the Hebrews is not Paul's because it is not inscribed with his name and because of its difference in language and style. It is an epistle of Barnabas according to Tertullian, of Luke according to others, or of Clement, a disciple of the apostles and ordained bishop of the Roman Church after the apostles. To this we respond: If it is not Paul's because it does not have his name, then it will be nobody's since it is inscribed with no name. An epistle that shines with such eloquence of his teaching should be considered his even if it is discordant and dissimilar from the rest. But since in the Jewish congregations Paul was falsely suspected of being a destroyer of the Law, he wished to give an account of the Law's figures and Christ's reality without mentioning his name, lest hatred of the name inscribed at the beginning should block the usefulness of its reading. It is not surprising if he seems more eloquent writing in Hebrew, his native language, than in Greek, a foreign language in which he wrote the other epistles.

Some wonder why the Epistle to the Romans is placed first when it is clear that it was not written first. For he testifies that he wrote it as he headed to Jerusalem, when earlier he had exhorted the Corinthians and others in writing that he would collect an offering to carry with him (1 Cor. 16:1–3; 1 Cor. 8:1–4). Some would have it understood that all the epistles are so arranged that Romans is placed first, even though it was sent later, so that more perfect things are reached in steps through all the epistles in order.

Most of the Romans, surely, were so ignorant that they did not understand God's grace towards them and that they were not saved by their own merits. Two groups fought among themselves over this. Therefore he asserts that they need to be corrected, reminding them of the prior vices of the Gentiles. But in the Epistle to the Corinthians the apostle says that the grace of knowledge had already been granted to them. And he does not rebuke all of them, but blames them for not rebuking sinners, saying: *Fornication is heard to be among you* (1 Cor. 5:1); and again: *When you have assembled with my spirit to hand this man over to Satan* (1 Cor. 5:5). In Second Corinthians they are praised and encouraged to advance more and more. The Galatians are accused of no other crime than that they believe the most cunning false apostles. The Ephesians rightly deserve no criticism, but are worthy of much praise, because they kept the apostolic faith. The Philippians are praised even more since they would not listen to the false apostles at all. He awards the Thessalonians all praise because they not only kept the true faith unshaken, but were also found constant in the persecution of their members. The Colossians were such that, although the Apostle did not see them in the flesh, he still considered them worthy of praise: *Although absent in body,* he says, *I nevertheless rejoice with you in spirit and see your order* (Col. 2:5). And what should be said of the Hebrews, of whom the Thessalonians, greatly praised themselves, are said to have become imitators, as he says: *And you, brothers, have become imitators of the churches of God that are in Judea, for you have suffered the same things by persecution from your own people that they have from the Jews* (1 Thess. 2:14). He mentions the same to the Hebrews when he says: *For you also have shown compassion to those in chains and have accepted with joy the confiscation of your goods, knowing that you have a better and permanent possession* (Heb. 10:24).

PROLOGUE TO THE EPISTLE TO THE ROMANS

The Romans are made up of both Jewish and Gentile believers. The former, out of proud contention, wanted to subject the others to themselves. The Jews were saying: We are the people of God whom God loved and nourished from the beginning; we are circumcised from the race of Abraham, we have descended from holy stock, and formerly God was known in Judea alone. We were liberated from Egypt with signs and the power of God; we crossed the sea on dry feet while terrible waters overwhelmed our enemies. The Lord rained down on us manna in the desert as though serving celestial food to his own children. He went before us night and day in a column of cloud and fire to show us a path in the wilderness. And to leave unmentioned his other immense blessings towards us, we alone were worthy to receive the Law of God, to hear God's voice speaking, and to know his will. In this Law was the messiah promised to us, and he himself testified that he had come for us, saying: *I have come only for the lost sheep of the house of Israel* (Matt. 15:24), when he called you dogs rather than people. Is it just, then, that you who are forsaking idols today should be compared to us who have forsaken them from the beginning? And you would not be deserving of this if the generous mercy of God were unwilling to allow you to imitate us.[2]

On the other hand the Gentiles were responding: The more you tell of God's great blessings towards you, the more you show yourselves to be guilty of sin, because you were always ungrateful for them all. You frolicked before graven idols with the same feet by which you crossed the dry sea. You asked for images to be made for you with the same mouth from which you had sung to the Lord a short time before of the destruction of your foes. You gazed at images with the same eyes by which you were accustomed to look upon God, worshiping him in the cloud and fire. Manna became irksome to you and you murmured continually against the Lord in the desert, longing to return to Egypt from which he had driven you with a mighty hand. Why say more? Your fathers so aggravated the Lord by repeated provocation that they all died in the desert;

no more than two of their elders entered the land of promise. But why reiterate antiquities when even if you had not done these things, from this alone no one would judge you worthy of grace: that you not only refused to receive the Lord Christ, promised to you by unceasing words of the prophets, but you even put him to death in the worst kind of way, while we immediately believed when we came to know him, although he had not been prophesied to us before. Hence it is shown that we served idols not with obstinacy of heart, but out of ignorance. We, then, who followed him immediately when he became known, surely would have followed before if we had known him then. Thus you boast of your noble race, as if he makes you children of the saints more from the birth of the flesh than the imitation of morals. Finally Esau and Ishmael, although they came from the same stock of Abraham, were not both considered sons.

The apostle puts himself in the middle of this argument and destroys the accusations of both sides. He confirms that neither of them had merited salvation by their own righteousness, but that both peoples had sinned knowingly and grievously: the Jews dishonored God by disobeying the law, and the Gentiles, although recognizing the creator from creation and knowing that they should worship God, changed his glory into manufactured images. He also demonstrates with a most convincing argument that both are equal in obtaining grace, showing in particular that both Jews and Gentiles were to be called to faith in Christ as was prophesied in the Law itself. Wherefore, humbling each in turn, he encourages them toward peace and concord.

Introduction to All the Epistles of Paul

In the epistles there are some general points that are applicable to all of them and some particular points that pertain to each epistle separately. First the general points are to be considered and then we will look at the particular points. Under the general it is asked why the epistles were written after the Gospel when there is a fullness of doctrine in the Gospel as well as a perfect rule of life and a full pattern for good works and morals. Then are answered the questions of why they are called epistles, what is their subject matter, and what is the common intention of them all; and finally the significance of their number is treated. These general points are applicable to all the epistles. Under particular considerations it asked to whom each was written, the reason for writing, and what is specifically intended in each.[3]

The first question is answered in this way: The epistles were written after the Gospel so that at the beginning of the newborn church Paul might warn us beforehand against the crafty assaults of heretics; that he might cut back burgeoning vices and answer questions that would surface later. Some things in the Gospel are expressed in such a way that uncertainty and error might easily arise in the minds of those understanding them wrongly. For example it is said that Christ was baptized at age thirty, from which some heretics tried to maintain that no one is rightly baptized before age thirty. Besides, in the Gospel there are certain sayings so obscure that even the faithful are uncertain about them. Therefore this apostle wrote his epistles to root out these heresies and other teachings that were sprouting up in the church at the time. These are the reasons the epistles were written after the Gospels. They are not superfluous, but like the Prophets who come after the law, the epistles too are very useful and necessary after the Gospels. Although a complete teaching is found in the law, nor is there anything else in the Prophets that is not contained in the law, nevertheless some things were expressed under a veil, which are elucidated and explained more clearly in the Prophets.

It should be observed that some have called the Epistles additions and discussed them in terms of the Gospel parable that says: *A certain man was going down from Jerusalem to Jericho and fell among thieves.* In other words, humanity descended from its homeland in the heavenly Jerusalem into the world and fell among wicked enemies. *They robbed him and after beating him went away, leaving him half-dead*, i.e., they subjected humanity to the errors of various teachings. *It happened that a certain priest and a Levite, as they went down the same road and saw him, passed by.* For the Law and the Prophets were unable to heal the human race. *But a Samaritan*, that true protector, namely Christ, *making the journey*, i.e., assuming human flesh, *was moved with compassion. And taking him he bound his wounds, pouring on oil and wine.* In other words, he pours out the grace of the Holy Spirit and the teaching of the New Testament, which so inebriates humanity that it makes it forget earthly desires. *And setting him on his own beast, he led him to an inn and offered two denarii, telling the innkeeper: Take care of him, and if you spend anything more I will repay you when I return* (Luke 10:30–35). For he gave the apostles and other teachers the two Testaments, New and Old, while Paul and many others have spent an additional amount.

The Epistles may also be signified by that ladder upon which Jacob saw angels ascending and descending. Paul bore their image when he was taken up to the third heaven, *where he saw hidden things*, etc. (2 Cor. 12:4); and he also descends so far to humanity and weakness that he says: *Let a husband give what he owes to his wife* (1 Cor. 7:3).

The Epistles are called additions because they were added to the Gospel. There are fourteen Pauline Epistles, ten to churches and four to individuals. By this number the apostle wished to show that he was in harmony with the Gospel and the Law, for the ten refers to the Decalogue of the law and the four to the Gospels.

In this Epistle to the Romans the apostle writes to address a controversy among them. And this was the controversy: the Jews were saying that they were of the race of Abraham, that they had received the Law and the Prophets, and that they had never worshiped idols, but only the one true God. They were calling the Gentiles unclean dogs. On the other hand, the Gentiles were saying that they had become obedient when they first heard the Gospel, ascribing this to their own good intelligence and nature. And they were saying that the Jews were not only disobedient to Christ, but had even condemned him to a most horrible death. Thus there was pride on both sides and no humility. The apostle placed himself between them in the center, refuting both sides in order to bring them to humility, that they might attribute everything to the grace of God.

He follows the custom of letter writers when he sets down a greeting at the beginning in order to build goodwill—with respect to himself when he says: *Paul an apostle* (Rom. 1:1), namely of Christ; to the subject matter when he says: *which he had promised beforehand* (Rom. 1:2); to the divine author when he says: *who was born to him* (Rom. 1:3); and to his hearers when he says: *among whom you also are called*, etc. (Rom. 1:6).

Having given reasons for the structure,[4] number, and order of the epistles, and having explained why the apostle wrote to the Romans, it remains to discuss the matter, intention, and mode of treatment. The doctrine of the Gospel is the general subject matter of all the epistles. The intention is the urging of obedience to the Gospel teaching. But beyond these we must investigate the particular intention and subject matter of the individual epistles.

Thus the first epistle has as subject matter the sins of the Romans and the gifts of God's grace to which Paul exhorts them. Its intention is to rebuke their sins and to humble them under the hand of grace toward true fraternal peace and harmony. Concerning the mode of treatment, he first puts down a greeting in the manner of letter writers. Here he wins favor, commending his own person, the subject, and its divine author. <u>Haymo</u>: After the salutation he reproves the sins of both sides, showing that they had each gone astray, arguing from natural reason with the Gentiles and from the law with the Jews.[5] Then he shows in many ways that there is righteousness and salvation for both, not through the law but through faith in Christ. In this way he hopes to take them away from the law and establish them in the faith of Christ alone. Moral instruction is added near the end, and the epistle ends in the giving of thanks.

Paul uniquely excels all other writers of letters in three ways: in the depth of his works, because they are longer and more difficult to understand than others; in the declaration of faith, because he brings forth fitting testimonies from the Law and the Prophets to declare the catholic faith; in the commendation of grace, because he wisely and forcefully fights for God's grace and argues against the arrogant and proud who presume on their own works. No doubt divine grace stood out more evidently and clearly in him because, having vehemently persecuted the church of God, he was worthy of severe punishment, but found grace instead of malediction; in place of condemnation he received mercy. And this lifts high our own hope.

ARGUMENT OF PAUL'S EPISTLE TO THE ROMANS

Romans are from areas of Italy. They were approached by false prophets and, under the name of our Lord Jesus Christ, had been introduced to the Law and the Prophets. The apostle calls them back to the true and evangelical faith, writing from Corinth.[6]

Romans. The word means the heights or the thunderers, because at the time in which the apostle sent this epistle to them they dominated all peoples. Thus they were higher than all other peoples and would thunder public and private laws and their fame resounded in the mouths of all people.[7]

From Corinth. <u>Origen</u>: That he wrote this from Corinth is clearly shown when he says: *I commend to you Phoebe, our sister, who is in the ministry of the church at Cenchrae* (Rom. 16:1). And Cenchrae, it is said, is a place near Corinth, indeed a port of Corinth itself. This is seen also when he says: *Caius, my host, greets you* (Rom. 16:23), whom he mentions when he writes to the Corinthians, saying: *I give thanks to my God that I baptized none of you except Crispus and Caius* (1 Cor. 1:14).[8] But Haymo says that the apostle wrote from Athens: The apostle wrote the Epistle to the Romans from Athens, a Greek city. And neither Paul nor Peter nor any of the twelve apostles had instructed them before. For they had only been taught by certain Jewish believers who, after receiving instruction from the apostles, came to Rome, where the prince of the world was living, whose subjects they were. And the Gospel they had been taught in Jerusalem they preached to the Romans.[9] Yet in Ecclesiastical History it is read that in the time of Claudius the mercy of divine providence brought Peter to the Roman city. Entering the city of Rome first, he opened the gates of the heavenly kingdom with the keys of his Gospel.[10] Commenting on Romans, where it is written, *that I might impart to you some spiritual* joy (Rom. 1:11), Jerome says: Paul wished to confirm the Romans in the faith they possessed from the preaching of Peter; not that they were lacking anything from Peter, but that their faith might be corroborated by the testimonies and teachings of the two apostles.[11]

To resolve the conflict of these authorities we may say that Peter was the first of the apostles to preach to the Romans although not first among all believers. And we may say that Paul wrote part of the epistle in Athens but finished it at Corinth, and from there sent it to the Romans. He writes to the Romans because of a controversy among them, confuting now the Jews, now the Gentiles, teaching them to be humble so that they might attribute everything to the grace of God. The Jews were attributing salvation to their race and the Gentiles to their intelligence and nature. This epistle is placed first because it destroys the first level of error. He commends his person, the subject, and its divine author, by which he properly wins favor.

Chapter 1

1:1 Paul, a servant of Jesus Christ, called to be an apostle; separated for the Gospel of God,

Paul. <u>Bede</u>, *On the Acts of the Apostles*, says that Paul had come to the faith in the year of the passion and resurrection of Christ, but that in the thirteenth year after the passion of Christ he received the name Paul and, with Barnabus, the apostolate to the Gentiles.[12] Earlier he was called Saul after the persecutor Saul, because just as the one persecuted David, so the other persecuted the Church. Then in the fourteenth year, as agreed upon by the apostles, he was commissioned to instruct the Gentiles. <u>Augustine</u>: He chose this name for no other reason than to show that he was small and the least of the apostles.[13] Without any boasting he went from being Saul to Paul, i.e., from proud to small, for Paul means small and calm, while Saul means restlessness or temptation.[14] <u>Ambrose</u>: It is said that he did this in the manner of the holy apostles, who were called by a changed name after advancing in virtues, so that they were known by a new name, such as Cephas and the Sons of Thunder.[15] <u>Jerome</u>: He is called Paul from the first spoils he brought to the Church. In other words from Sergius Paul, the proconsul whom he converted at Cyprus, he took this name for himself.[16] <u>Origen</u>: In the Scriptures we find others with two or three names, such as Solomon, who is also Ecclesiastes and Idida, and Matthew, who is also Levi. Thus according to this custom it seems to us that Paul also was called by two names, as is clearly shown in Acts, where it is written: *Saul who is also Paul* (Acts 13:9).[17] <u>Jerome</u>: Paul means remarkable or chosen.[18] The Lord himself called him a vessel of election and both his life and teaching made him remarkable.[19]

a servant. From a servant and humble man God made an apostle and lofty man; so you too should be humble: *for he who humbles himself will be exalted* (Matt. 23:12). <u>Haymo</u>, <u>Origen</u>: A servant in filial love and

9

humility, not in fear:[20] *For you have not received a spirit of servitude* (Rom. 8:15), etc. Again: *And so he is not a slave, but* a free man (Gal. 4:7). And again: *I shall no longer call you servants, but friends* (John 15:15). ***Jesus Christ.*** Ambrose: Christ in Greek, Messiah in Hebrew, anointed one in Latin. Christ was certainly anointed king and priest with an invisible oil—with the fullness of spiritual grace.[21] Thus: *Your God has anointed you*, etc. (Ps. 44:8; Heb. 1:9). Augustine, Haymo: By using both names, he testifies that he is one person of both divine and human natures.[22] He employs one name for the Jews, the other for the Gentiles. For the title of Christ was known to the Jews, by which they understood the appointed Son of God, whom they heard promised in the Law. And if Paul should preach another to them, they would not believe. But to the Gentiles, because they had not read about Christ at all, he puts forward a savior, i.e., Jesus. Although Christ is not a proper name, but a sacramental title like prophet and priest, it is properly used because it is known to the Jews. And if these names are given to many others, they are only figures, for he alone is the true king and priest.

apostle. See how he has been lifted from low to high. ***called.*** Not called by himself but by God; or called such by people and addressed with the privilege of the title. ***separated.*** Separated from the teaching of the scribes and Pharisees, he stands against the Jews. Or separated from the other apostles in body but not in mind. Hence: *Separate for me Barnabas and Paul for the work to which I have called them* (Acts 13:2). ***the Gospel.*** Haymo: Good news is what pertains to prosperity, but this is of things pertaining to faith and morals.[23] ***of God***, not of human invention.

> ***Paul***—a Hebrew name, meaning calm in Greek and small in Latin
>
> ***a servant***—a term of humility, so that he might incite others to the same
>
> ***Jesus***—the savior to whom all are rightly servants; to serve him is to reign
>
> ***Christ***—king and priest
>
> ***called***—by eternal election and in temporal mission
>
> ***apostle***—sent as a legate and nuncio
>
> ***separated***—from the womb of the Synagogue in which he was as though dead
>
> ***for the Gospel***—for preaching the Gospel; this is his office

1:2 which he had promised before through his prophets in the holy Scriptures,

before. Before its fulfillment. He does not come unexpectedly, but was promised long before. Hence the saying is true, that there is one who sows and another who reaps. *through the prophets*. Haymo cites Jeremiah[24]: *Behold days are coming and I will establish a new covenant with the house of Israel and the house of Judah* (Jer. 31:31). And again: *I will make with you an everlasting covenant* (Jer. 32:40), as well as others. *holy*, not heathen scriptures. Holy because they condemn sins and because they also contain, in the sacraments of the one God, the incarnation of the Son of God.[25]

> *which*—here begins a commendation of the Gospel for four reasons
> *he had promised*—the divine author, God the Father, had promised; freely; as something beneficial and necessary
> *before*—temporally; before its fulfilment
> *through his prophets*—by witnesses; they were great because of God, not themselves
> *in the holy Scriptures*—not only in spoken words, but recorded lest they fall into oblivion

1:3 concerning his Son, who was made for him from the seed of David according to the flesh,

his. His own, consubstantial with himself, coeternal and coequal. *made*, only with regard to the flesh. Augustine: Although not made according to his divinity, so close is the union of nature in both that the whole is called God and the whole man, and in turn man is called God and God man, which is not the case with human nature.[26]

who was made for him. Who was made of the Virgin according to the flesh by the work of the Holy Spirit; in other words: who was born. This is opposed to the impiety of heretics, who, understanding this chapter with a dull heart, accept Christ as merely a man. By adding *according to the flesh*, his divine dignity is kept intact, whereby Christ is the Word of God through whom all things have been made. Origen: God incarnate was made according to the flesh. Even in the assumption of the flesh he did not cease being God but remained unchanged when he assumed changeable humanity, the assumed human nature not diminishing his divine nature.[27] <u>Augustine</u>: He who had been was made: he who had been the Word, who had been the Son of God, was made Son of Man. He took on humanity but did not lose divinity.[28] Born of God according to the reality of that nature he is Son of God, and born of man according to the reality of that nature he is Son of Man. Thus not by adoption or a title granted, but truly in both births he has the name of son by being born.[29] Again: Therefore he is Son of God, equal in nature to God the Father, but lesser in position. In the form of God the Word was born from God; in the form of a servant he was made from woman. In the form of God he made humankind; in the form of a servant he was made human. In either form, each is God and each is human.[30] Again: *The Word was made flesh*, yet not in such a way that he was converted and changed, but in flesh he fittingly appeared clothed as a person of flesh.[31] <u>John of Damascus</u>: Both forms are in Christ because each is a real and full substance in Christ.[32] They are mutually in a unity of nature without being changed or altered. The divine form did not separate from its own divinity, nor was the human form converted into the nature of deity or into non-existence, nor was a single composite nature made from the two.[33] <u>Augustine</u>: Christ, then, is one person of two substances, yet neither God nor humanity can be called parts of this person, otherwise the Son of God, before he took on the form of a servant, was not complete and he grew when humanity was joined to his divinity.[34] <u>Ambrose</u>: To be made does not always refer to a creation, as in the verse: *Lord, you are made a refuge for us* (Ps. 89:1) A definition or statement of creation is not expressed here, but he is said to be a refuge for us, which he was not previously.[35] <u>Augustine</u>: *Who was made*, etc. This phrase signifies that the Lord's flesh was not compounded with human seed in the womb of the Virgin and made into a body, but by the action and power of the Holy Spirit. This is why the apostle says *made* rather than *born*.[36] Again: Although the seed of man did not intervene in the Virgin's conceiving, nevertheless, because Christ was formed from that flesh which existed from seed, it says correctly: *made from seed*. Yet he was not then a creature, for *all things were made through him* (Col. 1:17). He says simply *all things were made*, i.e., every creature. Hence it is clearly seen that the one through whom all things were made was not himself made.[37] <u>Hilary</u>: For he is the true and proper Son, by origin not by adoption, by fact not by pronouncement, by birth not by creation.[38]

from the seed of David. <u>Augustine</u>, <u>Haymo</u>:[39] Because Mary was from David. The promise was made to Abraham and to David, but he preferred to speak here of David, who was also sinful, and not of the just man Abraham, so that his birth from him may be considered as coming through grace, not merit, and so that his birth may be shown to derive from a king according to the flesh, just as he was born a king from God before all ages.

concerning—for which they were written

his—his own. Commendation of the Gospel from its subject matter

Son—because all the Scriptures lead to the Son

was made—lest he be thought merely a man and not according to his divinity

for him—to his honor

from the seed of David—the author's praise of Christ is fourfold: first because of his origin

according to the flesh—because the Word was made flesh, etc.

1:4 who was predestined as the Son of God in power according to the Spirit of sanctification by the resurrection of the dead of Jesus Christ our Lord,

who was predestined. Predestination is the preparation of grace whereby from eternity God prepared blessings without merit for the human Christ and for all whom he knew beforehand would be conformed to the image of his Son. Foreknowledge is of both good and bad people; predestination is only of the just. Predestination is not foreknowledge, which pertains equally to the good and the bad, but is properly called an ordination and preparation to help those whom divine providence has found worthy of blessing. Ambrose: Who was predestined—he that lay hidden in the flesh is what was predestined, that is, the Son of God was foreknown from eternity to be manifested in the power of rising again, namely when the dead rise again.[40] It does not say, by the resurrection of Christ, but by the resurrection of the dead, which is a greater power, because his own resurrection causes the general resurrection. This shows that he has destroyed death in order to redeem us. And thus he also calls him our Lord, who gave such grace and power of apostleship in his stead. Augustine: That transporting of human nature was predestined, and it was so great and so excellent and high that our nature could not be raised any further, just as for our sake the divinity could not have humbled itself any lower than by receiving human nature with the weakness of the flesh, even to death on the cross.[41] Haymo: The apostle does not speak here of the Word, but of the man who did not exist before he was made.[42] The humanity that did not exist before is what was predestined. Augustine: The brightest light of predestination and grace is the very mediator between God and man, the man Christ Jesus. This man was predestined so that, having been assumed by the coeternal Word of the Father into the unity of his person, he might be the only-begotten Son of God. How did he merit this? What kind of good in him came before, that he might obtain this ineffable excellence? With the Word of God making and receiving him, that man begins to be the only Son of God from whom he received existence. The woman full of grace conceived of the Holy Spirit: from the Virgin Mary the only God was born, not by the desire of the flesh, but by the gift of God alone. The will in that man was free, and so much the freer as he was not able to sin.[43] Again: Surely it is right that he be called the predestined Son of God, but not according to that which is the Word of God in God, for otherwise something would be predestined that already existed, for he was already everlasting, without beginning or end. But that had to be predestined which did not yet exist, so that it might come into being in its own time. Somehow, before all times, it was predestined that he should come into being. Therefore whoever denies that the Son of God was predestined denies that he was the Son of Man.[44] Jesus was predestined, then, in such a way that he who was going to be the Son of David according to the flesh was already the Son of God in power.[45]

according to the spirit of sanctification. This should be connected with the phrase: *who was made for him from the seed of David according to the flesh—made*, certainly, *according to the spirit of sanctification*, i.e., according to the operation of the Holy Spirit, who sanctifies people, and who sanctified the man Christ in the virginal womb. Augustine: Or he is proved the Son of God because he gave the spirit of sanctification to his own, beginning from the resurrection of the soul, that is, by the remission of the sins of those dead in their sins who belonged to Christ, namely those whom no one else was able to cure.[46] For there is a twofold resurrection: of the soul and of the body. Concerning the resurrection of the soul the apostle says subsequently: *Wake up, O sleepers, arise from the dead and Christ will shine upon you* (Eph. 5:14).

of the dead of Jesus Christ. He says "of Christ" in place of "his" or "of him," following the Hebrew custom of using the proper name instead of the pronoun. This locution is often seen, especially in ancient scriptures; for example: *Moses did as the Lord commanded Moses* (Josh. 11:15).

> *who was predestined as the Son of God in power*—according to which a person is elected by grace alone that he might be a son of God in the same power and strength of divinity with the Father through union with the Word. Commendation from power.
>
> *according to the Spirit of sanctification*—in this he was also shown to be Son of God, which can be seen from the fact that he was conceived by the Holy Spirit. Commendation from grace.
>
> *by the resurrection of the dead*—because he made the dead to rise again with him, those who were his, those to be revived by him: *Many bodies of those who had fallen asleep rose again* with him (Matt. 27:52)

1:5 through whom we have received grace and apostleship unto the obedience of faith among all the Gentiles for his name's sake,

among all the Gentiles. Not only among Jews. Because they were called apart from the Law, the Gentiles were not obliged to be under the Law. *for his name's sake*. For his glory, not your own, as you are claiming.

> *through whom*—see what the divine author means to him. Commendation from generosity
>
> *grace*—forgiveness of sins, the supporting of works, and other gifts
>
> *apostleship*—the authority or mission to preach
>
> *unto the obedience of faith*—that I might cause them to obey the faith
>
> *among all the Gentiles*—Jews are included among the Gentiles through intermarriage[47]
>
> *for his name's sake*—in place of simply "for him"; or for his name to be spread

1:6 among whom you too were called of Jesus Christ,

called of Jesus Christ, i.e., by him, namely Jesus Christ, the genitive used for the ablative in the Greek manner.

> *among whom*—among which Gentiles
> *you too*—you Romans; in order to instruct them in a more
>   familiar tone he turns from himself to them
> *were called*—by him through grace by an internal calling, or
>   that you might be his through an external calling

1:7 to all who are in Rome, beloved of God, called holy: grace to you and peace from God the Father and our Lord Jesus Christ.

beloved of God. He loved us earlier, before all merits, that we who are loved might also love him. *called holy.* Not called because they were holy, but rather made holy because they were called; and called because they were loved. *grace to you and peace.* Augustine: In this salutation the Trinity itself as well as its unchangeable unity, is acknowledged:[48] unity when it says: *from God.* Haymo:[49] He does not express the name of the Holy Spirit since he includes him in his gifts of grace and mercy.

> *to all who are in Rome*—he writes to them and not to others,
>   first wishing them well
> *beloved of God*—by God, i.e., those whom God has loved
> *called holy*—that he might call them to holiness
> *grace*—forgiveness of sins
> *peace*—reconciliation and tranquility of mind
> *from God*—towards God
> *the Father*—from him who wills and is able
> *Jesus Christ*—without whom no blessings come to us

1:8 First indeed I give thanks to my God through Jesus Christ for all of you, because your faith is proclaimed in all the world.

I give thanks. To give thanks is to perceive that all things have been given by God and to praise him from the heart in word and deed. *my God.* This utterance is not without meaning, for it can only be said of the saints, that God is their God, as the God of Abraham, Isaac, and Jacob. For although there is one God of all by nature, in a proper sense he is said to be theirs by grace, who are proven to be his worshipers through the merit of faith and righteousness. *for all of you.* Although I give thanks for other things, first I give thanks for you, and the tremendous blessing that has come from you through Christ the mediator, by whom God has given you all good things. *because your faith.* Ambrose: He rejoices in the good begun in them, which shows his love toward them; and he encourages them toward perfection. He tells them to do this above all else, because their faith is profitable to many people.[50]

> *First*—at first he is gentle, then later he will severely rebuke them
>
> *my God*—whom I call mine because you do not
>
> *Jesus*—he is the mediator between God and humanity; not through the Law, not through the Prophets
>
> *Christ*—since he is the minister of God's benefits
>
> *for all of you*—which you also should be doing
>
> *because your faith*—he does not praise their faith as perfect, but praises their readiness and desire to follow Christ, even if not perfect
>
> *in all the world*—because Rome is the head of the world, and many people traveled out from there

1:9 For God is my witness, whom I serve in my spirit in the Gospel of his Son, that I make mention of you without intermission,

witness. I assert that you have faith in the Lord, for I pray that it will be preserved by him. Or he is referring to when he gives thanks in prayers and, as it were, without intermission. *witness*. An oath should be made in necessity, when people are slow to believe what is useful to them. An oath is not good in itself, but it is not evil when it is necessary, even though it arises from the evil of weakness in those to whom something is said. Jerome: On Jeremiah, chapter two: It should be noticed that an oath holds these companions to truth, judgment, and justice. But if they fail in these things, there will be no oath at all, but perjury.[51] *I make mention of you*. He says this so that they might love him and desire to listen to him.

> *witness*—the authority about whom I have just been speaking, and therefore it is not safe to lie
>
> *in my spirit*—in my will or by my faith and love in spiritual matters; not in the flesh, i.e., by following carnal things
>
> *in the Gospel of his Son*—in which Gospel, not by preaching the law or circumcision or the things handed down by the servant Moses, but by preaching what the Son handed down, not in writing, but by inspiring hearts.

> ***I make mention***—<u>Ambrose</u>: God is mindful when he gives,
>   forgetful when he ceases to give[52]
> ***without intermission***—without neglecting you

1:10 always entreating in my prayers that somehow I may at last sometime have a favorable journey in God's will of coming to you.

entreating in my prayers. A prayer is to obtain good things; an entreaty is a distinct prayer for something needed and it is through a holy oath to God, as when suffering death or birth or similar things.

> ***always***—he had set hours for praying
> ***entreating***—striving; I not only pray, but even entreat
> ***in my prayers***—which are on behalf of myself and others
> ***that somehow***—I hope for or aspire to this; by whatever easy or
>   difficult means
> ***at last***—after long waiting
> ***sometime***—in winter or summer
> ***favorable***—which I do not think it will be unless I come to you
> ***in God's will***—not as the wicked say in their own evil; but
>   because then my coming will be profitable

1:11 For I long to see you that I may impart to you some spiritual grace to strengthen you,

For I long to see you, so that what I was unable to persuade you of in words I may convince you of when I am present by the power of miracles.

> ***I long***—and therefore I entreat
> ***to see you***—since the things I write can be taken wrongly, and
>   that I may urge you to grow in virtue
> ***impart to you***—i.e., I make you participants
> ***some spiritual grace***—the free gift of God; teaching
> ***to strengthen you***—because you already have some grace

1:12 that is, that at the same time I may be comforted with you by that which is mutually your faith and mine.

that ... I may be comforted. Now I am without comfort, and you as well, even if you do not think so; but in this way we may be comforted together.

> *that is*—he spells out the meaning of "to strengthen you": and
> this strengthening is therefore pleasant, in other words:
>
> *at the same time*—as if to say: my comforting will take place at
> the same time as yours
>
> *that . . . I may be comforted with you*—because he is saddened
> by their mistaken faith; or, *that is, that we may be comforted
> with you* in another letter[53]
>
> *by that which is mutually your faith and mine*—not a new faith,
> but mine and yours, which is common to each other, that
> is, if we are of one and the same faith in Christ; or that
> which is produced through love

**1:13 Now I do not want you to be ignorant, brothers, that I have often
intended to come to you, but have been prevented until now, so that I
may have some fruit among you as I have among the other Gentiles.**

brothers. Because they are born again, and some are upright; likewise,
above, he said they are *called holy* (Rom. 1:7).

> *Now I do not want you to be ignorant*, etc.—Haymo:[54] Why
> then are you not coming? Because I am prevented from
> doing what I wish. And you should realize and consider
> that the delay arises from your own fault, so that you may
> now make yourselves worthy. I desire it because I have
> planned to come and have not simply wished it.
>
> *but have been prevented*—from coming, as God brought this
> about through various impediments
>
> *until now*—up to the present time
>
> *some fruit*—i.e., that you may bear fruit through my preaching;
> or, that I may gain a reward for you, which I therefore
> desire to see
>
> *among the other Gentiles*—the example of others should chal-
> lenge them

**1:14 I am a debtor to Greeks and barbarians, to the wise and the un-
learned,**

debtor. Because sent to all. *to Greeks*. He is silent about the Jews because he is the teacher of the Gentiles. He names the Greeks because
all worldly philosophy had its origin from them. *barbarians*. He calls

barbarians those who are, as it were, without law: they are neither Hebrews nor Greeks nor Latins. This preaching is owed to none of these more particularly than to others.

> *debtor*—to evangelize; and just as I owe this to others, so also to you, because I am a debtor to all
>
> *to Greeks and barbarians*—this is what I desire because I am a debtor to all Gentiles
>
> *to the wise and the unlearned*—so that no one of either people may be excluded. Haymo: to the educated in worldly sciences and to others ignorant of those sciences.[55]

1:15 and so on I am eager to evangelize you also who are in Rome.

> *eager*—as if to say: Since I am prepared for this, the fault of another has come into play

1:16 For I am not ashamed of the Gospel, since it is the power of God unto salvation for everyone who believes, to the Jew first, and to the Greek.

For I am not ashamed of the Gospel, like those who preach false things; or those who consider the cross of Christ to be shameful. Therefore *I am not ashamed of the Gospel, since it is the power*, i.e., because it proclaims God's power, not weakness, God's wisdom, not foolishness: *For the weakness of God is stronger than people and the foolishness of God is wiser than people* (1 Cor. 1:25). Or, it is the power by which sin is pardoned for the one who believes. And when the case requires, miracles are performed by which the teaching is commended. *since it is the power of God*, because the preaching is confirmed with wondrous signs, which is not the case among false preachers. *to the Jew first*. Hesychius: As if to say: to the Jew especially and before all others. He places the Jew first for the sake of the fathers, yet the Jew also needs the Gospel. What is the necessity, then, of being under the law?[56]

> *I am not ashamed of the Gospel*—*I am eager to evangelize you* (Rom. 1:17). He has in mind those who had handed down incorrect teaching.
>
> *power of God*—for us, not others. He connects this to faith: God gives salvation to everyone who believes; he forgives sins, justifies, and preserves from the second death.

unto salvation—the power of God is able to bring salvation
to the Jew first, and to the Greek—he indicates what he meant
    by everyone; to the one who believes; by Greeks he
    includes all Gentiles

1:17 For the justice of God is revealed in it from faith to faith, as it is written: The just person lives by faith.

the justice of God. Haymo, Ambrose: That by which he freely justifies the ungodly through faith without the works of the law, as elsewhere: *that I may be found in him, not having my own righteousness that is from the law, but that which is from faith* (Phil. 3:9).[57] The Gospel reveals this when it gives faith by which a person is justified who believes that God is just and true to his promises. This is spoken against the Jews who deny that he was the messiah whom God promised.

is revealed. Augustine: He addresses the Gentiles in regard to their earlier condition, because they were boasting of their good nature and excusing their wickedness through ignorance.[58] But, on the contrary, the apostle says that earlier they had knowledge and had lost it through their own fault and, left to themselves by God, their good nature hastened into all evils. By commending the devotion of faith, whereby we are made justified and acceptable to God, and by deploring the contrary, he implies that they were puffed up in themselves and for this reason fell into idol worship.

from faith to faith. From the faithfulness of God who promises to the faith of the person who believes in God. Or *from faith to faith* in terms of all the parts of faith: from the faith of the Old Testament, where there is one God, to the faith of the New Testament, where there is the Father and the Son and the Holy Spirit; from the faith of the first advent to the faith of the second; from the faith of the first resurrection to the faith of the second; from the faith of the promise to the faith of the fulfillment; from faith of preachers to faith of people; from faith of sowers to faith of reapers. There is justice for him who crosses from faith to faith, so that the Jew or anyone else might cross over from the faith of the Old to the faith of the New Testament, and from a faith of words and hope to a faith of reality and vision. Augustine: Faith is that by which things that are not seen are believed. Faith is also when one believes not in words but in present things, which will be when God allows himself to be seen.

Therefore he says *from faith* of words, by which we believe what we do not see, *to faith* of things, by which we will obtain what is believed.[59]

as it is written. In Habakkuk, where it reads: *But the just person will live by his faith* (Hab. 2:4). But this and many other testimonies that he cites seem to differ from the translation of the Hebrew Scriptures which we use now, because sometimes he quotes from the Septuagint translation, sometimes, as though speaking in the same spirit, he only takes up the prophet's meaning, using his own words in his own arrangement.

> *justice of God*—for the believer it is unto salvation, because it is for him unto justice, which is clearly shown in the Gospel itself
> *as it is written*—justice, and thus salvation, is from faith, as Habakkuk says, and not from the law
> *The just person lives by faith*—Augustine: He is just by faith and so he lives in eternal life, which is the reward of faith[60]

1:18 For the wrath of God is revealed from heaven upon all impiety and injustice of people, of those who hold the truth in injustice,

the wrath of God is revealed from heaven. From faith comes justice, and from justice salvation, since from impiety comes injustice, and from injustice wrath, i.e., punishment; and this very thing is revealed in the Gospel. Or it is revealed from heaven in that it accuses them, since it has disclosed to them the creator, or the savior. For from the very structure of heaven God is shown to be angry with them. God created such beautiful stars so that from them it may be known how great and praiseworthy their creator is, and so that he alone might be adored. *upon all impiety*. Impiety is to have sinned against God; injustice is to have sinned against people. Or the impious person is unfaithful, such as an idolater, while the unjust person is one who is opposed to justice from the depravity of his works. *of those who hold the truth*. As if to answer the question: Why does wrath come upon them for impiety when they did not know God? To which he responds: They were certainly able to know him, but they have removed him from themselves, preferring to stay unjustly in their own pleasures. They *hold the truth* of God, and therefore it is said: what can be known of God is in them. In other words, they have in themselves that from which they may know God, namely natural reason. *who hold the truth in injustice*. What they hold is good, but how they hold it is bad; for they hold the truth, but in injustice. You have found God, you have found the truth, but you hold it in injustice. And what you have known through the works of God, you lose through the works of man. Augustine: You have considered the whole order of reality and have not cared to notice that the world is a work of God and an idol is the work of a craftsman. If a craftsman should give a heart to an idol, as he has given it a shape, let the idol adore him. Who, then, is your God? Is it the one who made you?[61]

> *wrath of God*—to come at judgment
> *upon all impiety*—not upon all the wicked, but upon all the
>   areas of ungodliness and injustice. Upon all idolaters.
> *injustice of people*—which comes from their sins
> *who hold the truth*—who have true knowledge of God
> *in injustice*—remaining in their evil works; when he willingly
>   offers himself to them

1:19 because what is known of God is manifest in them, for God has manifested it to them.

what is known of God. Gregory: This is what we are able to attain from the arrangement and natural order of this world.[62] What is unknown of God is what is concealed from every creature, such as the essence of his substance or nature and the mystery of human deliverance. *is manifest in them*. Augustine: Because natural reason alone cannot attain this, but God must also assist our reason daily, lest we imagine that nature were enough by itself.[63]

> *what is known of God*—i.e., the knowable in God; for there are
>   many things that cannot be known about God through
>   nature, such as the mysteries of redemption and the incar-
>   nation
> *is manifest*—by the guidance of reason
> *has manifested*—another reading: *has revealed*; through his
>   handiwork, not by teaching or inspiration

1:20 For the invisible things of him are perceived, understood from the creation of the world[64] through the things that have been made, even his everlasting power and divinity, so that they are without excuse.

invisible things. Haymo: He is describing what was able to be known about God. He speaks in the plural because God is known in many ways, namely that he is eternal, omnipotent, and such.[65] These invisible attributes are perceived through things made, because through heaven and earth and other creatures, which they knew to be immeasurable and perpetual, their minds have perceived that the creator is incomparable, immeasurable, and eternal. *from the creation*. From humankind on account of its excellence, because humans excel other creatures, or on account of the congruity that he has with all creatures: for he exists locally in a place like corporeal things; he has senses like animals; and he understands like angels. Hence: *Preach the Gospel to every creature* (Mark 16:15).

> *invisible things*—the Father; this verse explains how *what is known of God is manifest in them*
>
> *are perceived*—not with corporeal or imaginary vision, but with an intellectual vision
>
> *understood from the creation of the world*—understood by humankind, not only by angels[66]; or, *from the foundation of the world*
>
> *through the things that have been made*—through these if not through the law
>
> *his everlasting power*—the Son; that which governs all things is perceived
>
> *divinity*—the Holy Spirit;[67] his goodness which fills all things
>
> *without excuse*—for their injustice

1:21 For although they knew God, they did not glorify him as God or give him thanks, but they became futile in their own thoughts and their senseless heart was darkened.

although they knew, etc. Augustine: They saw from whom it must come, but were ungrateful to him who gave them the ability to see. They wished to attribute to themselves what they were seeing and, having become proud, they lost even what they were seeing. What they found by curiosity they lost through pride. For what God had graciously given they ungratefully received.[68] *darkened*. Ambrose: Clouds of error covered their heart, for although they had come to know the creator from his creatures, they had not glorified him as God, and were further darkened.[69]

knew God—through natural reason and the revelation of
   creation, so that they might confess him to be the one
   principle of all things
they did not glorify him as God—by living well and worshiping
   him
or give him thanks—for their knowledge, but attributed it to
   themselves, whereby they became vain and false
they became futile in their own thoughts—which was due to
   themselves, not God, by considering themselves to be
   something when they were nothing
and—therefore
heart—i.e., reason, because they believed reason resided in the
   heart
their senseless heart was darkened—gradually their heart was
   brought down to utter senselessness, as the swelling of
   pride overshadowed it

1:22 For claiming to be wise, they became foolish,

they became foolish. See how their heart was darkened, which is a punishment. They were *wise* about the natures of things but *foolish* in regard to God.

claiming—by their mouth or in their heart
to be wise—from themselves, not from God; see how they
   became futile
they became foolish—see how their heart was darkened toward
   God

1:23 and changed the glory of the incorruptible God into the likeness of an image of corruptible man and of birds, beasts, and serpents.

and changed, etc. Augustine: Here he condemns the images of the wicked: some were venerating the earth, others the sun and the like.[70] *in the likeness of an image*. He exaggerates the foolishness to show the depth of their stupidity. *of corruptible man and of birds, beasts*. From of old the Romans had the custom of praying to the images of people, such as Romulus, Jove, and others, especially since the coming of Aenaeus to Italy, and to the images of birds and beasts and serpents when Alexandria was conquered by Augustus and subjugated to Rome.

> *and changed*—they sinned not only in thought but also in
> deed. The change is in themselves, not God's glory.
> *glory of the incorruptible God*—the worship owed to the incor-
> ruptible God
> *into the likeness of an image*—into an image like that of which
> it was an image: idolatry, in other words
> *corruptible man*, etc.—first the human image, then moving on
> to beings with lesser intelligence

1:24 Therefore God delivered them over to the desires of their heart, to uncleanliness, so that they dishonor their own bodies among themselves,

God delivered them over, because nothing happens without his permission: first *to the desires of their heart*, God having left their heart to itself; then *to uncleanliness* in act, and such uncleanliness that by a kind of violence they were joining naturally repugnant bodies and making them more disposed to sin. Augustine: It is clear that God works in the hearts of people to incline their wills either to good on account of his mercy or to evil on account of their merits. He does this, certainly, according to his judgment, which is sometimes hidden, sometimes open, but always just.[71] *they dishonor.* Gregory: Sin that is not diluted by penance soon, by its own weight, delivers itself over to another sin.[72] Thus it happens that sin is not simply sin but also the cause of sin. Subsequent sin indeed arises from sin. And the sin that arises from sin is not only sin, but also the punishment of sin, because in his just judgment God darkens the heart of a sinner so that from the merit of a preceding sin he also falls into other sins.

> *delivered them over*—by removing his grace God permitted
> them to be delivered over
> *to the desires of their heart*—behold the punishment, which
> was prepared by themselves and not by God
> *to uncleanliness*—then desire is brought into act
> *so that they dishonor their own bodies*—an act, and also a pun-
> ishment, that is dishonorable according to nature
> *among themselves*—nothing else than engaging in sexual acts
> by themselves or with another of the same sex

1:25 because they exchanged the truth of God for a lie, and worshipped and served a creature rather than the creator, who is blessed for ages. Amen.

Because they exchanged.[73] He describes more fully the stages of sin and its punishment, that he might correlate them. *exchanged.* He shows the stages by which they exchanged the glory of God and believed in a god who did not exist, and *worshiped and served a creature rather than the creator.* Then he describes the stages of uncleanliness, that of women to women and men to men, which he matches as punishment to their sin of idolatry: just as they sinned against the creator of nature, so they were punished in their own nature. Thus he concludes: *and they received the reward that was due their error* (Rom. 1:27). *they exchanged the truth.* Ambrose: When they gave the name God, who is truth, to those that are not gods.[74] Augustine: The truth of a creature is from God, but it is not God, which truth they converted into a lie, worshiping creatures as the creator.[75] *and worshiped.* But lest they should say: I do not worship images but the realities behind them such as the sun, he adds: *and served a creature*, where he condemns the things that were understood in the images. *Amen.* As if to say: This is true, that the true God is blessed forever, while impiety pays temporal respect to the gods of the Gentiles. What they say, therefore, is untrue.

> *because they exchanged*, etc.—a repetition of: *they dishonor*, etc.
> *the truth of God*—this is what above he called *the glory of God*; that which is true of God they gave to an idol, namely being divine
> *worshiped*—by carefully adorning
> *served*—in deeds
> *rather than*—as though the creature were better than the creator
> *who is blessed*—although they deprived him of his honor; nevertheless he is exalted above all things
> *for ages*—without end

1:26 Wherefore God delivered them over to passions of ignominy, for their women exchanged natural use for a use that is against nature.

passions. Sexual pleasures, in other words, which, even if they give delight, are nevertheless passions better left unmentioned. *of ignominy.* Haymo: As if to say that they are without any dignified name. An ignominious person is one who ceases to have a dignified name after being caught in some crime.[76] ***natural use***. Do you suppose with Julian that the apostle praised lust here, because he said that the use of a woman is natural? Are you really forced to praise every use of a woman? And by this will you also praise those fornications that are committed with women, because therein is certainly natural use? Such natural use must be condemned, however, because it is not legitimate. That is why the children who are born from it are not called legitimate, but natural. The apostle, then, did not praise concupiscence of the flesh in his words, but called it natural use, that use from which human nature can subsist by reproducing. Nor did he say conjugal use, but natural use, meaning what happens in the members created for this, so that by them both sexes are able to be joined for reproducing. Ambrose: And thus when by the same members someone is also joined to a harlot, it is natural use, though not laudable but culpable; but when it is by that part of the body that was not instituted for generating, even if someone uses a wife, it is against nature and shameful.[77]

> ***Wherefore***—because they had sinned so grievously against the
>   creator of nature; the punishment is repeated, correspond-
>   ing to the previous sin
> ***delivered them over***—he permitted them to be delivered over
> ***to passions of ignominy***—first to the ardor of lust, which is a
>   passion of nature not to be named, then to the act itself
> ***for***—and truly

1:27 And likewise men, having abandoned the natural use of women, burned in their desires for one another, men with men, performing disgraceful things and receiving in themselves the reward that was due their error.

men with men. Augustine: They were handed over (either by God forsaking them or by another explicable or inexplicable way) to a most just judgement of God, to the passions of shamefulness, so that sins are avenged with sins. The punishment for sins is not only torments, but also the increase of sins.[78] ***and receiving in themselves the reward***. Augustine: But few people view these as punishments, and therefore the apostle mentions them in particular, carefully enumerating what they are and how they are penalties for sin. For within the very sin of apostasy, and its ultimate punishment of eternal fire, there are means which are both sins and punishments.[79] *that was due their error*. Here is shown unambiguously the reason for which they were delivered over.

> *likewise*—acting among themselves
> *burned in their desires*—see here the sin of the will or desire;
>   the desires come from themselves, not from God
> *performing disgraceful things*—not only did they burn but
>   they also sinned in act
> *receiving in themselves*—vindicating God in their own nature,
>   i.e., receiving God's punishment in their own sex
> *reward*—and so they received a worthy punishment that
>   befitted their sin

1:28 And just as they did not approve to have God in their understanding, God delivered them over to a reprobate mind, so that they do things that are not proper,

And just as. Again, since they have not yet come to their senses, they fall from these sins into others. And in saying *just as*, he fits the punishment to the sin, so that just as they sinned in their understanding of God, so they were punished in their own understanding. ***And just as they did not approve***. Because they did not know God so as to have him in their understanding, when their reason itself offered proof of God; or because they thought God did not know or was unconcerned with their evils, he ***delivered them over***, etc.

> *just as*—or because
> *God delivered them over to a reprobate mind*—so that they
>   understand nothing except what is distant from goodness
> *do*—perform
> *not proper*—not proper to reason

1:29 full of all iniquity: malice, fornication, avarice, worthlessness; full of envy, murders, contention, deceit, malignity;

full of all iniquity. He enumerates the parts so that he may rebuke them more explicitly. ***Malice*** is when someone strives to harm another. ***Worthlessness*** is rashness, when a person attempts what he is incapable of or what is intemperate in itself. ***Contention*** is the impugning of truth through a proclivity to bicker. ***Malignity*** is ill will, when a person is unable to carry it out in action, or when he does not render thanks for favors.

> *full*—they are filled, as though possessing a large amount of sin
> *malice*, etc.—he enumerates this by its parts
> *fornication*—every use beyond a legitimate spouse
> *avarice*—to acquire many things and not to donate superflu-
>   ous goods to the poor
> *envy*—sorrow at another's good
> *murders*—plural as a whole, both act and will
> *deceit*—when one thing is pretended and another done

1:30 being gossipers, detractors, hateful of God, contumelious, proud, haughty, devisers of evil, disobedient to parents,

detractors. Those who deny or undermine the good of others. *hateful of God*. Lest gossip or detraction be considered slight offenses, because they are in words, he adds that they are *hateful to God*, so they may understand that they can incur eternal damnation by gossip and detraction alone. The *haughty* are those who are unwilling to bear anyone above or equal to themselves.

> *gossipers*—who sow discord among friends
> *contumelious*—who bring forth insults and outrages in words
>   and deeds
> *proud*—in honors
> *devisers of evil*—in word and deed; who devise new types of evil
> *disobedient*—more unmanageable than beasts
> *parents*—both natural and spiritual

1:31 foolish, disorderly, without affection, without a sense of duty, without mercy.

disorderly. Disorder of the body indicates a quality of the mind.

> *foolish*—not discerning between good and evil
> *disorderly*—in dress and comportment
> *without affection*—without love of neighbor
> *without a sense of duty*—in society
> *without mercy*—they are not compassionate toward the needy

1:32 And although they knew the justice of God, they did not understand that those who do such things are worthy of death, not only those who do them, but also those who consent to those who do them.

are worthy of death. Lest they think that they will only be afflicted with those penalties in which they delight, he adds the final penalty: eternal death. *also those who consent.* To consent is to keep silent when you can reprove; or they are those who encourage them in their error.

> *they*—again they fall deeper
> *knew*—earlier, with reason as a guide
> *the justice of God*—that God is just
> *they did not*—nevertheless they did not
> *death*—eternal death
> *those who consent*—so that none may be excused

Chapter 2

2:1 Therefore you are inexcusable, O man, every one of you who judges. When you judge another, you condemn yourself, because you do the same things you judge.

Therefore you are inexcusable. Here he speaks to Gentiles and Jews in common. The Jew is judging the Gentile, and the Gentile the Jew, on the basis of their former states. Neither of them is judging in the Spirit, since the Jew judges the Gentile for idolatry, while he is himself an idolater, and the Gentile judges the Jew for breaking the law, while he is himself a breaker of the natural law. *inexcusable*. Because you are witnesses to your own condemnation when you judge another. And why? *because you do the same things*.

who judges. Whereby someone shows that he is not just himself.[80] He is speaking of the Jews although he does not yet mention them by name. They boast in the law, but do the things they condemn. And because he does not yet mention them by name, he says: *the wrath of God upon every soul of humankind who works evil, Jew and Greek; and glory to everyone who works good, Jew and Greek* (Rom. 2:9–10). *you do the same things*. The apostle destroys the empty excuses of the Gentiles and Jews by their own authorities. The Jew might offer an excuse for his own sin: Although I do the same things, the Jewish race defends me, and the law. And the Gentile might say: Ignorance defends me. The apostle refutes these excuses.

> *Therefore you are inexcusable*—because all who do and consent
>   to these things are worthy of death
> *every one of you*—both Jew and Gentile

2:2 For we know that God's judgment is according to truth toward those who do such things.

who do such things. <u>Haymo</u>:[81] who do such things that are faulted in others; who in their judgment pay attention to persons of power, to the rich and to relatives.

> *For*—or, moreover
> *we know*—as if to say: You believe this, but we know it. Or we
>   truly know that you are inexcusable because, etc.
> *according to truth*—according to impartiality, not according to
>   persons
> *toward*—against
> *those*—whether Jews or Gentiles

2:3 But do you think, O man, each of you who judge those doing such things while you also do them, that you will escape the judgment of God?

But do you think. This chapter is commonly interpreted as directed against Jews and Gentiles, yet it can also be read particularly against any superstitious prelate of the Church. *that you will escape*. When you claim impunity you sin more grievously because you despise God's goodness and do not realize that you are despising it. And do you do this?—a reproach as though he were surprised.

> *do you think*—a sarcastic reproof: we know about God's judg
>   ment, but do you think, do you believe otherwise?
> *O man*—O carnal man
> *who judge*—<u>Augustine</u>: Because this power has been given to
>   you and there is no one in the world who may judge you.[82]
>   He is addressing prelates.
> *such things*—which he has mentioned above
> *that*—do you think this, namely that
> *you will escape*—in any way whatsoever

2:4 Or do you despise the riches of his goodness and patience and long suffering? You are unaware that the kindness of God is drawing you to repentance.

the riches of his goodness. <u>Ambrose</u>: Abundant is the goodness that is full or that supplies many good things to many sinners, coaxing them toward repentance. Abundant is the patience that endures so many and such great sinners, not punishing them at once. And it is long suffering because he waits not for an hour, but at length through an extensive period.[83] A person despises these things when he does not use them to seek repentance, as God intends, but subverts them to claim impunity. ***patience and long suffering.*** Augustine: Patience is when God does not immediately punish those who sin through pride and with an impudent spirit. Long suffering is when he bears for a long time those who sin through weakness and not through a deliberate malice of soul, waiting for their repentance.[84] ***you are unaware.*** Three grades of sins are noted in these three verses: first when you presume impunity (*But do you think . . .*); second, and more serious, when you despise God's goodness (*Or do you despise the riches . . .*); third, and the most serious, when you are unaware that you are despising it (*You are unaware . . .*).

> *Or do you despise*—Why, then, does he not punish you now?
> Because his goodness waits, which you are not aware of.
> *riches of his goodness*—his abundant goodness
> *patience and long suffering*—These are the riches of his mercy.
> Augustine: Because now is the time of his mercy.
> *You are unaware*—He speaks sharply because the soul is not
> called back except through fear. Behold, you do not know
> that God is merciful.
> *is drawing you*—in so far as it depends on him
> *to repentance*—or, to patience

2:5 But according to your hardness and your impenitent heart, you are storing up wrath for yourself on the day of wrath and of the revelation of the just judgment of God,

But according to your hardness. There are some for whom the evil things they do are displeasing and, having been led in repentance of heart, in so far as it is given to them they strive to depart from these evils. He is not speaking about such people here. There are others for whom evil deeds are pleasing and, presuming too much on God's mercy, they continue stubbornly in their sins. By this they show forth God's patience and load down their own burden by sinning more. And there are still others for whom evil deeds are displeasing, but because they understand them to be serious, they think they cannot now be forgiven, like Cain who said, *My iniquity is greater*, etc. (Gen. 4:13). Those with too much hope assert that God is not just, while those in despair believe that God is not good. Therefore they will be in danger on each side, both by hoping and by despairing, and they will perish as they toil in opposite directions and with opposite feelings. *you are storing up*. You are piling up punishment on yourself by sinning further. Such impenitence is blasphemy against the Holy Spirit. These two, despair and improper hope, kill souls; by these two blasphemy is made against the Holy Spirit. Thus in the Gospel: *Whoever sins or speaks a word of blasphemy against the Holy Spirit, it shall not be forgiven him here or in the future life* (Matt. 12:32). Concerning this John writes in his canonical epistle: *There is a sin unto death; I do not say that someone should pray for him* (1 John 5:16). The sin against the Holy Spirit comes about in two ways, namely through obstinacy or through despair. Obstinacy is the stubbornness of a hardened soul in evil, whereby a person becomes impenitent. And such impenitence is a sin against the Holy Spirit. Despair is when someone has absolutely no trust in God's goodness; and this too is called a sin against the Holy Spirit.

Ambrose: Truly he sins against the Holy Spirit who thinks that his own wickedness comes from the goodness of God.[85] Haymo: God should not seem to you so merciful that he does not seem just, nor so just that he does not wish to be merciful.[86] Augustine: Some call that sin unforgivable because those who sin in this way are unable to repent, having hearts hardened like stones. Concerning such a one Job says: *His heart was hardened like a stone* (Job 41:15). Others call it unforgivable because those sinning in this way never repent, although they are able, and so they are never forgiven for it.[87] This is what is said above in Matthew. So great is the stain of this sin that someone cannot attain the benefit of praying with humility, even if his bad conscience is forced to acknowledge and declare it a sin.

In the Gloss on Mark it is said that such a sinner is unable to repent worthily. But it seems this should be understood as a shortened way of saying he is scarcely able to repent or unable except rarely and with great difficulty. Hence Augustine: He punishes the guilty as though unwillingly, for from the beginning he brought people into life, not into death. Again: This impenitence or impenitent heart cannot be judged as long as someone remains in this life, for no one should be despaired of as long as God's patience is leading to repentance.[88]

> ***But according to your hardness***—but because you are hard and
> stubborn in your evil, from which you do not repent in
> your heart

> *wrath*—that will be wielded
> *on the day of wrath*—when all things are laid bare and when
>   what is now unknown to us shall be revealed

2:6 who will render to each one according to his works:

who will render to each one. At present he does not render to those whom he forgives, for his goodness is now immense even toward the wicked. But in the future he will render evil for evil since he is just, good for evil since he is good and just; yet he will not render evil for good since he is not unjust. It pertains to justice that they should never be without punishment whose soul in this life never wanted to be without sin. It also pertains to justice that no end of retribution should be given to a wicked person who, while alive, was unwilling to make an end of sin. Therefore it is not improper for a person to be punished eternally for temporal sin. <u>Ambrose</u>: No evil goes unpunished, etc. For this reason some hold that the bad will in the reprobate is only a punishment and not sin itself, since it merits nothing; others hold that it is both sin and punishment even if it merits nothing, just as the good will in the upright. Nor does the bad will remain unpunished since it is a punishment in itself. Or they say that this is understood only with regard to the state of the present life.[89]

> *who*—with just judgment
> *his works*—or, his own works

2:7 eternal life to those who, according to patience of good work, are seeking glory and honor and incorruption,

> *patience of good work*—having made good use of God's
>   patience, they perform good works
> *are seeking*—who have worked with a good intention and not,
>   like hypocrites, in order to be seen
> *glory*—because *the just will shine like the sun in the kingdom
>   of their Father* (Matt. 13:43)
> *honor*—when they are placed at the right hand of God
> *incorruption*—because what they possess shall endure

2:8 but wrath and indignation to those who are contentious and do not submit to the truth, but assent to iniquity;

Indignation. Lest he seem to be angry and not to punish. *wrath and indignation* come after judgment.

> *wrath*—punishment after judgment
> *indignation*—this will be on the day of judgment, when they
>   shall be indignant at themselves
> *to those*—as you Romans
> *who are contentious*—or who contend with God, being unwill-
>   ing to repent
> *do not submit to the truth*—when it is spoken to them
> *but assent to iniquity*—they cling to impunity, not believing in
>   a future judgment

2:9 tribulation and distress upon every soul that does evil, of the Jew first, and of the Greek;

Before judgment there is only *tribulation and distress* in the soul. *upon every soul.* Above he spoke indefinitely (*but to those* . . .) while here he speaks universally so that he might include Jew and Gentile. He speaks of the soul because he is dealing with an unbeliever, whose soul will be afflicted with spiritual punishment for its faithlessness. *of the Jew first.* Ambrose: He always places the Jew first because the Jewish believer is more honorable on account of Abraham, but the unbelieving Jew should be considered worse since he has rejected the promises made to his fathers.[90]

> *tribulation*—before judgment, which is the wrath spoken of
>   above (Rom. 2:8)
> *distress*—which is indignation
> *upon every soul*—of both Jew and Gentile
> *of the Jew first*—of the Jew especially, since he also had the
>   written law
> *Greek*—Gentile

2:10 but glory and honor and peace to every one who does good, to the Jew first, and to the Greek.

> *peace*—which is the incorruption mentioned above (Rom. 2:7)

> *to the Jew first*—first in time, or he does more good because he
> has been better instructed
> **Greek**—Gentile

2:11 For there is no partiality with God:

For there is no partiality with God. God considers Jew and Gentile the same in regard to punishment and glory, because God does not judge according to persons, but according to merits; and he condemns both according to the manner of sin. <u>Ambrose</u>: He does not take into account family privilege, so that he would accept a faithless person for the sake of his ancestors; nor does he reject a believer because of the unworthiness of his parents; but he rewards or condemns each one on his own merits.[91]

> *For*—because

2:12 all who sin without the law will perish without the law, and all who sin under the law will be judged by the law.

without the law. <u>Augustine</u>: The apostle is speaking here about the law that Moses gave to the people of Israel. Therefore he says that the Gentiles were without the law because they had not received this written law, which the Jews were boasting that they had received.[92] *under the law.* <u>Augustine</u>: They are those who knew the divine commandments. Any excuse that others have from ignorance will be taken away from them. But neither shall these others be without punishment. And while it is worse for a person to sin knowingly than unknowingly, one should not therefore flee to the darkness of ignorance, for it is one thing not to have known and another not to have wanted to know.[93]

will be judged. Not that they may be saved as through fire, as some say, but that they shall actually perish. For Christ says that it will be more tolerable for Sodom at judgment than for the Jews who do not believe in Christ, and also that they will have no excuse from the sin of unbelief because he came and spoke to them. Others have an excuse, to whom he did not speak either through himself or through his spokesmen, yet they will not escape condemnation, because *all who sin without the law will perish without the law*; nevertheless they are going to suffer lighter punishments, since more is required of him to whom more is entrusted, because *the servant who knows the will of his master and does not do it*, etc. (Luke 12:47).

> *all who sin without the law*—without the written law, i.e., the Gentiles
> *will perish without the law*—will be condemned, but not for transgression of the written law
> *all who sin under the law*—i.e., the Jews who have the written law
> *will be judged by the law*—for transgression of the law, which makes their sins worse

2:13 For the hearers of the law are not just before God, but the doers of the law shall be justified.

For the hearers. <u>Ambrose</u>: Does not the law alone save? No, because it does not make people just.[94] Justice comes not from hearing *but the doers of the law*, which surely is through grace. *but the doers of the law*, i.e., all those that believe in Christ, whom the law promised, and such belief only happens through grace, *shall be justified*, i.e., they shall be accounted just; or they shall be made just by God so that they may be doers. It is not that those who were doers before shall be justified later; for we could say in a similar vein that the doers of the law shall be human in the sense that they are already human by creation itself. Thus those who were not doers before shall be justified, even the Gentiles, and so he continues:[95]

> *hearers of the law are not just*—i.e., not just from hearing the law
> *before God*—even if they are considered just before people
> *doers of the law*—i.e., grace justifies them so that they may fulfill the law, because they are not doers of the law in order to be justified but are justified in order to be doers of the law
> *shall be justified*—shall be considered just. The doers shall be justified, even Gentiles, as is explained in the next verse.

2:14 For when the Gentiles, who do not have the law, do by nature those things that are of the law, not having such a law, they are a law to themselves,

For when the Gentiles. He had said that a Gentile is condemned if he has acted wickedly and saved if he has acted well. But since he does not have the law and does not know, as it were, what is good or what is evil, it would seem that neither should be imputed to him. On the contrary, the apostle says that even if he does not have the written law, he has the natural law, because he understands and knows in himself what is good and what is evil. Therefore he must be credited with acting well or wickedly, of being saved or condemned by his merits. To act well, I say, and to be saved does not happen except through grace and faith, which renew the natural image of God in a person, bringing him out of the sleep of sin and decrepitude. Without this renewal he acts wickedly and is condemned, with his conscience accusing him. Corruption of nature is the very thing that grace heals. For the image in the human soul has been so worn away by the stain of earthly desires that no features have remained in it. But what was impressed there by the image of God at creation has not been completely blotted out. Thus when the defect is healed by grace, the things that are of the law are done by nature. Not that grace is denied by naming nature here, but that nature is restored by grace. The law of justice, which sin had destroyed, is impressed upon the interior person renewed by grace.

> *the law*—the written law
> *do by nature*—Origen: illumined by natural reason, they distinguish between what should be done and what avoided, which the law also did[96]
> *those things*—which the law commands, namely, to believe in God and in Christ
> *not having such a law*—although not having the written law of Moses
> *they are a law to themselves*—they are able to be a law to themselves

2:15 who show the work of the law written in their hearts, with their conscience bearing them witness, and of thoughts within them in turn accusing or defending them,

the work of the law written in their hearts. This is faith which they have in their hearts, i.e., in their innermost being, where faith works through love.

who show—by the signs of their works, when some works
praise and others condemn them

written in their hearts—firmly fixed in their reason

their conscience—even if it is not seen by others

bearing them witness—whence they will be witnesses to themselves of good and evil, knowing from this that they are
rightly condemned or saved

of thoughts—the conscience is not only in regard to works but
also in regard to thoughts, both good and evil; or the genitive is used for the ablative in the manner of the Greeks[97]

accusing—this is said of those who do not believe

defending—this is said of those who believe

**2:16 on the day when God will judge the hidden works of people ac-
cording to my Gospel through Jesus Christ.**

on the day—of judgment

God will judge the hidden works—the things that are now
hidden will be revealed

my—i.e., Paul's, namely the Gospel that Paul preaches

according to my Gospel—which is fully certain according to
the Gospel, etc.

through Jesus Christ—because the Father judges no one, but
has handed over all judgment to the Son

2:17 But if you are called a Jew and rely on the law, if you boast in God

But if you are called a Jew. Here he addresses the Jews, accusing them of
graver sin because they had more divine assistance.

a Jew—The Gentile has only the natural law, but you, a Jew,
have more. Your name comes from the patriarch Judah,
from his relationship to you.

rely on the law—you do not wander into errors as those who
are without the law

you boast in God—concerning your knowledge of God

**2:18 and know his will, and if you approve of more beneficial things,
instructed by the law,**

> *and know his will*—concerning the redemption that he
>   announced to you through the prophets
> *you approve of more beneficial things*—among beneficial things,
>   you know to choose the more beneficial

2:19 you trust yourself to be a leader of the blind, a light to those that are in darkness,

a leader of the blind. He calls the Gentiles blind and living in darkness, and they are blind, deprived of reason; although they know something, they are in darkness.

> *the blind*—i.e., those who do not understand
> *a light*—because you are also able to enlighten them

2:20 an instructor of the simple, a teacher of children, having a form of knowledge and of truth in the law.

having a form of knowledge. So that you might be an example to others of the knowledge of the law. *and of truth*. For some people have a certain knowledge and understanding of a book, and so they believe as the author himself believes, but they do not know how it is true nor even if it is true. But the Jew boasts that he has understanding of the law and knows that this understanding of the law is true. Thus he should be an example to others who desire to have this knowledge.

> *the simple*—not yet mature Jews
> *children*—Jews who do not know how to discuss the law
> *form of knowledge*—i.e., the perfection of knowledge

2:21 Therefore you who teach another, do you not teach yourself? You who preach not to steal, do you steal?

> *Therefore*—since you have all these things
> *do you not*—why do you not?
> *not to steal*—as the law says
> *do you steal?*—do you steal the understanding of Christ that is
>   in the law?

2:22 You who say not to commit adultery, do you commit adultery? You who abhor idols, do you commit sacrilege?

> *do you commit adultery?*—do you take away the truth of Christ
> from the law and insert a lie?
> *do you commit sacrilege?*—by denying Christ; by giving the
> worship of God to idols, which the Jews often did

2:23 You who boast in the law, do you dishonor God by transgression of the law?

> *dishonor God*—i.e., you are the reason the Gentiles dishonor
> God, which is true
> *by transgression of the law*—when you disregard the Law's
> meaning concerning the incarnation and divinity of Christ

2:24 For, as it is written, *The name of God is blasphemed by you among the Gentiles.* [Isa. 52:5]

The name of God, etc. The Jews blasphemed the name of God among the Gentiles when they tried to persuade believers that Christ should not be called God. Or this happened at the time of the prophet, when the Gentiles were unaware that the Jews had been handed over to them on account of the Jews' own offenses, and the Gentiles were giving glory to their own idols for the victory as if they had defeated the God of the Jews along with the Jews.

> *as it is written*—by Ezekiel (Ezek. 5:15) about his contempo-
> raries; Paul uses the words of the prophet Ezekiel as his
> own
> *The name of God is blasphemed*—today, because in blaspheming
> Christ the Father is blasphemed, as he himself says: *He
> who receives me, not only receives me, but him who sent
> me* (Mark 9:36); just as before, when it seemed to the Jews
> that the Gentiles had defeated God

2:25 Now circumcision is an advantage if you keep the law, but if you are a transgressor of the law, your circumcision has become foreskin.

Now circumcision. Above he showed that the law does not benefit them; now he shows that neither does circumcision. *is an advantage*. Because to him that obeys God circumcision provides a sign of the truth, when the unlearned are guarded under the fear of God. He speaks of an advantage here; and later he says: *If you are circumcised, Christ is of no advantage to you* (Gal. 5:2). He would have this be understood according to the condition of different times. For according to the dispensation of the Old Testament, circumcision was advantageous at that time, but not advantageous unto salvation without the keeping of the spiritual law. But now, namely in the time of grace, after which the truth has been manifested, it is of no advantage at all. *if you keep the law*. <u>Ambrose</u>: That you may lay aside all shameful practices, that you may circumcise your heart and believe in Christ.[98]

> *an advantage*—but since you are such as you are, circumcision
>   is of no advantage to you who are of the race of Abraham
> *if you keep the law*—if you believe in Christ you keep the law
>   spiritually
> *if you are a transgressor of the law*—if you do not fulfill what
>   circumcision demands, namely, that you believe in Christ
> *circumcision*—fleshly circumcision
> *foreskin*—circumcision is of no more advantage than foreskin

2:26 Therefore if foreskin keeps the justice of the law, will not foreskin be considered as circumcised?

will not foreskin. By comparison with himself, the Gentile shows that you are to be condemned. For you do not know through nature, nor through circumcision, but through the law, that which the Gentile knows through nature, i.e., through Christ.

> *if*—if on the other hand
> *foreskin*—any Gentile
> *justice of the law*—the commandment by which a person is
>   justified; or the faith of Christ which the law foretold was
>   going to come for justification
> *be considered as circumcised*—so that he is a son of Abraham,
>   the father of faith, and no one, as it were, can deny this

2:27 And foreskin, completing the law by nature, will judge you who through the letter and circumcision are a traitor to the law.

foreskin . . . will judge. In the present place, then, he seems to be speaking of the Gentiles that have come to faith in Christ in the foreskin of their flesh. He compares them to those keeping the spiritual law and he considers them superior to the Jews, who through the letter and circumcision are traitors to the law and who, he also says, will be judged by the Gentiles.

> *And foreskin . . . will judge*—And will not foreskin judge?
> *completing*—carrying out
> *by nature*—nature restored through grace
> *who through the letter*—although you have been taught
>   through the written law
> *circumcision*—which is a sign of the removal of sins

2:28 For he is not a Jew who is one outwardly, nor is circumcision what is done outwardly in the flesh;

For he is not, etc. Hence a Gentile can become a Jew, and a Jew can become a Gentile. *Jew* means one who confesses, and thus the one who truly believes and rightly confesses is a genuine Jew.

> *a Jew*—truly a Jew
> *outwardly*—he is a Jew in name and nationality only, who
>   confesses with his lips while his heart is distant
> *circumcision*—true circumcision
> *outwardly in the flesh*—which is made by a removal of skin

2:29 but he is a Jew who is one inwardly, and circumcision is of the heart, in the spirit not in the letter, whose praise is not from people but from God.

circumcision is of the heart. <u>Origen</u>: It is what purifies the soul and cuts away the stain of sins.[99] *whose praise.* <u>Ambrose</u>: God praises the one who believes, not the one who is circumcised in the flesh. The praise of the Jews is from people; when they do what the law commands, it is without spirit, in fear of punishment, not out of love of justice, and so what appears before people is not the same as what appears before God.[100] *not from people but from God.* <u>Augustine</u>: This is that circumcision by which illicit desires are cut off, which does not happen when the letter teaches and assists, but when the Spirit helps and supports.[101]

> *he is a Jew*—he is a true Jew
> *inwardly*—confessing in his heart
> *circumcision is of the heart*—true circumcision is a cleansing of the heart
> *in the spirit*—brought about by the Holy Spirit
> *not in the letter*—not with stone knives as the letter teaches
> *whose praise is not from people but from God*—i.e., what is truly praiseworthy is not from people but from the grace of God

Chapter 3

3:1 What advantage then is there for a Jew? Or what is the benefit of circumcision?

What advantage then. He presents what he sees may be an objection, so that he might answer it, inasmuch as a Jew becomes a Gentile, and vice versa. *What advantage then is there for a Jew,* who is one of God's chosen people, more than for a Gentile, who is called an unclean dog? Or what follows from circumcision? To which he responds: There was certainly a value once, but this does not mean Jews are more worthy in the faith.

> *What advantage*—according to their earlier dispensation, in terms of the law and legal observances

3:2 Much in every way. First indeed because the oracles of God were entrusted to them.

The Jew has *much* according to his earlier state, and *in every way*: in every provision of temporal things or in every revelation of spiritual things. In both ways God did many things for the Jews, which he did not do for the Gentiles, and thus they are worthier according to their earlier dispensation. *First indeed because*. As if to say: In order to skip over other and lesser temporal blessings, I am laying down first and foremost that the oracles of God, i.e., the Law and the Prophets, were entrusted to them as to friends, through which they could come to an understanding about future redemption. You will say, then, that there is no advantage, because some of them did not believe the oracles so as to receive the promised messiah. To which it is answered: Yet thus it was not less profitable for those who believe, as is declared: for if some have not believed, faith is not therefore nullified.

47

> *Much in every way*—according to their earlier dispensation,
>> but nothing more in relation to the faith of Christ
>
> *the oracles*—the Law and the Prophets

3:3 For what if some of them have not believed? Has their unbelief nullified the faith of God?

Has their unbelief. Because some were unwilling to believe, shall that prejudice God against the other Jews so that they are judged unworthy to receive what God has promised to the faithful? Indeed the promise was made that it might be profitable to those who believe. *the faith of God.* Either in the sense that some believed in God or that God is faithful to the promises he made to people.

> *For what*—thus there is an advantage
>
> *their unbelief*—but no disadvantage is made for those who
>> believe
>
> *nullified the faith of God*—rendered it unfulfilled

3:4 May it never be! Nevertheless God is true while every human is false. As it is written: *That you may be justified in your words and prevail when you are judged*. [Ps. 50:6]

while every human is false. He adds this to show that God's promise was made and fulfilled not because of any human worthiness but because of his own mercy. For grace is given to the unworthy that grace may be more commendable. God is called *true*, i.e., unchangeable both in his essence and in his promise; a human being is called *false* because he does not hold on to true being and he falls away through sin.[102] Every human is false who denies that God has fulfilled his promises, especially the Jew, whom God prevails against when he grants what was promised.[103] Every human is false, including the Jew, so that no one is considered more worthy in the new dispensation.

That you may be justified. As if David were saying to God: I have sinned, so that by sending a Son from my lineage as you promised you are proven to be just and to have fulfilled it by the justice of the promises alone and not by my merits. And you *prevail* by fulfilling your promises *when you are judged*, when they say you should not fulfill them on account of my sins; or, against you alone I say that I have sinned so that when I sin (and we all sin), you alone may appear just in all your promises, and you may surpass all in justice when you are compared to others. Or the God-Man prevailed when he was judged since, on account of his humility, God has given him a name that is above every name. This does not relate to the argument above, but was added by way of ampleness. *That you may be justified . . . and prevail.* The just judge was judged by sinners and nevertheless prevailed. It is surely to this one, who has no sin, that David says: *Against you alone have I sinned . . . that you may be justified* (Ps. 50:6), you who surpass all judges, who alone are unjustly judged.

> *May it never be!*—that it was nullified; but rather
> *Nevertheless*—for
> *true*—fulfilling his promises; he is true in and of himself
> *false*—and thus unworthy of the promise
> *As it is written*—But God is true
> *your words*—concerning the promise of a Son, or concerning
>   forgiveness of the repentant
> *when you are judged*—either not to have sent a Son or not to
>   grant forgiveness

3:5 But if our iniquity commends the justice of God, what shall we say? Is God unjust when he inflicts wrath? (I am speaking in human terms.)

But if our iniquity. He has said that God is true and every human false, and that he gives good things to the unworthy, whereby his justice and grace appear more commendable. Hence the carnal person, asserting that God uses the wicked as an instrument for his own glory, deduces that he may call God unjust since he punishes sins that are beneficial to himself. The apostle refutes this, saying: *Is God unjust when he inflicts wrath?* God is true and the human being false. But if this is so, and thus our iniquity commends the justice of God, what seems to follow? That God is unjust. But is God, who inflicts punishment, unjust?

> *the justice of God*—the holiness of God
> *our iniquity commends the justice of God*—this meaning is
>   drawn without warrant from the words of David
> *he inflicts wrath*—on account of sins he inflicts punishment
>   and damnation
> *in human terms*—i.e., this question is brought up by carnal
>   people

3:6 May it never be! Otherwise how shall God judge this world?

> *May it never be!*—but may it never be that he is unjust
> *Otherwise how shall God judge this world?*—If he is not just,
>   no judge can be just. If he is unjust he will judge badly,
>   namely giving bad things to the good and good things to
>   the wicked.

3:7 For if the truth of God in my falsity has redounded to his glory, why am I still judged a sinner?

For if the truth. After inserting his refutation, he returns to the argument of the carnal person, that God would be unjust to punish iniquity. For if God is more glorious from it, then why am I even now, and not just in the future, judged as a sinner, which I am not? Or *why am I still judged*, i.e., after conversion, after he has given gifts to the unworthy? For before conversion God was not more glorious from my sins. In other words: What could be considered before forgiveness should not be considered afterwards, namely that I be judged a sinner, since it is now certain that the truth of forgiveness would not have redounded to God's glory had I not sinned. Or *For if the truth*, etc., may be construed more properly: How shall he judge if he is unjust? And this means that God shall not judge correctly because he judges me unjustly now as a sinner, which I am not.

> *For*—because
> *the truth of God*—God's justice. Truth is used here because
>   truth includes justice.
> *my falsity*—through my sin, because iniquity includes falsity
> *has redounded to*—has increased
> *his glory*—i.e., if he is more glorious on account of my sin

3:8 And why should we not do evil that good may come? Thus we are blasphemed and some claim that we say this, whose condemnation is just.

And if my falsity redounds to his glory, then *why should we not do evil that good may come? Thus we are blasphemed*. We are accused of thinking this way, which is blasphemy, and even of preaching it on occasion with words such as these: *Where sin abounded, grace abounded all the more* (Rom. 5:20).

> *that good may come*—i.e., that God's justice and glory may increase
> *Thus we*—we apostles
> *and some*—the blasphemers
> *that we say this*—that we think and preach this
> *whose condemnation is just*—therefore they should not be believed

3:9 What then? Are we better than they? By no means! For we have argued that Jews and Greeks are all under sin.

What then? Because he did more for the Jew in the earlier dispensation, and because he satisfied them with good things, not because of any merit of theirs: *What then? Are we better than they?* Or, since every human is false, therefore we are not better than the Gentiles in this dispensation, although we were better in the earlier dispensation. *By no means!* Because there is no respect of persons with God, but *in every nation, he who fears God is acceptable to him* (Acts 10:35).

> *Are we better than they?*—are we Jews better in regards to this grace than the Gentiles?
> *we have argued*—we have shown by argument
> *are all under sin*—before grace, and thus none is better than another

3:10 As it is written: Because no one is just;

> *it is written*—concerning the Jews, of whom it would seem less applicable
> *no one*—no one who does not come to faith in Christ

3:11 there is no one who understands; there is no one who seeks God.

there is no one who seeks God. From his works they were able to seek and find out that Christ was God.

there is no one who understands—they are not just because they
    do not understand that Christ is God
there is no one who seeks God—they do not understand on
    account of their own sin, because they do not seek God,
    but turn away from him

**3:12 All have turned aside, together they have become useless. There is
no one who does good; there is not even one.**

All have turned aside. He does not mean absolutely all people, but a part
of the people, for there are always two people within the one people, as
is found in Jeremiah: At that time all rose up against the prophet of the
Lord, wanting to kill him (Jer. 26:8). And it continues: But all the people
did not permit them (Jer. 26:16). It says that all rose up, i.e., the wicked,
and that all the people did not permit, i.e., the good. *there is not even one*.
Christ alone does good in himself and in his people.

turned aside—from God to evil
together—with this turning aside
useless—because they have caused others to turn aside
There is no one who does good—they have turned aside because
    there is no one who does good, or they have turned aside
    and so there is no one who does good; no one because
    none of them, or none besides Christ[104]
not even one—i.e., no one, because none except Christ

**3:13 Their throat is an open tomb; they acted deceitfully with their
tongues, the venom of asps under their lips.**

an open tomb—because the stench of their words and works
    corrupts others; because their throat opens to receive the
    dead; this happens when they dare to act openly
acted deceitfully—speaking good words but planning evil in
    their heart
with their tongues—the tongues of the wicked; when they dare
    not do evil openly
venom of asps—incurable hatred
under their lips—i.e., in their heart

3:14 Their mouth is full of cursing and bitterness;

Their mouth—and their mouth
is full—overflowing
of cursing—i.e., of curses such as, *you have a demon* (John 7:20;
    8:48, 52), and the like
bitterness—i.e., bitter threats

3:15 their feet are swift to shed blood;

their feet are swift. Of them the Lord laments: *Jerusalem, Jerusalem, who kill the prophets* (Matt 23:37; Luke 13:34); and again: *evil and adulterous generation* (Matt 12:39, 16:4). And Isaiah: *Woe to a sinful nation, a wicked seed*, etc. (Isa. 1:4).

their feet—and their feet; their emotions
to shed—i.e., by deliberate murder
blood—the blood of Christ and his people

3:16 crushing and misfortune are in their paths

crushing and misfortune. They do such things and so they are crushed in this world by Titus and Vespasian, and they will suffer misfortune, punished in soul and body.

crushing—temporal afflictions
misfortune—eternal damnation
paths—works

3:17 and they do not know the way of peace,

way of peace—i.e., Christ; hence: Much peace to those who
    love your name, O Lord (Ps. 119:165)[105]

3:18 nor is the fear of God before their eyes.

nor is the fear of God, etc.—The fear of God is the beginning of wisdom; but not even the fear of God turned them from evil. Thus far these are words of David (Ps. 14:1–3, 53:2–4).

3:19 But we know that whatever the law says it says to those who are under the law, so that every mouth may be shut and that the whole world may be subject to God.

under the law. The Old Testament is sometimes called the Law in a general sense, as in the verse: *The Lord opened the disciples' understanding, that they might perceive the things which had been written of him in the Law and the Prophets and the Psalms* (Luke 24:44–45). Sometimes the Psalms are called the Law, as when the Lord says: *It is written in your Law: I have said you are gods and all children of the Most High* (John 10:34; cf. Ps. 81:6). And in another place: *That the word may be fulfilled, which is written in their Law, that they hated me for no reason* (John 15:25; cf. Ps. 35:19, 69:4). *so that every mouth may be shut.* Even the mouth of the Jews, who were boasting in their own glory, saying that they came to faith on account of their own merits; or thus the mouth of the Jews is shut just as the mouth of the Gentiles, who were boasting of natural gifts, had been shut above.

> *we know*—we apostles know, so that the Jews might not twist
>   this to another meaning
> *the law*—the Psalms are called law because they give instruction
> *to those who are under the law*—for their correction
> *so that*—thus
> *every mouth*—even of the Jews
> *may be shut*—from claiming its own glory
> *the whole world*—not only the Gentile without the written
>   law, guilty of impiety, but also the Jew, guilty of trans-
>   gressing the law
> *subject to God*—attributing all to God

3:20 Because from works of the law no flesh shall be justified before him. For through the law comes knowledge of sin.

from works of the law. Just as he has removed the pride of circumcision, so also he wishes to do the same concerning the other works of the law. And this is a new sentence even though it is joined to the preceding with a "because." The works of the law are those that were instituted with the law, and they were ended since they were ceremonial and figurative. They were never able to cleanse the conscience, even if they were performed with love and devotion, because they were not instituted for justification but for signifying things to come and for showing the infirmity of sin.

For the law did not come to take away sins but to show and punish them. *no flesh shall be justified*. Understand this according to the ceremonial, not the moral laws, which certainly justify and are perfected in the Gospel. *before him*. Before him who sees the inmost thoughts that people do not see, whether something is done out of love of justice or out of fear of punishment.

For through the law. Here he begins to discuss the law to show that justice does not come from it. *For through the law comes knowledge of sin*. Not that sins were completely unknown before, but the fact that they were going to be punished by God was unknown. Some sins were known before the law, as when Joseph was accused of the crime of adultery before Pharaoh and was sent to prison. And his brothers said: We rightly suffer these things because we have sinned against our brother. But some sins, which were unknown before, came to be known through the law, such as concupiscence and original sin. And some sins were known through the law to be more serious than they were thought before. *knowledge of sin*. If they know something to be sin and do not avoid it, this is transgression and thus brings wrath.

> *works of the law*—what one is obliged to do
> *no flesh*—no corporeal being
> *before him*—before God, even if someone is justified before
>   people

3:21 But now the justice of God has been manifested without the law, testified to by the Law and the Prophets:

testified to by the Law and the Prophets. Because the law prefigured God's justice in many sacraments. Or it means the law bore witness to God's justice because no one is justified under the law, and the prophets announced beforehand that which the coming of Christ has fulfilled.

> *but now*—with the coming of Christ; i.e., in this time of grace
> *the justice of God*—not of human justice
> *has been manifested*—not only granted; not disputably but
>   with miracles; with the Lord cooperating and confirming
>   the word
> *without the law*—without the command or help of the law

    testified to—or bearing testimony to; he adds this so that
        others might have a surer basis for belief

**3:22 the justice of God through faith in Jesus Christ to all and over all
who believe in him. For there is no distinction:**

the justice of God—not the justice by which God is essentially just but
that by which he clothes an ungodly person, when he mercifully changes
him from unfaithful to faithful. He speaks of justice, and not mercy, because God has fulfilled what he had promised in the Law and the Prophets, namely the coming of Christ.

    justice—the justice by which we are justified; this justice, as I
        have said, comes from God
    of God—from God
    through faith—faith obtains what the law demands; a faith by
        which one believes in Christ, the justifier of the ungodly
    and over all—that it might be expressed more precisely: a
        justice given from heaven over Jews and Gentiles
    there is no distinction—between Jew and Gentile; it is truly
        for all

3:23 all have sinned and need the glory of God.

and need the grace [glory], i.e., mercy and forgiveness of sins.

    all—both Jews and Gentiles
    have sinned—either in themselves or in Adam; previously and
        still daily
    glory—justice which is God's glory, because by it God appears
        glorious
    of God—not their own glory

**3:24 They have been justified freely by his grace and through the re-
demption that is in Christ Jesus,**

freely. Not by the law, not by their own will, but by the grace of Christ,
which is a gift of God. And the greatest gift of God is the Holy Spirit.
Yet it is not that this happens wholly without the will, but through the
law our will is shown to be weak, so that grace might heal our will, and

that our healed will might fulfill the law, although our will is not established under the law and does not need the law. No merits precede the reception of this grace. For the merits of the wicked deserve punishment, not grace, nor would it be grace if it were not given gratuitously.

> *They have been justified*—because all have sinned, therefore
>   *they have been justified freely*, etc.
> *freely*—without merits
> *by his grace*—by his gratuitous gifts
> *through the redemption*—i.e., the price paid for us; hence: *not*
>   *with corruptible gold or silver but with the precious blood of*
>   *the only begotten Son of God* (1 Pet. 1:18–19)
> *in Christ Jesus*—and nowhere else

3:25 whom God made a propitiation through faith in his blood, to show forth his justice by forgiveness of former sins

whom God made a propitiation. In order to manifest that he is true to his promises. This manifestation was necessary, not only for forgiveness of present sins, but also of those sins that came before in the forbearance of God, namely with God enduring and not punishing them at that time, so that he might show in this time of Christ what could not have happened at any other time, namely that he justifies and saves. *through faith in his blood*, i.e., faith in his passion; or through faith and through his passion, for neither avails without the other. *by forgiveness.* There are two effects of forgiveness: to be free of punishment and to enjoy glory. The just had the first before the death of Christ, because they did not experience actual punishment. But after the death of Christ the glory of the divine vision was granted to them, from which they were kept back when God was bearing with their sins.

> *whom God made*—long before he predicted or revealed Christ
>   to all
> *propitiation*—mercy
> *through faith*—without which nothing is pleasing to God
> *in his blood*—of the passion
> *to show forth his justice*—that he might be just in his promises
> *by forgiveness of former sins*—not only of present sins but also
>   sins committed before the advent of Christ

3:26 in the forbearance of God; to show forth his justice in this time, that he might be just and the justifier of him who has faith in Jesus Christ.

in the forbearance of God. God bore patiently with the sins of those who lived before the law and under the law. He did not punish them, nor pardon them in such a way that they could have glory, until he should come who, by the price of his own blood, would absolve the sins of those who came before and of those who came after.

> *in the forbearance of God*—he endured their sins and did not take them away at that time, but reserved them until his coming
> *to show forth his justice*—that he might justify
> *in this time*—of salvation, in this time of Christ's death
> *that he might be just*—in his promises; otherwise he could not help us
> *of him*—of the one that believes in him
> *who has faith*—not by the law

3:27 Where is your boasting? It is excluded. By what law? The law of works? No, but by the law of faith.

It is excluded. That is, it is clear what you should boast about, namely not in the law of works, but in the law of faith. Thus he can speak of praiseworthy boasting, which is boasting in the Lord. And he says that it is excluded, i.e., that it might stand out clearly. So also certain silver craftsmen are called excluders. In the Psalm this word is understood in the same way: *that they may be excluded*, i.e., might stand out, *who have been tried with silver* (Ps. 68:30), i.e., by the word of the Lord.

> *Where is your boasting?*—because justice is from faith without the law, therefore, O Jew, you are not able to boast
> *It is excluded*—it has been removed, and he shows how: not by the effort of works, but by the facility of faith

3:28 For we consider that a person is justified by faith without the works of the law.

a person is justified. Not that a believer is not bound to work afterward through love, as Abraham was even willing to sacrifice his son. Works indeed come after someone has been justified and not before he is justified; but a person is made just by faith alone without preceding works. Thus they who have done works of the law out of fear are not more just, since faith is not working through love in the heart if it does not go outward in works. Hence the justice of faith does not come from the merits of earlier works, as the Jews used to pride themselves in. And good works done before faith are empty: like runners who seem to have great strength and a fast pace, yet are running outside the track.[106] For intention makes a work good, and faith directs intention. *without the works*. Without preceding works, not without subsequent works, apart from which faith would be empty, as James says: *Faith without works is dead* (James 2:17, 26); and Paul himself: *If I should have all so as to move mountains, but do not have love, I am nothing* (1 Cor. 13:2).

> *we consider*—we apostles consider that faith justifies; he
>   declares this by his own authority
> *a person*—whosoever, also a Gentile
> *works of the law*—carnal works

3:29 Or is he only the God of the Jews and not also of the Gentiles? No, but also of the Gentiles.

> *and not also of the Gentiles*—as he is of the Jews? We hold that
>   any person is justified by faith, which must be believed
>   since he is also the creator of the Gentiles.

3:30 For surely there is one God, who justifies the circumcision from faith and the foreskin by faith.

> *there is one God*—surely of both peoples; as if to say: although
>   I can prove this in other ways, I need only assert this
> *who justifies*—since there is one God of all, he justifies all on
>   the same basis
> *foreskin*—unclean Gentiles
> *by faith*—from faith and by faith have the same meaning

3:31 Do we therefore destroy the law through faith? By no means! Rather we establish the law.

By no means! The law is not destroyed but, when fulfilled according to the Spirit, it ceases to operate according to the letter. ***we establish***. Because we have shown that what the law says has been fulfilled; or we establish, i.e., we strengthen the law since without faith it would be weak. This is the grace of faith by which the law is fulfilled, for the dispensation of the law is strengthened since the mystical and ceremonial laws are fulfilled spiritually. And the Gospel adds to what the law included in a lesser way in its moral precepts. And what the law promised would come, the faith of the Gospel now testifies to having arrived. Therefore the mystical meanings and promises of the law are fulfilled in the Gospel according to a spiritual understanding, while the letter that kills is removed.

> ***Do we therefore destroy the law through faith***—because we say
>   that all are justified by faith?
> ***we establish the law***—i.e., the moral precepts of the law

Chapter 4

4:1 What, then, shall we say that our father Abraham found according to the flesh?

What, then, shall we say. What he had said above, that a person is justified by faith, he now shows through Abraham, in whom all trust, and who through faith obtained justice, the promise, and paternity. *according to the flesh,* i.e., from works of the law. As if to say: You will ask whether he is just from these? No, because if he were just from carnal observance then he has eternal glory, which follows justice, from himself and not from God. Or such justification is in human opinion and not justification before God. Thus it follows that he was justified by faith, which he goes on to prove, if you listen to what Scripture says.

> *What, then*—because no one is just without faith
> *Abraham*—whom we should imitate
> *according to the flesh*—i.e., circumcision

4:2 If Abraham was justified by works of the law, he has reason to boast, but not before God.

> *was justified by works*—was only justified by works
> *he has reason to boast*—concerning this justification
> *but not before God*—which is contrary to the verse:
> > *Let him that boasts boast in the Lord* (1 Cor. 10:17)

4:3 For what does Scripture say? *Abraham believed God and it was reputed to him as justice.*

For what does Scripture say? As if to say: Listen to what Scripture says. *Abraham believed.* Believing was a sufficient cause of justice for him and for others. Yet a reward will not be given according to grace alone to someone that has the opportunity to work,[107] but also according to what is owed for his own work. But to him who does not have an opportunity to work, if he believes, then faith alone suffices for justice and thus for salvation, according to the grace made available to all, or according to what God laid down earlier in the law.[108]

> ***what does Scripture say?***—but he had justice before God, for Scripture says, *Abraham believed*, etc.
> ***Abraham believed God***—who said: *In your seed shall all the Gentiles be blessed* (Gen. 22:18, 26:4, 28:14), and other prophecies of this kind
> ***was reputed to him as justice***—i.e., was a sufficient cause of justice for him, as it is for others too

4:4 Now to him who works, a reward is not imputed as grace, but as debt.

Now to him who works. As if to say: Abraham was just by faith, but to him who performs those carnal works, or any good works, in order to merit grace, then if he has a reward, it is not from grace but from what his own merit deserves. But to the one who does not do these carnal works or any good works but only believes, his faith suffices for justice. And so he attributes to others what he has said of Abraham, namely, that if he is just from works he has reason to boast, but not before God; and therefore justice is by faith. ***But as debt***. Augustine: Do not flatter yourself concerning merits when you hear that he renders you a reward as a debt for works, as if the grace of the one rendering a reward were not as much in your works as the grace of the one justifying is in your faith. For I am far from convinced that anything may be called a work requiring God's remuneration from debt, since even when we are able to accomplish or think or say anything, we do it from God's gift and generosity.[109]

> ***who works***—who has an opportunity to work
> ***a reward***—justice
> ***is not imputed***—will not be given
> ***grace***—the grace of faith alone
> ***debt***—owed for his work, from his works

4:5 But to him who does not work, but believes in him who justifies the ungodly, his faith is reputed as justice according to the purpose of God's grace.

But to him who . . . believes in him. It does not say "who believes him," for a person believes him when he accepts what God says as true, which even the wicked do. Nor is it to believe that God exists, which even the devils do. But to believe in God is to love him in believing, to go to him in believing, and to be incorporated into his body. *according to the purpose.* In other words, an ungodly person is justified without preceding works, and this happens according to the purpose of God's grace, i.e., according to God's grace intended for believers, or according to what God determined long before.

> *who does not work*—who does not have an opportunity to work as Abraham had
> *him*—Christ
> *who justifies the ungodly*—who freely forgives the sins of the ungodly; then he shows how:
> *his faith*—which works did not merit
> *is reputed*—i.e., is what suffices
> *justice*—salvation
> *according to the purpose of God's grace*—as God has determined, so that when the law came to an end, then faith might justify

4:6 Likewise, David speaks about the blessedness of a person to whom God credits justice without works:

> *Likewise, David speaks*—I am saying the same thing that David says
> *about the blessedness*—here and in the future life
> *of a person*—that he has blessedness
> *credits*[110]—at the acceptable time, that is in the time of Christ; or acceptably, that is freely; God carries in, as it were, a person who is unable to approach on his own
> *justice*—the remission of sins and good works
> *without works*—without preceding works

4:7 Blessed are they whose iniquities are forgiven and whose sins are covered;

iniquities. Original sin, namely the inclination to sin, which is called concupiscence or passion or the law of one's members or the debility of nature, and other such terms. Before baptism it is sin and punishment, but after baptism it is punishment and not sin; it makes a child prone to concupiscence but not concupiscent. An adult, however, is also concupiscent, which indeed is forgiven in baptism and left behind as far as guilt, but remains as far as act. It is called original because it is incurred from the corrupt condition of our origin, whereby we have been conceived out of the corrupt law of conceiving that resulted from the sin of the first man, i.e., from concupiscence of the flesh. It has caused three degrees of sin: iniquity or impiety, when the creator is not acknowledged; sinful works; and slight sin, which he does not impute. *are forgiven*. To forgive is to cover; the words mean the same thing.

> *Blessed*, etc.—David speaks in these words
> *are forgiven*—by God, that sin may not rule in his mortal
> body; through baptism without the work or labor of
> penance
> *sins*—that are in act
> *are covered*—they are so covered in baptism that they are no
> longer seen to deserve punishment

4:8 blessed is the person to whom the Lord has not imputed sin.

> *has not imputed* (or will not impute)—for punishment
> *sin*—original sin, which is from another, or venial sin

4:9 Does this blessedness, therefore, abide only in circumcision, or also in foreskin? We say that faith was reputed to Abraham for justice.

> *this blessedness*—About which David speaks and which Abraham possessed. Since it is established that blessedness is from grace through faith, now it is asked among whom it exists, whether among the Jews alone or also among the Gentiles.

We say—speaking according to the meaning of the law
faith—not circumcision

4:10 How, then, was it reputed? In circumcision or in foreskin? Not in circumcision, but in foreskin.

in circumcision. In other words, was the faith of Abraham reputed as justice at the time of circumcision? *but in foreskin*. Or at the time of foreskin?

> *How . . . was it reputed?*—In what condition? Therefore I ask this, in other words: Since we know that Abraham was just by faith, and this is certain, then in what condition was he? Was it after he was circumcised or before? And what is seen in him can be believed about others.
> *in circumcision*—when he was circumcised
> *or*—or also
> *in foreskin*—before he was circumcised
> *Not,* etc.—here he gives the answer
> *in circumcision*—i.e., this blessedness is not only for Jews
> *in foreskin*—it is also for Gentiles

4:11 And he received the sign of circumcision, a seal of the justice of faith that is in foreskin, that he might be the father of all who believe through foreskin, so that it may also be reputed to them for justice.

the sign. Exterior circumcision is called a sign of interior circumcision. And such a sign becomes a seal which bears a likeness to the thing signified. Thus, just as a man is stripped of the flesh in the member of sexual desire, so he should be stripped of all filthiness of his first birth. And because he had not yet said of what it was a sign, he adds *of the justice* which is *of faith*. Or it is a seal that conceals a certain mystery, because it should be concealed from enemies, i.e., the unfaithful, and be kept for friends, i.e., the faithful, according to the likeness of a seal. Thus just as a male is circumcised on the eighth day, so on the eighth day, after the end of the world's seven days, all decrepitude of sin and punishment will be taken away.

The circumcision of Abraham was commended so that, living under the law of commandment, his obedience might be proved. Now first it was instituted for the sake of obedience; second for a sign of Abraham's great faith; third that this people might be distinguished from other nations; fourth that chastity of mind and body might be shown for preserving purity, and for this reason it was made in the male member; fifth because there was no better way to signify that original sin is taken away by Christ. And circumcision used to be performed on the eighth day with a stone knife because in the eighth age, which will be the age of all the resurrected, the corruption of flesh and spirit will be cut away from the elect by Christ the rock. These, then, are the realities behind this sacrament, namely the cutting away of sins in the present life and of every corruption in the life to come. Moreover circumcision used to confer in its time the same things that baptism confers in our time. Again, what the water of baptism does for us, faith alone accomplished for children and the power of sacrifice for adults among the ancients, and the mystery of circumcision for those who are of Abraham's lineage. But it was changed to baptism because the sacrament of baptism is more perfect, more common, and more full of grace, for it remits sins, increases virtues, confers the grace of cooperating, and is common to both sexes, which circumcision is not.

through foreskin, i.e., through what was given to him at the time of foreskin, i.e., through faith. Or through foreskin, i.e., in foreskin, i.e., in the time of foreskin.

> *he received the sign of circumcision*—And since he was just before, why then was he circumcised? It was not superfluous, but he received the sign of circumcision, not to make him just, but to show that he was just.
> *of the justice*—already obtained
> *in foreskin*—of Abraham himself before he was circumcised
> *that*—and this is true in order that
> *the father*—the founder of faith
> *so that*—and indeed that
> *that it may also be reputed*—that believing in God may be reputed
> *for justice*—for the remission of sins and good works

4:12 And thus he might be the father of circumcision, not only to those who are of circumcision but also to those who follow in the footsteps of the faith that is in the foreskin of our father Abraham.

the father—the founder of justice
circumcision—which is done by faith through example
of circumcision—i.e., of the Jews, of carnal circumcision
but also—since faith is reputed for justice
who follow in the footsteps of the faith—that they may believe
    as fully as he did
in the foreskin—in the time of his foreskin
our father Abraham—the father of all who believe

4:13 Indeed the promise to Abraham and to his seed, that he would be heir of the world, was not by the law but by the justice of faith.

Indeed the promise. The promise made to Christ was different than that to Abraham. The promise made to Abraham was that all who should imitate him would be blessed by Christ; but the promise to Christ was different: that he would not only be the exemplar and form in the establishment of morals and good works but that he would also bless those imitating him with an eternal blessing. *to his seed,* i.e., to all believers who are the seed of Abraham, not in flesh but in imitation; or to Christ, to whom the promise is said to have been made because it was to be fulfilled in him. *not by the law.* Abraham is the heir of the world according to the proposed example because all are his children through faith. Christ is the Lord of the world according to the power by which the blessing is bestowed on the children of Abraham. To him the Father gave the nations and the ends of the earth (Ps. 2:8).

    to Abraham—to him or of him, in the sense that the promise
        regards the work of his seed
    his seed—Christ
    that—this is the promise, namely that:
    he would be the heir of the world—the possessor of those peo-
        ple from the whole world who imitate him; and he that is
        born of Christ will possess all things in him
    was not—was not made
    not by the law but by the justice of faith—in other words, Abra-
        ham is our father by faith because the promise is through
        faith, not through the law nor through a circumcision that
        did not yet exist

4:14 For if those who are of the law are heirs, then faith has been nullified, the promise has been abolished.

For if those, etc. Abraham is not the heir of the world through the law because people are not his children through the law. His children are called heirs because what he has they also possess. For if it were through the law, absurdities would follow: faith, by which it is certain that Abraham was just, would be rendered null and the promise would be unfulfilled, so that there would be no heirs. Indeed the law makes no heirs but rather works wrath, and wrath works transgression. For transgression comes from it and without it there is no transgression. Because these absurdities follow if the promise were from the law, they are therefore heirs by faith, and in this way the promise is firm.

> *if those*—if only those
> *are heirs*—are said to be heirs
> *then*—then these absurdities follow, namely that:
> *faith*—by which it is certain that Abraham was just
> *has been nullified*—has been made of no effect
> *the promise has been abolished*—left unfulfilled, so that there
> are no heirs

4:15 The law indeed works wrath; for where there is no law, there is no transgression.

The law indeed works wrath. It is not that the law makes transgressors guilty as an efficient cause but that it does not provide helping grace; or to make them liable to temporal punishment the law works wrath because it causes transgression. And how this is so he reveals, saying: *for where there is no law, there is no transgression.* He does not say there is no sin, for everyone that trespasses against the law is sinful, but not the other way around. Those who have not received the law can be called sinful but cannot be called transgressors.

> *The law ... works wrath*—the law was given for this reason,
> that it might make people guilty; in other words, the law
> does not make people heirs but rather assigns punishment
> *no law ... no transgression*—since grace has been given to
> those who have been removed from the law, and there is
> no transgression for the justified

4:16 Therefore it is of faith, so that according to grace the promise may be firm to all the seed; it is not only to him that is of the law but also to him that is of the faith of Abraham, who is the father of us all.

it is not only to him that is of the law. Because such a one departs from grace; and *therefore*, on account *of faith*, one must withdraw from the law, so that *the promise may be firm.* For without the grace of the promise, the law not only cannot take away sin but even increases it.

> *it is of faith*—namely, the inheritance, which is a gift of mercy, was given on account of faith
> *according to grace*—which assists us through faith; not according to the merits of legal works
> *the promise*—of God's Son
> *may be firm*—the promise to the guilty is not firm from the law
> *to all the seed*—to those who imitate Abraham, both Jew and Gentile
> *it is*—it comes
> *him that is of the law*—i.e., who presumes on the works of the law
> *to him that is of the faith of Abraham*—who follows Abraham's faith
> *the father*—the founder by example
> *of us all*—who believe

4:17 Thus is it written: *I have made you a father of many nations*, before God in whom you have believed, who brings the dead to life and calls things that are not as things that are.

Who brings the dead to life, or, in another reading: who calls the dead. *things that are not as things that are.* These are things that are predestined or ordained, for things that are going to be are already present to him, in which grace alone is manifest.[111] Hence it says in another place: *Who made the things that are to come* (Isa. 44:7); and again: *Who chose us before the foundation of the world* (Eph. 1:4). They are chosen who do not exist; nor does he who chooses make a mistake or choose to no effect. Nevertheless he chooses them and considers them to be his elect, whom he was going to create to be chosen; whom he considers to be with him, not in his own nature, but in his presence. They did not yet exist to whom it was being promised, but those to whom it was being promised were themselves also promised.[112] And in this way he calls things that are not as though they are. In other words, for those who do not exist he ordains and prepares from eternity the grace of justification and glorification to be provided in time. *things that are*, i.e., as though they are in those who are already with God through predestination. Or, *who . . . calls*, i.e., he knows the things that exist in potentiality as though they existed in actuality, etc.

> *Thus is it written*—Scripture confirms this in Genesis
>   (Gen. 17:5)
> *you*—O Abraham
> *a father*—a founder according to faith
> *many nations*—which are not circumcised
> *before God*—you who are before God, who are pleasing to God
> *in whom you have believed*—to whom you are pleasing
>   through faith
> *who*—of whom it should be believed that he exists
> *brings the dead to life*—or calls the dead; through faith and grace
> *the dead*—in their sins; the Jews
> *things that are not*—i.e., the Gentiles who seemed to be nothing
> *things that are*—i.e., the Jews who seemed to be something

4:18 He believed with hope against hope, so that he became the father of many nations, according to what was said to him: *Thus your seed shall be like the stars of heaven and as the sand of the sea.*

He believed. He begins to commend the faith of Abraham so that we may imitate him. By faith he received justice and the great promise. *against hope*. Against his earlier hope: when he was young he naturally hoped for a child from his young wife, but did not have one; now he hoped against this hope that by God's power he would beget as an old man from his old and sterile wife. *Thus your seed shall be*. It should be understood that Abraham was the first to know that God was three in one, and by the merit of this faith he obtained forgiveness of all his sins. But after obtaining justice he received the promise from God that he would be the father of many nations; then the promise was made to him again, that his seed would be like the stars.

> *He*—Abraham
> *with hope*—expecting with certitude

against hope—of nature
the father of many nations—historically, or according to faith
according to what—he believed so completely
was said to him—in Genesis (Gen. 22:17)
like the stars of heaven and as the sand of the sea—that is, innumerable good people, who are signified by stars, will be
   born from you, while evil people are signified by sand

4:19 And he was not weakened in faith, nor did he consider his own decrepit body, although he was then nearly a hundred years old, or the decrepit womb of Sarah.

he was not weakened. Those who were puffed up from knowledge of the world were not mindful of God, and therefore God did impossible things so that, believing in these, they might be saved.

and—and afterwards
he was not weakened in faith—although he had reason, namely
   his old age and Sarah's sterility; yet he was not weakened
   in faith
decrepit—in terms of the capacity for procreation
although—knowing that the power of the one that promised
   him exceeded every impossibility

4:20 At the promise of God he did not waver in unbelief, but was strengthened in faith, giving glory to God,

at the promise, etc. Isaac, who was promised contrary to the natural course of human generation, was meant as a sign that God's Son was going to be born of woman against human reckoning, and that human children were going to be generated by the Spirit of regeneration from sinners into children of God, from mortals into immortals.

the promise—when the angel promised again: *At this time I*
   will come and Sarah will have a son (Gen. 18:10)
he did not waver in unbelief—even though the promise was
   delayed
was strengthened—was confirmed
giving glory to God—for the constancy of faith

4:21 knowing full well that God is able to accomplish whatever he has promised.

> *knowing full well*—by deep reflection on God's power
> *is able to accomplish*—as easily as to promise
> *whatever*—the Gentiles should imitate these things, believing
>   *God is able to accomplish whatever*, etc.
> *he has promised*—it does not say he predicted because he him-
>   self brings it about; if another should accomplish it, it
>   would not be to promise but to predict

4:22 And therefore it was reputed to him for justice.

> *therefore it was reputed to him for justice*—because, strength-
> ened in faith, he accepted the promise and was made just

4:23 Now it was not only written for his sake, that it was reputed to him as justice,

> *Now*—as if someone has asked what is this to us?
> *for his sake*—for his praise alone

4:24 but also for our sake, to whom it will be reputed, who believe in the one that has raised Jesus Christ our Lord from the dead,

> *for our sake*—for instructing us
> *the one*—namely God the Father
> *who raised Jesus Christ our Lord*—as if to say that what he did
>   is beneficial for us
> *from the dead*—i.e., from the grave, which is the proper place
>   of the dead

4:25 who was delivered up for our sins and who rose again for our justification.

was delivered up. The death of Christ signifies the destruction of the old life; and his resurrection signifies the new life that begins at justification and is perfected in immortality. Christ's death and resurrection in us are the same in terms of effect, because they free us from sins and the yoke of the devil, but their significations are different. For his death signifies that we should die to the old life while his resurrection signifies that we should so walk in newness of life that we shall at last rise to the newness of immortality, as Christ already has.

> *was delivered up*—to death; by God the Father, by Judas, and by Pilate
> *for our sins*—taking them away, when the jurisdiction of the devil was destroyed
> *who rose again*—in which new life is signified
> *for our justification*—so that we might live justly, which otherwise we could not do

Chapter 5

5:1 Therefore, having been justified by faith, let us have peace towards God through our Lord Jesus Christ,

having been justified, etc. Because justification is by faith, have peace with God, as though to say: This dissension among yourselves is against God. *by faith*. Earlier he said, *having been justified freely by his grace* (Rom. 3:24), lest they be proud of faith itself. For *what do you have that you have not received* (1 Cor. 4:7)? *peace towards God*. Because we are reconciled to him through Christ, the minister of grace.

> *by faith*—not from the law nor from ourselves
> *peace*—which you do not have when you are arrogant toward
>   one another
> *through our Lord Jesus Christ*—through his help and grace

5:2 through whom we have access by faith to that grace in which we stand, and we boast in the hope of the glory of the children of God.

through whom. He enumerates the blessings that we have from Christ.

> *through whom*—through whose works
> *we have access*—not only to God but also to grace
> *that grace*—the observance of a good life
> *we stand*—we who fell in Adam stand erect in the hope of
>   supernal glory
> *we boast*—about that for which we hope, the glory that the
>   children of God possess
> *the children of God*—the angels or the saints of God

5:3 And not only this, but we also boast in tribulations, knowing that tribulation works patience,

tribulation works patience. Because love, which is a gift of the Spirit, keeps tribulation from destroying patience.

> *not only this*—not only do we boast about the hope of glory
> *we also boast*—through his grace
> *in tribulations*—which we suffer for Christ's sake; by which we attain glory
> *knowing*—Why do we boast? Because we know, etc.

5:4 patience works testing, and testing works hope.

hope, i.e., certainty of future glory, which seems vain to human reason but is confirmed by the testimony of truth, namely of patience and of miracles.

> *testing*—purification

5:5 Moreover hope does not disappoint, because the love of God has been poured out into our hearts by the Holy Spirit who was given to us.

Moreover hope does not disappoint. Because it is hope in God who does not deceive and not hope in deceitful humanity; and God's pledge of hope is his Spirit. It is read: May the fountain of your water be your own and may no stranger partake of you.[113] This is the Spirit whom the wicked cannot receive, and it is love which someone cannot possess and be evil. But an evil person is able to have the name of Christ and baptism, to eat the Lord's body and have the other sacraments, and still be evil. Love, then, is a particular gift and singular fountain of the Spirit.

the love of God has been poured out. Or God has loved us profusely. And we have this in our hearts through the Spirit, who causes us to understand God's love towards us.

> *hope does not disappoint*—it does not cause embarrassment since it is fulfilled

by the Holy Spirit—It is not from ourselves. It is certain that our hope will be fulfilled because we already have the Spirit as a pledge.

who was given to us—he is God and the gift of God

5:6 For when we were still weak, why did Christ die for the ungodly for a time?

when we were still weak. Behold, while he hated us on account of sins, he loved us on account of his work that he did even before the foundation of the world. How much he loved us had to be expressed so that we might not despair. And what kind of love it was had to be expressed so that we would not be proud. There was another way possible for God, who can do all things, but no other way was as suitable for the healing of our misery. For what lifts us up and frees us from despair more than the fact that he held us in such esteem that he died as a man for our sake?

why did Christ die? Since God loves us, or since we love him through the Spirit, then our hope will be fulfilled. For if this were not true, then Christ suffered in vain. And this is the reason Christ died *for the ungodly*, i.e., for love of the ungodly, or in place of the ungodly. Not for those who were formerly ungodly and then changed, but *when we were still weak* in our sins. *for a time*, i.e., for three days only, so that you may not despair of his power, whose kindness appears in death. And from him we have received strong pledges in that he offered his death for the ungodly and preserves his life for the just.[114] He died for you, O mortal, that you might live with him. He accepted our death that he might give us his own life. He received from you the cause whence he would die for you. He clothed himself that he might die for you; he will clothe you that you might live with him. He clothed himself with mortal flesh in the virginity of his mother; he will clothe you with everlasting life in the equality of the Father.[115]

> *still weak*—so weak in sins, as though needing a physician
> *why*—unless our hope were going to be fulfilled
> *did Christ die*—did he perform so great a deed
> *for the ungodly*—for love of the ungodly, or in place of those that should die

5:7 Scarcely will anyone die for a just person, for perhaps someone may venture to die for a good person.

He says *scarcely* will anyone die for a just person and *perhaps* for a good person, showing that both are difficult and rare, but the first is more difficult and rarer. *for a just person … for a good person.* A good person is also called just from the practice of goodness; but there is also a good person who is not just, i.e., someone that was born in simplicity or an innocent person that has not yet labored to develop himself in good works, such as a child cleansed in baptism. And while a just person is better, the cause of innocence is more pitiable than the cause of justice, because justice of this kind is not without severity.[116]

> *scarcely*—i.e., hardly
> *die for a just person*—and the deed was truly great, for rarely
> will someone die for a just person, i.e., for love of a just
> and good person, let alone for an ungodly person
> *for*—I say scarcely, *for perhaps someone may venture*, etc.
> *perhaps*—i.e., rarely
> *a good person*—a simple and innocent person, for perhaps one
> can be found

5:8 But God commends his love in us since if Christ died at the proper time for us, when we were still sinners,

> *God commends*—he commends his love in this way, that it is
> for sinners; and if this is true, then he will save the just,
> which means that hope is not disappointed
> *his love*—namely of Christ for sinners, in whom love is more
> praiseworthy
> *in us*—who were unworthy
> *if*—or without "if"
> *Christ died*—just as Christ died

5:9 how much more then, now that we are justified in his blood, shall we be saved from wrath through him?

how much more. It is harder to die for sin and to take away sin than to save those who are already just and cooperating with grace. *in his blood.*

Thus the devil is overcome by justice, not power. It was justice because the devil, while he had the right to destroy others, killed someone that did not deserve it, namely, Christ. It was not power because the devil is a lover of power and deserter of justice, in which way people most imitate him. Therefore it pleased God to rescue humanity, conquering not in power but in justice, leaving him an example to imitate. But later power followed in the resurrection, because the dead Christ arose never to die again.

> *from wrath*—the cause of which is nothing besides sin, which
> has been taken away
> *through him*—i.e., through him that lives

5:10 For if, when we were enemies, we were reconciled to God through the death of his Son, much more, having been reconciled, shall we be saved in his life.

enemies. Not sinners in every way.[117] **we were reconciled**. Before this we were justly under the devil's power, our nature corrupted by sin.

> *through the death of his Son*—this has the same meaning as the
> phrase above: *in his blood*
> *reconciled*—not only freed from wrath, but also reconciled
> *shall we be saved*—It is certain that he that now lives will
> be able to save the friends that were made because,
> having died, he was able to justify them. By that deed
> those who were enemies because of sin were reconciled
> and are now God's friends.
> *in his life*—through the life by which he rose again from the
> dead

5:11 And not only this, but we also boast in God through our Lord Jesus Christ, through whom we have now received reconciliation.

> *not only this*—not only shall we be saved
> *we also boast*—already in hope of what we shall be
> *in God*—we boast that we shall be like him, not by nature, but
> by love and will; or in the present we boast in God and
> not in ourselves

through our Lord Jesus Christ—not through ourselves but
    through Christ
now—already in the present
reconciliation—to God, since we separated from God in
    Adam's sin

5:12 Therefore, just as by one man, in whom all have sinned, sin entered this world, and through sin, death, so death passed to all people.

Therefore. He said above that Christ is justice and life; and what can come through him Paul intends to prove in the syllogism's minor through a similitude: For *just as by . . . sin . . . and . . . death*, etc. *by one man*, namely Adam; the apostle did not say by one woman, Eve. He was following common convention when he attributed to man, not woman, the succession of human posterity which succumbed to sin and to death that came from sin. For it is customary that posterity be named not from the woman but from the man. Or it may be because the woman came from the man and both were one flesh, therefore one may say by Eve or by Adam since both pertain to the first man. And by this the apostle wished to be understood the original sin of propagation whose source is Adam, not the sin of imitation whose source is the devil, from whose envy death entered into the earthly world.[118]

to all people. Because even before the law, when it would not seem so evil, since the law was not providing instruction, it was surely accounted sin in the sight of people. Yet they did not realize that sin was going to be punished in the sight of God, since it was not known that he was going to judge the world. But when the law was given they knew that God was concerned with human affairs and judged them.[119] Before the law it was not imputed; nevertheless death reigned, with the devil holding people in his power, but it was not considered as punishment until Moses, through whom the knowledge of the one God returned. Death also reigned,[120] however, over those who were like the transgressor Adam, who neglected God and served the creature, just as Adam consented to the devil instead of God. And this is how almost all lived until the coming of the law. A small number served the one God like Abraham, and death did not have dominion over them, but they were preserved under hope in the coming of Christ to liberate them. Books that maintain otherwise, says Ambrose, have been corrupted. They say it means that bodily death reigned until

Moses even over the worshipers of the one God. But in that case why not until the end of the world?[121]

in whom all have sinned. <u>Augustine</u>: They have sinned in his material substance, not only by his example, and all were that one man or all were in that sin; for other sins are their own.[122]

> *Therefore*—Through Christ justice and life come to all who have been regenerated by his grace. Life comes through one man just as death came from one man.
> *one man*—Adam, from whom we have been propagated
> *sin*—original sin
> *this world*—which is miserable on account of sin; sin came to all people, in other words
> *death*—death came to Adam himself, i.e., the dissolution of soul and body
> *to all people*—born through corrupted flesh

5:13 Sin indeed was in the world up to the law, but sin was not imputed since the law did not exist.

in whom all have sinned . . . up to the law. For the law, whether natural law or written law, was not able to take away sin but rather increased it. And *sin was not imputed*, i.e., it was not recognized. Nevertheless sin reigned up to Moses, i.e., the law, since the law could not remove the reign of death. Death reigns when it does not allow the guilty to reach eternal life but pulls them down to Gehenna. Only the grace of Christ destroyed this reign, which was also true among the ancient faithful. Over all except them death reigned, even over those who did not sin by their own will, as Adam had, but who were being held by original sin, such as children. *up to the law* (or up to Moses). This includes the law, because also at that time existed sin and death, i.e., damnation. And therefore "up to" is not exclusive as it is in other places. *up to the law.* Because at that time a remedy was given to people by which they were able to be free. Under the law, however, when they were like Adam in transgression, death reigned over them. But the law was given at the beginning of their departure from Egypt. It taught about the one God so that death might not reign; and the kingdom of death first began to be destroyed in Judea, which is now being destroyed everywhere.

sin—although it was not seen as such

in the world—i.e., in the human race

up to the law—i.e., before the law, the written or the natural
law; also under the law

not imputed—in the sight of people since they were blind.
Judgment of sin was imputed in the sight of God:
*Those who have sinned without the law shall perish without
the law* (Rom. 2:12). In God's sight sin appeared just as it
existed in the wicked.

the law did not exist—the law which prohibits sin; the law of
reason in a child or the written law among the people,
which make sin known by reproving it

**5:14 Yet death reigned from Adam to Moses, even over those who did
not sin in the likeness of Adam's transgression, who is a figure of the
one to come.**

Yet death reigned. Sin was not being imputed but its effect, death, revealed it, because corporeal death reigned every day in certain passions
and finally by destroying the body. *to Moses*, when it seemed to be weakened. *Yet death reigned.* It should be noted here that most manuscripts
omit "not" and read: Death reigned from Adam to Moses over those who
sinned in the likeness of Adam's transgression. Thus they understand the
words, *who sinned in the likeness of Adam's transgression*, to refer to those
who sinned in Adam.[123] In this way they were created like him, namely
just as they were human from a human, so they are sinners from a sinner,
mortal from a mortal, condemned from a condemned one.

who is a figure. Adam is a figure of Christ because, just as Adam is the
father of all according to the flesh, so Christ is the father of all according
to faith; and just as Eve was formed from Adam's side, so the sacraments
by which the Church is saved flowed out from the side of Christ. Therefore just as Adam was able to communicate sin to his children, and death,
so Christ is able to communicate his own justice and life to his children.
Truly Christ is able to confer more good to his children than Adam
conferred death to his, and thus he is able to save more than Adam lost.

death—of the body, of the soul

to Moses—i.e., up to the law promulgated from heaven
through Moses

even over those—not only over those who through their own
sins appeared to deserve death but also over children who
of themselves deserved nothing from transgressing any law

in the likeness of Adam's transgression—i.e., resembling the
transgressor Adam

a figure—a likeness, referring to Adam

of the one to come—of Christ

**5:15 But the transgression is not like the gift: for if many died in the
transgression of one, much more did the grace and gift of God abound
to more in the grace of the one man Jesus Christ.**

There are similarities between Christ and Adam, but the offense is not
similar in the sense that Adam's sin is not effective to damnation in the
same way that Christ's grace is effective to salvation. In other words,
their causes are not equal, nor are the effects equal. As we read: *the transgression is not like the gift*. The causal principle that comes from Christ
is abundant grace by which a person has all good things, and without
which he has nothing good. The causal principle that comes from Adam
is that sin of which all who are generated carnally are guilty. They have
many other sins from themselves, but they are prone to sin from that
original sin. And rightly is this causal principle from Christ beneficial
to all his own because, if the causal principle from Adam is harmful to
all his descendants, then also Christ's causal principle was able to be
beneficial to those that are his. And this is what it states: *for if many died
in the transgression of one*. For the effect of Adam's causal principle, i.e.,
the effect of the sin which he brought in, is not total condemnation but
a condemnation that is owed because of that one man, since there are
also other condemnations from our additional sins. The effect of Christ's
gifts, after all sins have been taken away, both original and actual, is total
justification and eternal life. And rightly did this come through the one
Christ to his own, because if condemnation came through one Adam
to his own, then this was also able to come through Christ to his own.
Adam, it says, *is a figure of the one to come*, because already at that time
God had decreed in a mystery to repair through the one Christ what had
come through the one sin of Adam. Hence in the Apocalypse it says that
the lamb was slain before the beginning of the world (Rev. 13:8).

the transgression is not like the gift. The figure is in this: One man sinned,
one man repairs. But the causal principle from Adam is not qualitatively

the same as the causal principle from Christ, for there is one transgression of Adam by which many died who similarly transgressed; but the grace of Christ comes to more because it comes both to those who similarly transgress and to those who do not. *For if many died in the transgression of one.* <u>Ambrose</u>: Death reigned then, but no longer reigns, because those who through the law feared God when his judgment was made known were lifted up from the kingdom of death; but before the law death was dominant in the likeness of Adam. And if death reigned at that time, how much more should grace reign, which has passed over to more people and which confers life. When he says "all" later (Rom. 5:18), he likewise means all who sin and all who believe, for there is no general condemnation or justification for all. Hence he says afterward: *many* (Rom. 5:19).[124] *in the grace.* By grace he means the perfection of virtues in the man Christ.

> *But the transgression is not like the gift*—it is a figure, but the gift of Christ is greater than the transgression of Adam
> *many*—namely, all his descendants, who imitate his transgression
> *died*—were made sinners
> *in the transgression*—indeed by that single transgression
> *of one*—of the one man, Adam
> *grace*—gratuitous gift or grace, i.e., forgiveness of sin, which is bountiful, greater, and better than all his other gifts
> *gift*—the lofty gifts of the Holy Spirit
> *abound*—because it also absolves additional sins
> *to more*—not comparatively but absolutely, as if to say "to many"; grace abounds to more, i.e., it passes down to all his children
> *in*—i.e., through

5:16 And what was through the one transgression is not like the gift: for the judgment from one is unto condemnation, but the grace from many transgressions is unto justification.

> *was*—came about
> *transgression*—or sin
> *is not like*—because those who are in the one man Adam are condemned like him
> *for*—but rather

the judgment—of God

from one—proceeding from one man, from his original transgression

unto condemnation—of corporeal and of eternal death, if it is not forgiven

grace—of Christ

from many—not from one

is unto—results in

justification—it not only forgives but also justifies in this life

5:17 For if in the transgression of one man death reigned through the one man, much more through the one man Jesus Christ shall they reign in life, receiving an abundance of grace and blessing and justice.

death reigned through the one man. Because the powers that were in him he exercised for all his posterity, of whom he was the matter; and likewise it was his guilt alone that was transfused into all. *much more* shall they reign in life, because they shall reign eternally; more than death reigned in them, because it reigned temporally and with an end.

For—because

if—and this is possible because it leads even to eternal life

the transgression of one man—even if their own sins were not added

death—dissolution of soul and body

reigned—even before death, the passions produce death

through the one man—Adam

much more—because there is greater power here than is in the kingdom of death

shall they reign—eternally in incorruption

life—eternal life

receiving—possessing these from God, not from themselves

abundance—because their own sins are also forgiven

grace—forgiveness

blessing—charisms

justice—good works

5:18 Therefore, just as through the transgression of one unto condemnation to all, so also through the justice of one unto justification of life to all.

through the justice of one. Not that all born from Adam are regenerated by Christ, but just as there is no carnal generation except through Adam, so there is no spiritual generation except through Christ. If anyone were generated apart from Adam, or if anyone were regenerated apart from Christ, he would not say "all" and "all." But just as no one is outside of that generation, so no just person is outside this regeneration. In the following verse he will call the same people "many."

> *Therefore*—seeing that Adam is a figure of Christ, therefore
>   . . . ; and because the gift of Christ is greater and confers
>   more
> *just as*—how deservedly
> *unto condemnation*—condemnation of body and soul came
>   from a man; or the sentence of God resulted in condem-
>   nation
> *to all*—who likewise sin; being passed along, not by imitation
>   but by propagation
> *justice*—sufficient for all
> *unto justification*—it came from a man; or the sentence of
>   God resulted in justification, as above
> *of life*—justification is the cause of life
> *to all*—if they be willing

5:19 For just as by the disobedience of one man many were made sinners, so also by the obedience of one man many will be made just.

For just as. He compares the transgression of one man and the justice of one man, so that just as one brought us to ruin by the merit of his sin, so the other may be seen to have liberated us by the merit of his justice. *so also by the obedience of one man.* Of a man, he says, and not of God or of the Word, lest you think that the ancients who were righteous were freed in God's Word alone, i.e., only by faith in the Word without faith in the incarnation.

> *one man*—Adam
> *many*—i.e., all who are his and not Christ's
> *so*—rightly
> *one man*—Christ
> *many*—all who are his

5:20 Now the law entered so that transgression might abound, but where transgression abounded, grace abounded all the more.

Now the law. He has shown that Christ forgives all sins, both original and actual; here he adds that Christ also frees from the sin of the law, i.e., from transgression, so that the Jews might be more answerable to Christ. *the law entered.* <u>Ambrose</u>: Here the apostle is speaking about what happened after the law was given, rather than about what the law did.[125] For it had been given to help nature: seeds of justice were planted in nature, after a manner, so that from them justice might grow. But the people, following their custom, sinned more, the devil turning the good law to evil. To counter this evil God has pardoned all sins. *Now the law entered.* To those who are born in sins the law is given to conquer pride. It is not as though he fails who commands the law, but he fails who would fulfill the law; since he is born in sin he cannot fulfill the law. This is the reason Christ was born, i.e., the grace that might bring healing.

so that transgression might abound. Great was God's counsel, that through the law transgression might abound so that, in the harshness of the law, the weak who understood their own infirmity might flee to the remedy and seek the help of grace. *but where transgression abounded.* Here he is discussing the power of grace and how much it accomplishes. *grace abounded all the more,* both because the grace of Christ is also effective for those whom the devil was unable to conquer,[126] and because sin reigned for a time while grace reigns forever.

> *the law*—justification is through Christ
> *entered*—it entered secretly[127] after sin, or after the natural law
> *that transgression might abound*—if it were more abundantly known
> *but where transgression abounded*—but the Jew should not therefore be despised; but Christ heals this also; or, sin abounded through the law
> *grace abounded all the more*—pardoning all sins

5:21 Thus, just as sin reigned unto death, so also grace will reign through justice unto eternal life through Jesus Christ our Lord.

just as sin reigned unto death. He does not add "through one man" or "through Adam" because he is not only discussing the fact that people have contracted sin from Adam but also that they have added sins by their own will. When he says, **grace will reign**, however, he adds **through Jesus Christ**, because through him is accomplished not only the forgiveness of original sin but also the forgiveness of voluntary sins.

> *Thus*—meaning: let no one entrusted to grace think he may sin safely; rather, let grace be vigorous and through justice let it lead him toward life, just as sin had been vigorous, leading to death
>
> *sin*—which is in addition to Adam's sin
>
> *reigned unto death*—leading to eternal death
>
> *grace*—of the remission of sins
>
> *will reign*—in the elect
>
> *through justice*—good works
>
> *unto eternal life*—bringing them to eternal life
>
> *through Jesus Christ*—without whom there is no justice

Chapter 6

6:1 What, then, shall we say? Shall we remain in sin that grace may abound?

Shall we remain. The perverse take it in this way from the words above: *where transgression abounded, grace abounded all the more.* To say this is to be ungrateful for grace. And the fact that grace flourishes where transgression has abounded does not mean someone should remain in sin, as some think, for the sake of greater grace. For grace abounded more where transgression abounded not from the merit of the sinner but from the help of the one assisting.[128] Therefore we should not remain in sin but rather ought to be and are able to be as though dead and buried to sin by this very grace, and to rise to righteousness and afterwards to eternal life.

6:2 May it never be! For we who have died to sin, how shall we still live in it?

we who have died to sin. Who have, in other words, been freed from sin through baptism so that, through grace, sin may no longer rule in us. To die to sin is to be free from sin. *how shall we still,* etc. For when grace accomplishes this, that we die to sin, then what else are we doing when we live in sin but showing that we are ungrateful for grace?

> *May it never be!*—For truly sin must not remain
> *For we*—namely, now that we have grace; because we have
>   died to sin; or, if we have died to sin
> *died to sin*—so that, through God's grace, sin may no longer
>   have dominion over us
> *how*—by what means

how shall we still live in it?—how shall we give back power to
    the enemy
still—after so great a blessing

6:3 Or do you not know, brothers, that all of us who have been baptized in Christ Jesus have been baptized into his death?

Or do you not know. Having died to sin, which happened in baptism, we should not live in it again so that it is necessary to die again. *into his death*, i.e., in the likeness of Christ's death, for just as he once died in the flesh and lives forever, we, having once died to evil through baptism, should always live for doing good; or he says into death because death is the cause of this purification.

Or—having died
do you not know—he often accuses them of ignorance; as if to
    say: You should not be so ignorant
all—of any condition whatsoever
baptized—purified from sins
in Christ Jesus—in his institution of baptism, which is in the
    name of the Trinity; or in the operation of Christ, the one
    who truly baptizes

6:4 For we have been buried with him through baptism into death so that, just as Christ rose from the dead by the glory of the Father, we too may thus walk in newness of life.

buried with him. Whatever was done in the cross of Christ, in his burial, in his resurrection, in his ascension, and in his being seated at God's right hand, it was done in such a way that by these things understood mystically (not only things that were spoken but also things that were performed), the Christian life is signified. Look at each of the deeds of Christ. He lived to old age, not in terms of sin but in terms of suffering, of hunger and thirst and the like. And in this way he ended and put aside old age so that, bearing the pain of the cross, he might hold his members stretched out and fixed, lest they be moved to earlier acts. And being buried he rested from these, drawn away from human sight. Thus he requires of us that we should lay aside our old age of sin with the sorrow and groaning of repentance, and that our members should be fixed by continence and righteousness lest we return to earlier evils, from which we should rest so completely that no image or memory of them remains.[129] And he not only demands this of us in the sacrament of his passion but he also causes us to imitate him, if we are willing. *rose from the dead.* The death and resurrection of Christ are also sacraments.

> *we have been buried*—in baptism we are truly conformed to the death of Christ, because we have been buried with him by faith
> *with him through baptism*—drawn into a likeness of him
> *into death*—the absolution of sins
> *so that*—for this reason we died with him and were buried with him
> *from the dead*—far removed from the dead
> *by the glory of the Father*—through God's word or grace
> *we too may thus*—firmly rising up again from our sins to good works
> *walk*—from the good to the better
> *in newness of life*—placed there by the righteousness of faith and the hope of glory. As if to say: Let us walk in newness of life, which we are able to do.

6:5 For if we became planted together in the likeness of his death, at the same time we shall also be of the resurrection.

> *we became planted together*—in the image of a tree
> *in the likeness of his death*—if, having been removed from the old rite, we cling firmly to God who does the work himself, then we also resemble the death of Christ
> *at the same time*—soon
> *we shall also be*—we shall become planted together in the likeness of his resurrection
> *the resurrection*—of Christ, that we may walk in newness of life

6:6 We know this, that since our old humanity was crucified together, the body of sin is destroyed so that we might no longer serve sin.

our old humanity. Our old acts have been crucified, i.e., have died. *since our old humanity.* Our oldness, our curse, consists in two things: guilt and punishment. Christ destroyed his own single oldness and also our double oldness. For he rested in the tomb for one day and two nights: his single oldness is signified by one day, our double oldness by two nights. Hence Christ abolished our guilt, present, past, and future: our past guilt by forgiving it, our present guilt by drawing us back from sin, our future guilt by conferring grace to live. And likewise he destroyed our punishment by abolishing hell altogether so that the truly repentant do not experience it. He took away temporal punishment too, but not completely, since hunger, thirst, death, and the like remain. Yet he has cast out their rule and dominion, and ultimately he will put an end to them entirely. *the body of sin is destroyed*. Namely the flesh has been subjected to the spirit.

> *We know this*—he shows how this is possible; knowing this, let us walk, I say, in newness of life
> *our old humanity*—the inclination and habit of sin, which is from us and not from God
> *was crucified*—the old humanity was thus weakened in the crucifixion of Christ
> *together*—with Christ
> *the body of sin*—i.e., all sins, like a body or heap
> *is destroyed*—with reason now having dominion
> *so that we might no longer serve sin*—not that sin might not exist but that we might not be forced to serve it, because we have been justified

6:7 For he that has died is justified from sin.

> *For he*—surely we will not be compelled, because we are justified
> *that has died*—to sin, as we have
> *is justified from sin*—is just and free from sin

6:8 But if we have died with Christ, we believe that we shall also live together with him,

> *if we have died with Christ*—if we have thus died to sin as Christ once died for the punishment of sin; or if we have died with Christ, i.e., resembling his death, as was said above, then besides the aforementioned blessings we will also possess this: that we will live in eternal life
> *we shall also live together with him*—in such a life as he himself lives; not elsewhere but in the same place with him

6:9 knowing that Christ, who rose from the dead, dies no more; death shall no longer have dominion over him.

> *from the dead*—far removed from the dead
> *dies*—is dissolved by the division of soul and body
> *no more*—after this life
> *death shall no longer have dominion*—by any passion

6:10 In that he died for sin, he died once; but in that he lives, he lives for God.

In that he died for sin. Augustine: The apostle commends the mysteries of baptism, that in the same way Christ is preached—having died once by dying in the likeness of sin—so everyone who has been baptized in him, of whose reality baptism was a likeness, may die, i.e., to sin, and live by being born again from the bath just as Christ lived by rising again from the tomb.[130]

> *for sin*—for taking away our sin
> *he died once*—truly Christ dies no more because he died once
>   to take away sin; or he died once for sin, i.e., in the like-
>   ness of sin, i.e., in the flesh in which there was not sin but
>   the likeness of sin
> *in that he lives*—death will have no dominion over Christ, but
>   rather he lives
> *he lives for God*—in the likeness of God the Father: just as the
>   life of the Father receives no disturbance, so also the life
>   of Christ

6:11 So you too consider yourselves to be dead, indeed, to sin, but alive to God in Christ Jesus our Lord.

So you too. Here he ascribes to the Romans whatever he said above that people have by the grace of Christ.

> *So you too*—just as Christ died once, so sin died in you and
>   should not be repeated
> *alive*—in virtues
> *to God*—to the honor of God

in Christ Jesus—and this is by Christ's work, otherwise there is no hope

6:12 Therefore let not sin reign in your mortal body, that you should obey its desires;

Therefore let not sin. He said above that we have died to sin and should not live in it, but, since no one is without sin, he indicates what sins should be especially avoided, as though answering what was asked before: Shall we remain in sin? *that you should obey its desires.* Concupiscence sometimes means the desire of inclination, that is of innate vices; and sometimes the desire of interior act, which is in the first motion, where it is called propassion, or in the second motion, where it is called delight, or in the third motion, where it is called consent. Here he is not forbidding the concupiscence that is in the first motion since it is not within our power when it arises. But by God's grace we are able to restrain it so that it does not proceed to delight and consent, which he does forbid.

> *Therefore*—because you have died in this way to sin
> *let not sin*—the inclination to sin
> *reign*—even if it exists
> *in your mortal body*—through sin, because your body, now
> subject to your control, will become immortal in the
> future if sin does not reign in it; or by this he means that
> sin, which will have reigned, is going to die forever
> *that you should obey*—by consenting and performing
> *its desires*—even if you desire out of weakness

6:13 nor should you yield your bodies to sin as instruments of iniquity, but yield yourselves to God as those alive from the dead, and your members to God as instruments of righteousness.

> *nor should you yield your bodies*—but neither should you desire,
> which is to yield and adapt your members, which are then
> instruments
> *to sin*—to the sin of concupiscence
> *instruments of iniquity*—by which iniquity is carried out
> *but yield yourselves to God*—adapt yourselves to God, which
> you can do, because you who were dead should now
> be alive

alive—in virtues
from the dead—from vices and sins
and your members—even if you are unable or unwilling to
complete the work by which you will be adapted and
prepared, then yield your members, which you can easily do
as instruments of righteousness—by which justice is carried out

6:14 For sin shall not have dominion over you since you are not under the law, but under grace.

sin shall not have dominion over you—as it had at one time
not under the law—which did not give any help
but under grace—which refreshes and helps

6:15 What then? Shall we sin because we are not under the law, but under grace? May it never be!

What then? In other words, because the law is from God, he sins who dismisses it on account of grace. *Shall we sin because we are not under the law*, which brings fear, *but under grace*, which promises good things? *What then? Shall we sin?* Certain ones ask this, who preach the law as something that presses or coerces, and that it must be kept.[131]

shall we sin—with this assurance
the law—that brings fear
grace—that promises good things

6:16 Or do you not know that to what you yield yourselves as slaves to obey, you are slaves of that which you have obeyed: either of sin unto death or of obedience unto righteousness.

Or do you not know. Lest professing God in words we are devils in deeds, he reminds us that we are slaves of him whose will we do.

do you not know—that you should not sin but perform good
works, since *to what you yield*, etc.
to what you yield yourselves—to which desires you yield
yourselves
as slaves to obey—as those inclined to obey by consenting and
performing

> *you are slaves of that*—you will be forced to do its will by a
>   certain necessity which the habit of doing his will imparts
> *which you have obeyed*—after you have obeyed, even if not
>   before, when you first yielded yourselves
> *unto death*—leading to greater sin, or to eternal punishment
> *of obedience unto righteousness*—of righteousness leading
>   to greater righteousness, or to eternal life

6:17 But thanks be to God that you were slaves of sin but have become obedient from the heart to that form of teaching to which you were delivered.

form of teaching. Our teaching is a form which restores God's image that had been deformed.

> *thanks be to God*—you are his to whom you were given, and
>   I give thanks because you are no longer as you were at first
> *you were slaves of sin*—you once were, but are no longer
> *but*—but now
> *have become obedient*—by this you were made slaves of
>   righteousness, i.e., of Christ
> *from the heart*—not in outward appearance but in the spirit's
>   judgment, because now you are obedient by nature and
>   not by law; by will and not by fear
> *to that form*—holding to that form
> *teaching*—the gospel
> *to which*—to which or by which form
> *you were delivered*—not through yourselves, but through the
>   grace of God

6:18 Now, having been freed from sin, you have become slaves of righteousness.

> *now*—and through this
> *having been freed*—by another
> *from sin*—from the inclination to sin, that it might not reign
> *slaves*—by consenting and performing

6:19 I am speaking on the human level because of the weakness of your flesh. For just as you yielded your members to serve uncleanliness and

iniquity unto iniquity, so now yield your members to serve righteousness unto sanctification.

I am speaking on the human level. So far the apostle has shown that we should not sin. Here he says what should be done next, namely, that we should be slaves of righteousness. No one may excuse himself from this since there is no one who is not able to do good, at least in his will, which also happens through grace. *For just as.* Augustine: If not more, than at least just as much, lest faith be avoided as something harsh and unbearable.[132] Just as no fear impelled us at that time, but lust and the pleasure of sin drew us, so now the delight of mature righteousness, even if not yet perfect, should draw us. That is why he said, *I am speaking on the human level. so now.* Because righteousness ought to be loved now even more than iniquity was loved then, so that, for the sake of righteousness, a person might bear sorrows and despise all things, even death.

> *I am speaking on the human level*—and so about something
> less weighty; because you ought to pay more attention to
> righteousness than to sin
> *because of the weakness*—I would be speaking about greater
> things if you could bear them, but I am taking your weak-
> ness into account
> *of your flesh*—which comes from your flesh
> *For just as*—because this is human
> *your members*—which were subject to your control if you so
> willed
> *to serve*—by carrying out
> *uncleanliness*—of the body, which defiles the body, such as lust
> *iniquity*—and if it does not defile the body, it corrupts the soul
> *unto iniquity*—leading, I say, to the consummation of evil
> *so now*—similarly, since you are freed from sin
> *yield*—prepare
> *your members*—which are subject to your control
> *to serve*—by carrying out
> *unto sanctification*—leading to the consummation of good

6:20 For while you were slaves of sin you were free people in regards to righteousness.

you were free people in regards to righteousness. A slave has liberty when he delights to sin, which comes from his free choice. He serves as a free person who willingly does his master's will. Thus also he freely serves righteousness who loves it and who rejoices in it.

> *while you were slaves of sin*—therefore you should be slaves of righteousness
>
> *you were free people in regards to righteousness*—when sin had dominion over you, you were without the dominion of righteousness

6:21 Therefore what fruit did you have at that time from those things of which you are now ashamed? For their end is death.

Therefore what fruit. This recollection makes us abhor earlier works and be more submissive to grace. *you are now ashamed*. Augustine: For there is a certain temporal shame, a disturbance of the spirit considering its own sins, a shuddering in the consideration, an embarrassment in the shuddering, a correcting in the embarrassment.[133] *For their end is death*. Because death is a fitting retribution for sin; but eternal life, which is the end of the just, is given by grace alone through Christ, since merits are also from grace and grace will be rendered for grace.

> *fruit*—there was fruit of which you were ashamed, and its end was death; the fruit is greater disgrace in this life as a punishment
>
> *from those things*—in the depravities of sins
>
> *of which*—in the memory of which
>
> *you are now ashamed*—when you are of sound mind
>
> *For their end*—I ask about their fruit, for their end is clear: eternal death
>
> *death*—hence: *The beasts have rotted in their dung* (Joel 1:17)

6:22 But now, having been freed from sin and made slaves to God, you have your fruit unto sanctification and the end, eternal life.

But now, having been freed. Augustine: Above he said *free in regards to righteousness*, not *freed*; and now he does not say free people, lest they attribute this to themselves, but he intentionally says freed, according to the Lord's declaration: *If the Son has freed you, you will be truly free* (John 8:36).[134]

> *But now*—such it was then, but now, since you have been converted
> *freed from sin*—whose slaves you were then
> *and made*—as by another
> *slaves to God*—earlier you were free in regards to righteousness
> *your fruit*—suitable for you
> *unto sanctification*—brought to the consummation of virtues
> *and the end, eternal life*—and you have the end that is without end

6:23 For the wages of sin is death; but the grace of God is eternal life in Christ Jesus our Lord.

wages. That is, wages owed to the devil's army, which are rendered, not granted. The word "wages" (*stipendium*) comes from "gifts to be hung" (*stips pendenda*), i.e., payment to be weighed, for in ancient times money used to be weighed out rather than counted, and it would be given from the public treasury to those serving their country as soldiers. And he says the wages of sin is death to show that death was due to sin and not unjustly ascribed to it. It could also have been said that the wages of life is eternal life, but instead he said that *the grace of God is eternal life*, so that we might understand that God leads us to eternal life on account of his own mercy, not our merits. Thus eternal life—rendered by God in the end for preceding merits, which are not from us but have been made in us through grace—is also rightly called grace itself, since it is given freely. Yet it is not given freely in the sense that it is not given for merits, but in the sense that the merits for which it is given have themselves also been given. Therefore it should be confessed that eternal life is called grace because it is rendered for these merits that grace has conferred on humanity. Hence *we receive grace for grace* (John 1:16), namely the grace of glorification for the grace of justification.

> *wages*—they are like veterans' pay
> *death*—eternal death
> *grace of God*—given by God
> *eternal life*—which is only the end of the just
> *in*—i.e., through

Chapter 7

7:1 Or do you not know, brothers and sisters (for I am speaking to those who know the law), that the law in a person has dominion during the time it is alive?

Or do you not know. So far he has addressed the power of grace; now he treats the fact that the law is no longer to be kept. And here he discusses the end of the law and its earlier ineffectiveness. The Romans, then, should not be surprised when the apostle tells them, *You are not under the law but under grace* (Rom. 6:14). Above he said the law does not justify; here he says it must come to an end, since it was given only until Christ came. This, then, is the proper construction: *Or do you not know* this, namely, *that the law in a person has dominion during the time it is alive,* of which you should not be ignorant since you know the law *(for I am speaking to those who know the law)* and what I am saying is clear in the law if it is understood spiritually. Or: *the law* of Moses *in a person has dominion,* that it might be obeyed by him, and since you know the law of Moses, *for I am speaking to those who know the law,* etc. The sentence may thus be read in two ways, either concerning the natural law or the Mosaic law. *during the time it is alive.* For the law is said to be dead when its authority ceases.

> *Or do you not know*—Why it is said that justification is by
> Christ and not by the observance of the law? Because now
> he is discussing the results of the law; and it does not give
> life but increases sin.
> *that*—do you not know this? namely that
> *the law in a person*—natural law; the law of nature is general
> and not written
> *has dominion*—so that one must obey it
> *during the time it is alive*—as long as the law is in force

99

7:2 For a woman who lives under a husband is bound by law to her husband while he lives; but if her husband dies she is freed from the law of her husband.

For a woman. In order to bolster their understanding he uses an example from human law. The Romans know the law because they are not barbarians, but they took their understanding of natural justice partly from the Greeks, just as the Greeks took it partly from the Hebrews. By this example he teaches that a Christian is released from the law of works (although not from every law since he is still subject to natural law), just as a woman is released from the law of her husband. Thus he is no longer under the law, because if the law were alive for him he would be an adulterer and to be called a Christian would not benefit him.

> *For*—he draws a comparison from a particular law
> *bound by law to her husband*—so that she is not able to depart from him; so too the law must be kept as long as it is in force
> *freed from the law*—likewise a person is freed from the law when it loses its force

7:3 Therefore while her husband is alive she will be called an adulteress if she is with another man. But if her husband dies she is freed from the law of her husband, so that she is not an adulteress if she lives with another man.

Therefore while her husband is alive she will be called an adulteress. If someone wishes to be of the faith while serving the dead law then he is an adulterer to both and Christ is of no benefit to him. *but if her husband dies she is freed from the law.* With the law thus ended he does not transgress against it who crosses from discarded figures to Christ. <u>Augustine</u>: For when the law is dead those who are in Christ are not adulterers.[135]

> *Therefore while her husband is alive*—because she is bound by law to her husband while he lives
> *will be called an adulteress*—and likewise he sins who violates the law while it is in force
> *if her husband dies*—when the law is taken away and forgiveness of sins given

freed from the law—and the same is true for those who have
   been joined to the gospel and freed by grace
she is not an adulteress—since the law is dead, those who are
   with Christ are not adulterers

**7:4 And so, my brothers, you also were made dead to the law through
the body of Christ so that you might belong to another, who rose from
the dead that you might bear fruit for God.**

through the body of Christ. Because Christ was the realization and reality,
while the laws were figures and shadows of things that were fulfilled in
Christ.

And so—according to this comparison
my brothers—brothers of the apostle
you also were made dead—with your sins absolved, you have
   not only dismissed the law but have even become dead to
   it; you are no longer indebted to the law, which was given
   until the advent of Christ
to the law—to the figurative laws
through the body of Christ—i.e., through the mystery of the
   incarnation, or through the fulfillment of the law in the
   reality
to another—to Christ; and you should not be ashamed to
   belong to him because Christ himself belongs to another
who—to whom we also surely belong
that you might bear fruit—that you, or we, might bear fruit
   now, who were sterile under the law
for God—earlier we bore fruit for death

**7:5 For when we were in the flesh, the passions of sins, which were
through the law, were at work in our members to bear fruit for death.**

For when we were in the flesh. Augustine: There are three things in the
preceding comparison: husband, wife, and law; and again in the reality, to which the comparison refers, there are also three things: soul, sin, and law. In the comparison the husband dies and so the wife may marry again, because she is freed. But in the reality it is not sin that dies but the soul itself dies to sin, the soul which serves the law of God in the mind. The passions themselves, however, are not yet dead as long as the soul

serves the law of sin in the flesh. Therefore something of the passions still remains in him, but should not overcome him.[136]

> *when we were*—now we are in God and are not as we once were
> *in the flesh*—in carnal understanding, when we were doing things that are of the flesh, when we were under the law
> *passions of sins*—desires that are the causes behind the mortal sins of consent and action
> *which were through the law*—they became known or increased when our corruption or concupiscence acted through the law
> *were at work*—they were drawing our members towards evil works
> *in our members*—i.e., through their own instruments
> *to bear fruit for death*—that they might make our members worthy of eternal death

7:6 But now we are freed from the law of death, in which we used to be held, so that we may serve in newness of the spirit and not in the antiquity of the letter.

in newness of the spirit. In the works of the new nature, which we are unable to attain by our own powers or by the law but only by grace, namely, the grace of the Spirit. We should continue in these works in such a way that nothing is added from the works of the law, which are old.

> *But now*—when we are Christ's
> *we are freed*—after our sins have been forgiven
> *the law of death*—which is the cause of sin; or it is called the law of death because it kills sinners
> *in which we used to be held*—and from which we could never be freed except by the grace of God
> *so that*—having been freed
> *in newness of the spirit*—by the law of faith, which is in the renewed spirit, which also makes a person spiritual and so is a law of the spirit
> *in the antiquity*—for the law grew old because it came to an end
> *the letter*—which passes away

7:7 What shall we say, then? Is the law sin? By no means! But I would not have known sin except through the law. For I would have remained unaware of desire if the law did not say: You shall not desire.

What shall we say, then? Inasmuch as it is a law of death and has increased the strength of sin, holding people back from good works, it seems the law is sin, i.e., teaching people to sin; or the author of the law sinned since it was given for this evil purpose. No, on the contrary, the law is good, because it causes people to recognize sin. Before the law, some sins were not known to be sins, or to be so serious, or to be liable to punishment. *But I would not have known sin.* He shows that the law is not sin but an indicator of sin, so that the guilty soul, in solicitude, might be converted to receive grace. *I would have remained unaware of desire.* The apostle selects this general sin to speak of all sins. The law is good, which, when it prohibits this sin, prohibits all sins. Some understand general desire here while others understand the sin of covetousness found in the Decalogue: *You shall not covet your neighbor's possessions or his wife* (Exod. 20:17). General desire is that from which every evil comes. The apostle speaks in his own person here while he discusses the general cause.

> *What shall we say, then?*—here it is asked whether the law itself is evil, since it seemed that he was blaming the law
> *Is the law sin?*—i.e., an evil thing that teaches or causes us to sin, etc., as stated above
> *By no means!*—on the contrary, it is good
> *I would not have known sin*—I would not have acquired this knowledge from God through the law; or I would not have known that it was going to be punished
> *unaware of desire*—partly unaware that it was sin or that it was so serious
> *if the law did not say*—he gained knowledge but his way of life became worse as long as he was without grace[137]

7:8 But when the occasion arose, sin worked every desire in me through the commandment. For sin was dead without the law.

But when the occasion arose, etc. Because our carnality is such that it more ardently desires forbidden things, unmentionable things in which we used to lie as if asleep. And the devil, seeing the law given as a help to people, burned more fiercely and strove harder to turn the law to their ruin, while before he used to tempt them less, as though already possessing them securely. Or the occasion arose in the things themselves as when a women or gold is seen. ***every desire***. Ambrose: Saying this he signifies all sins, for there was sin before, but not every sin since the offense of deceit was still not present.[138] But every sin has now arisen including deceit. Augustine: For desire increased from the prohibition of the law when the grace of the liberator was still lacking.[139]

> ***when the occasion arose***—behold the law is good, yet evil came from it because sin, i.e., the inclination to sin, or the devil, found occasion in it
>
> ***sin***—concupiscence, namely the beginning of desire; or the devil as the instigator of sin
>
> ***every desire***—of consent and action[140]
>
> ***sin***—the devil, or the inclination to sin
>
> ***dead***—weak or unknown, it lay hidden and did not appear
>
> ***without the law***—*through the commandment*, I said, because it was when there was no law; here is noted the first human act before the law was given

7:9 Now at one time I was living without the law; but when the commandment came, sin revived.

I was living. It is clear that the apostle is not speaking of himself but in the person of humanity in general. Notice two people in the same individual: the interior person and the exterior person, i.e., the reason and the impulse that is in the flesh. He says that the interior person consents to the law, and by its testimony he proves that the law is good. But he says that the exterior person fights against the interior person and against the law and takes them captive; and the exterior person has greater power through the law. *I was living*. I was not afraid of death from sin because sin did not appear as such; in other words I was unaware that it was sin and so I was living in security. *but when the commandment came*. This is the second state: humanity under the law, i.e., here the apostle is speaking in the condition of a person placed under the law: Before *I was living without the law; but when the commandment came*, ***sin revived***. Sin began to appear and to rebel. He says it revived or lived again, not simply that it lived, for sin had lived at one time in paradise when it clearly appeared as a crime against the stated command. But when people who had been born sinners were living without the commandment, then sin lay hidden without recognition, as though dead, because it was without prohibition. But when the law was given then sin, which had once lived in the knowledge of the first human, lived again in human knowledge.

> *at one time*—in the time before the law
> *I*—the rational nature
> *was living*—I seemed to myself to be alive in comparison to this death
> *sin*—the exterior person, who was asleep before
> *revived*—appeared, became known

7:10 Moreover I died, and the commandment, which was meant to bring life, was found to be unto death for me.

was found. Before the sinner was ignorant of himself, but now the transgressor is made manifest to himself.

> *I*—the interior person
> *died*—when sin was increased and deceit added, I knew that I was dead
> *and*—thus
> *the commandment*—of the law, to me who did not observe it
> *was meant to bring life*—to the one obeying and observing it; because the law is good in the intention of the one who gave it
> *was found*—the same commandment and no other
> *death*—eternal death; not by the law's own fault but by reason of the occasion mentioned above
> *for me*—who was sinning and well aware of it

7:11 For sin, when it had occasion through the commandment, deceived me, and by the commandment killed me.

For sin. In other words, how was the commandment given to me unto death? I was seduced through it by a false sweetness. *when it had occasion through the commandment.* What is desired becomes more appealing when it is forbidden, and in this way sin beguiles through the commandment. Indeed when love is missing then desire for evil increases from its prohibition; and having been increased, what is prohibited becomes even more enticing. Thus it beguiles by a false sweetness, for that sweetness is false which entails more suffering and greater bitterness.[141]

deceived me. Sin pulled me from good to evil, thereby bringing me to eternal damnation. *killed me*. <u>Augustine</u>: By your sword that you carried the enemy killed you; he put you to death with your own weapons.[142] For you were armed with the commandment as with a sword in order to kill the enemy, which you cannot do if you rely on yourself. Therefore be humble and you will be able to conquer.

> *For*—this is how the law was found to be unto death
> *sin*—carnality or the devil
> *when it had occasion*—sin becomes appealing when desire is
> increased by the prohibition
> *deceived me*—because deceit arose
> *by it killed me*—with your own sword it slew you

7:12 Consequently the law indeed is holy, and the commandment is holy, just, and good.

Consequently the law itself *is holy*, since it teaches correctly, *and the commandment*, i.e., what is prescribed by the law, *is holy* in itself and *just*, i.e., justifying the sinner, *and good*, i.e., useful in gaining life.

> *Consequently*—because the law is unto life, and because it
> prohibits sin and makes it known, therefore it is good
> *the law indeed is holy*—because it commands and prohibits
> according to what is right
> *the commandment*—the works of the law; praise of the law[143]

7:13 Has what is good, then, become death to me? By no means! But sin, that it might appear to be sin, worked death in me through something good, so that by the commandment sin might become sinful beyond measure.

And since I am convinced that the law is good and yet that by it death comes to me, as was stated above, then *has what is good, then, become death to me*, i.e., is the law given to me by God in such a way that it becomes the efficient cause of death? No, rather concupiscence is the efficient cause, which turns something good into evil. *that it might appear*.

I do not say that it becomes sin, since it already was sin when it did not appear as such. Similarly, I said above that I was *unaware of desire* (Rom. 7:7) and not that I had no desire. *beyond measure*, because there was also deceit, or because there was more sin when the devil, who is provoked by good, urged the opposite. In this the enemy appears *through something good*, the law, surely not causing sin but rather demonstrating and prohibiting it. Or *beyond measure* because through the law sin did not slacken but rather increased in its habitual desires.

> *Has what is good*—here is asked whether the law, even if good,
>   is nevertheless blameworthy by what it does
> *By no means!*—for death is not from the law itself, but from
>   human corruption
> *sin*—the inclination to sin
> *appear to be sin*—it appears when it draws reason to consent
>   and action
> *death*—actual sin, which is the cause of death
> *something good*—namely the law
> *so that*—inasmuch as
> *the commandment*—without which it was not burning as
>   much, and by which deceit increased
> *sin*—concupiscence
> *sinful*—i.e., causing to sin
> *beyond measure*—more than before, not moderately, because
>   deceit also arose

7:14 For we know that the law is spiritual, but I am carnal, sold under sin.

that the law is spiritual. To the evil person whom it punishes, the law is just; to the good person it is spiritual because it prohibits sin and the worship of visible things. Therefore the law of Moses is spiritual since in it are things that are of God and since it must be understood spiritually. Now the law of the gospel, where God himself is found, is called the law of the spirit. God's words are in the law of Moses, his reality in the gospel. *but I am carnal.* To this point he has defended the law because the fault should not be laid on it; here he says that neither should it be laid on a person's principle nature, i.e., reason, being that which it has from God. And thus the fault should not be laid on the creator but on people, who of themselves have become so corrupt that they are unable to resist depraved impulses. *carnal.* The apostle is not speaking unsuitably of himself according to the flesh as long as he lives in this world and depends on the motions of the flesh. And every saint may properly say this of himself. *sold under sin.* This comes from the sin of the first man, who sold himself and all others for the delight of forbidden food.

> *For*—because
> *we know*—that the law is not death, but is good
> *spiritual*—nourishing the spirit when it instructs in spiritual
>   things
> *I am carnal*—impotent to resist my soul's corruption or the devil
> *sold under sin*—in my first parent, so that I am truly like a slave
>   under sin

7:15 I do not understand what I do, for I do not perform the good that I will, but I perform the evil that I hate.

I do not understand what I do. He establishes that he is a slave of sin: for I understand according to the interior person that I should not do what I do according to the exterior person, in neglecting good works or committing evil works. Truly I do what I do not understand because I forsake the good that I will and perform the evil that I do not will. I forsake and I perform—these I understand as parts of doing; I will and I do not will—these I understand as effects. His argument is from the parts and their effects, and it is this: I do not do what my interior self wills, for reason naturally wills the good; but this will always lacks an effect unless the grace of God adds its own will to love the good, so that it can be brought into effect. For there is a will of nature, a will of grace, and a will of sin; the will of nature is impotent of itself and does not merit a reward, but is overcome and carried away by the will of sin unless the will of grace assists. When the will of grace assists, then the will of sin flees and the will of nature is freed.[144] *I do not understand.* Because he sees one thing, knowing himself through the law, but he does another. *For I do not perform*, etc. Being subject to sin, I do not perform what I will. *I perform the evil.* Not that the apostle fulfills his desire; it draws him toward evil works, and he wrestles but is not overcome. He proposes this to you concerning himself so that you may not despair about this in yourself.

> *I do not understand*—i.e., I do not approve of
> *what I do*—according to the external person

the good—the good of not desiring
that I will—which the interior person wills

7:16 But if I perform that which I do not will, I agree with the law, that it is good;

But if I perform that which I do not will. He has shown that the flesh is a slave of sin, by which it is evil; here he shows the other side, namely, that the good nature is created by God, which agrees with the law and does not perform evil. Put simply: I do not do what I will and I do what I do not will. But if this is true, namely, if I forsake what I do not will to forsake, when the law commands the same thing I will; and if I perform what I do not will to perform, when the law prohibits the same thing I do not will, then I agree with the law that prohibits what I do not will and commands what I will; I agree with the law and am a witness to the fact that it is good.

I agree—I will the same as the law commands, according to
the interior person

7:17 but now it is no longer I who do evil, but sin which dwells in me.

but now it is no longer I who do evil. Now that I am redeemed, who had been sold under sin before, now that the grace of Christ has been received. The mind is free but the flesh is captive. *but sin which dwells.* Even though he lives by faith, not consenting to it. There are desires, but they do not reign. He himself does not perform evil, but he would perform it if he should consent to it. *sin which dwells in me.* How can it be said to dwell when it is not a substance but a privation of good? The body of the first man was corrupted by sin, and this corruption remains in the body through the condition of the offense, maintaining its force by the divine sentence given to Adam, and through association with the body, the soul is stained by sin. *sin.* The law of the flesh, with which the devil cooperates so that it might yield to his own law.

but now—I said that *I perform the evil*, and not that the interior person performs it, which now becomes clear, because in the interior person I am unwilling to perform the evil and I consent to the law

I—the interior person
no longer—under the law before the time of grace
sin—the law of the flesh
dwells—continually exists
in me—in my flesh, or *against me*, i.e., against my salvation

7:18 For I know that nothing good dwells in me, that is, in my flesh. For the willingness lies near to me, but I do not find the ability to complete the good.

For the willingness. The will is ineffective since *the willingness* to do good *lies near to me*, for it lies next to the flesh but it is inactive, unable to rise to doing good. It is near because it is natural in a certain way to will the good through reason, but it turns out that this willing is always overcome by the power of the flesh. Nevertheless God's will overcomes the flesh. *the willingness.* The things that the law commands are good, so that a person naturally loves them and wills to perform them, but the power to complete them is lacking. <u>Augustine</u>:[145] A good person always wills not to have any concupiscence at all, but he never completes this in this life. He does not say "to perform" but *to complete* because he does perform something: he does good in that he does not consent to concupiscence, but he does not complete the good of not having any concupiscence at all. And in the same way the enemy does evil when he arouses desire, but he does not complete it because he does not drag us by force into evil.

> *nothing good dwells in me*—sin dwells in me because good does not dwell in me
> *in my flesh*—in the sensual nature
> *I do not find the ability*—surely because it comes from God alone
> *to complete the good*—truly good does not dwell in me because neither to will the good nor to complete the good dwells in me

7:19 For I do not perform the good that I will, but I do the evil that I do not will.

For I do not perform the good that I will. I do not find the ability to complete the good because *I do not perform the good that I will*, *but* on the contrary, arguing from the lesser to the greater, *I* even *do the evil that I do not will.*

Or *I do not find . . . the good*, not because it is not there, for many foolish people do not find the good in anything even though it is there.

> **the good**—the good of not desiring
> ***I do the evil that I do not will***—namely forsaking good and
> doing evil

7:20 But if I perform what I do not will, then I no longer do it, but sin which dwells in me.

But if I perform what I do not will. He is concluding the sentence above: therefore *I no longer do it*, namely, the evil. And by this the matter is brought to a close, namely, that I agree with the law of God. *But sin which dwells in me.* Pressed by sin, he does its will, which nevertheless is a person's fault. He speaks in this way to indicate from what depravity God has rescued people.

> ***I no longer do it***—I am not consenting in my mind but desiring
> in my flesh
> **sin**—the inclination to sin; or carnal concupiscence out of
> which all sins arise

7:21 Therefore I find that the law does me good when I will, because evil lies near to me.

Therefore I find. He had said that the law is good, and that the nature which wills the same as the law and assents to it is good; here he joins the good law to the good nature as a helper. However the exterior person overcomes these two conjoined forces so that anyone, seeing that he can escape through neither, is wholly indebted to grace. *when I will.* When I will alone, because I am not able to complete the good, since evil is near to my reason. Evil lies in wait in the flesh like enemies at the gates,[146] and it compels me to do something other than what the interior person and the law will.

> ***Therefore I find***—because I do not do the evil, or rather
> because I do not will to do it
> ***that the law does me good***—it is good, i.e., useful, and a helper
> to my reason, when it teaches what is good and evil

when I will—by this I prove that it is good, because I will to
do what it commands
lies near—is close
to me—to my reason, the interior person

7:22 For I delight in the law of God according to the interior person,

according to the interior person. <u>Ambrose</u>: Because the flesh is derived
from Adam it has sin in itself. If the soul were derived from Adam then
it too would have sin because Adam's soul sinned. But if the soul had sin
in itself then a person would not know himself to be a sinner.[147]

> *I delight*—The law seems good to my reason. I will what it
> commands and rejoice to be helped by it.
> *according to the interior person*—whose liberty is partially
> restored

7:23 but I see another law in my members, fighting against the law of my mind and leading me captive to the law of sin that is in my members.

but I see another law. <u>Augustine</u>: This pertains to the body of death, so
that the law of the members fights against the law of the mind when *the
flesh lusts against the spirit* (Gal. 5:17). But the law of sin does not reign
when a person does not obey its desires.[148] *another law in my members.*
The inclination to sin is rightly called a law because it came to be in a
lawful way. Thus when a person did not obey his own higher nature, then
his lower nature, i.e., the flesh, would not serve the higher. *captive.* By
the flesh, but only partly captive since the mind fights against the flesh
and delights in the law of God. In this way it may be understood of the
apostle himself: my mind does not consent to sin; death contends but my
mind does not consent. There is in me a certain dead thing and a certain
living thing.[149] From this we should have hope.

> *but*—I delight in the law, however:
> *another law*—concupiscence which rules; weakness partially
> remains
> *in my members*—as in the eye unto desire and in the hand
> unto carrying it out
> *the law of my mind*—the law and my reason are in full
> agreement

> *leading me captive*—by the flesh, not by the mind; through
>   consent and action, because sin has dominion through use
> *the law of sin*—sin is a law because it has dominion
> *in my members*—all the more dangerous the nearer it is

7:24 Unhappy person that I am, who will free me from the body of this death?

Unhappy. Not in the mind but in the flesh. *who will free me?* I will be freed when this mortal frame is clothed with immortality, when no concupiscence will remain. But now, in the meantime, what will free me? *The grace of God,* etc. Or *from the body*, that is, from the crowd of attacking evils and sins.

> *Unhappy*—because I am captured, because I was born under
>   sin, because I am carnal, i.e., born of the flesh
> *I*—my spiritual self
> *who*—and since I am unable in myself, who besides someone
>   great?
> *from the body of this death*—from the dominion of the flesh,
>   in which is death

7:25 The grace of God through Jesus Christ our Lord. Therefore I myself serve the law of God in my mind, but I serve the law of sin in my flesh.

I myself serve the law of God in my mind by not consenting to *the law of sin in my flesh* in lusting. *Therefore I myself*, etc. Here is the third state: in the law of the spirit. But because he said that he was freed by grace, therefore, lest someone should rest secure as though sin could no longer harm him, he indicates how the liberation happens: if he remains in grace. For otherwise sin will overtake him again. *I myself.* The "I" in the flesh and the "I" in the mind are not two selves, but one self of both: I do not consent in the mind and I desire in the flesh.[150]

> *The grace*—not the law, not my own powers, but grace
> *Therefore*—because grace liberates
> *I*—the rational and interior person
> *myself*—having concupiscence as before
> *I . . . serve*—I am able to serve

> ***in my mind***—with my will
>
> ***in my flesh***—and therefore the flesh should not be treated
> more gently but must be guarded against lest it have
> dominion

From the verse, *For we know that the law is spiritual* (7:14), until the end of this chapter, it is not completely clear whether the words are better understood of Paul himself or in the person of universal humanity. Augustine says that at one time he had considered these words of the apostle to describe humanity under the law.[151] But, as he says, it is none other than the person of grace who delights in and consents to the law of God, who does not do or will evil, and who does not know it, i.e., does not approve of it. To such a person *there is now no condemnation*, as is shown in the following chapter, and yet he says that he is still carnal.

Chapter 8

8:1 Therefore there is now no condemnation for those who are in Christ Jesus, who do not walk according to the flesh.

Therefore there is now no condemnation. <u>Augustine</u>: Just as certain good things are not beneficial to evil people, so certain stains, if they are light and without which human life cannot be lived, do not prevent the good from receiving a crown.[152] *now.* Although there was condemnation before, now there is none when you are in Christ. *no condemnation.* Because through the grace of baptism and the washing of regeneration the guilt in which you were born is forgiven, as well as any sins you committed before.

> *Therefore*—because I serve the law of God in my mind
> *now*—in the time of grace
> *no condemnation*—because the stains of the flesh do not harm them
> *in Christ Jesus*—in whom all sins are forgiven
> *who do not walk*—who do not obey the flesh, even if they sometimes fall
> *according to the flesh*—i.e., there is no condemnation for those who do not walk according to the flesh

8:2 For the law of the Spirit of life in Christ Jesus shall free me from the law of sin and death.

For the law of the Spirit of life. Here he shows how grace frees us through the Holy Spirit. It is the Holy Spirit who teaches us what should be done and what should not be done, who is the giver of life, which comes through Christ who gives the Spirit. And he explains how this happens in Christ. Or the law of the spirit is the law of faith, which is said to be of the spirit because God, the object of faith, is a spirit. Or it means the law of faith by which we are brought to life, which the Spirit places in our heart. Or it is the law of the spirit of life because the spirit is unwilling to sin and because it calls us back from death. And in addition a person believes in the spirit, i.e., in the mind, the Spirit is what is believed, and it is the spirit of the one who has faith.

The law of Moses is called a law of the spirit, i.e., a spiritual law, because it prohibits sin, but it is not a law of life because it did not give life after sins were forgiven. This distinction is quite necessary: *the law*, he says, *of the Spirit of life*—here is one law; *from the law of sin and death*—here is another law. And he continues: *what was impossible for the law*—here is a third law, which is the law given through Moses on Mount Sinai. Therefore two laws are good, namely the law of faith that takes away sin and the law of Moses that makes sin known and prohibits it. But the law of sin is evil because it makes sinners. The law that the Spirit frees us from is the law of the flesh, which could not fulfill the third law, the law of Moses. The law of the flesh is not of God but of sin and death, and it makes sinners. The law of Moses is holy and of God; it makes evil known but does not take it away. The law of the Spirit, which is the law of faith and grace, takes away evil.

> *For the law of the Spirit*—As if someone should say: Are you able not to walk according to the flesh? I am, because *the law of the Spirit*, etc.; or there is therefore no condemnation because the law frees from sin.
> *shall free*—or has freed
> *from the law*—from the law of Moses which, by our consent and action, is the cause of deceit and death
> *of sin*—by consenting to sin and carrying it out

8:3 For what was impossible for the law, since it was weakened through the flesh, God did, sending his Son in the likeness of the flesh of sin, and from sin he condemned sin in the flesh,

For what was impossible. He shows how liberation was accomplished in Christ. *through the flesh.* Through carnality, which was in rebellion. And when the law was received, the flesh was further aroused. In this way the law of the letter was weakened through the flesh, and therefore it was not possible for it to liberate us from the law of sin and death.

sending his Son. <u>Augustine</u>: Not to where he did not exist, since he is everywhere, but he, who was in the Virgin before, came to the Virgin. He chose her whom he created; he created her whom he chose. He brought fertility to the Virgin; and as he came into the Virgin's womb he did not take away her virginity.[153] For he was there by a union of nature in a way that he was not there before. Likewise he was in the world and is said to have come into the world, because he was manifested visibly to the world.

in the likeness of the flesh of sin. Not in sinful flesh, because his mother did not conceive him in concupiscence, but in grace. Thus he was not sinful, because he was not conceived in the concupiscence of lust. He had no cause of sin in himself and did not sin in the flesh. Therefore he was like us in the punishment of sin, not in the condition of sin. *and from sin*, i.e., in the place of sin, *he condemned sin*, i.e., he destroyed the devil, which he accomplished in Christ's flesh. Or *from sin*, from the sin of Adam, *he condemned sin*, i.e., he weakened the concupiscence that proceeds from it.

> *For*—because he condemned sin
> *what was impossible*—to condemn sin
> *for the law*—for the natural or the written law
> *it was weakened*—in this regard, namely, to be fulfilled in justification
> *through the flesh*—it could not justify through carnal observances
> *sending*—making himself knowable through humanity
> *his Son*—consubstantial with himself
> *in the likeness of the flesh of sin*—not in sinful flesh, but like it by passibility and mortality
> *from sin*—because of which he became a sacrifice for sin
> *he condemned*—he destroyed
> *in the flesh*—in the flesh of Christ, in which our old nature was crucified

8:4 so that the justification of the law might be fulfilled in us who do not walk according to the flesh but according to the spirit.

that the justification of the law. Sin was condemned in such a way that the justice which the law of Moses promised might be fulfilled.

the law might be fulfilled—the law commands, the Spirit fulfills
in us—in people such as us
according to the flesh—in actions, even if we sometimes fall

8:5 For those who live according to the flesh know the things of the flesh; but those who live according to the spirit know the things of the spirit.

who live according to the flesh. The just person is not one who walks according to the flesh because he does not live according to it. And why not? Because he knows that the things of flesh are opposed to justice.

> *who live according to the flesh*—who consent to the carnal
> mind, who are not just
> *know the things of the flesh*—they are absorbed and inquisitive
> in carnal matters
> *who live according to the spirit*—he is just who walks according
> to the spirit, since he is also one who lives according to it;
> according to the Holy Spirit, or according to reason by
> consent
> *know*—are mindful to accomplish
> *the things of the spirit*—which the Holy Spirit teaches or reason suggests

8:6 For wisdom of the flesh is death, but wisdom of the spirit is life and peace.

For wisdom of the flesh. He that knows the things of the flesh is not just, for *wisdom of the flesh is death*.

> *wisdom of the flesh*—when a person eagerly fulfills the things
> of the flesh; or when he pursues physical things by striving
> for temporal goods and avoiding temporal evils
> *death*—eternal death
> *wisdom of the spirit*—when a person eagerly practices spiritual
> things
> *life*—the cause of life in the future
> *peace*—of mind here
> *life and peace*—i.e., life with peace which will be in the future

8:7 For wisdom of the flesh is inimical to God, since it is not subject to the law of God nor indeed can it be.

wisdom of the flesh. By enumerating these things he discourages us from obeying the flesh. *is inimical.* Because the flesh thinks that God cannot do anything besides what is seen in the course of nature.

> *wisdom of the flesh*—is death, being thus absorbed in carnal things
> *God*—whom it has not taken to itself as its end
> *it is not subject to the law of God*—it is not obedient to good practices
> *nor indeed can it be*—nor can it be subject to the law; after the fall, nature is unable to do what the physician urges

8:8 Now those who are in the flesh cannot please God.

> *Now*—Why should I dwell upon each and every thing?
> *those who are in the flesh*—who follow after its desires

8:9 You, however, are not in the flesh but in the spirit, if indeed the Spirit of God dwells in you. And if anyone does not have the Spirit of Christ, he does not belong to him.

if indeed. He expresses a doubt because they are not yet perfect in faith, but there is hope of advancing. *the Spirit of God* is the same as *the Spirit of Christ.*

> *You*—O Romans
> *are not in the flesh*—you do not do the works of the flesh; as if to say that such is not reported of you
> *in the spirit*—in those things that reason urges
> *if indeed the Spirit of God dwells in you*—here he teaches how a person walks according to the Spirit, namely, if he has the Spirit of God
> *if anyone does not have the Spirit of Christ*—here is shown how walking according to the flesh arises; when someone lives according to the understanding or deeds of the flesh,

when his mind consents to the flesh, or when he fulfills its
works in action
he does not belong to him—i.e., he is not a member of Christ

**8:10 But if Christ is in you, then the body is dead on account of sin
while the spirit lives on account of justification.**

then the body. Perhaps by "body" he means the entire person, as Ezekiel,
in a contrasting way, uses "soul" when he says that *the soul that sins shall
die* (Ezek. 18:4, 20). In which case it reads: *if* the Spirit of *Christ is in you*,
although *the body is dead*, i.e., although the person has died *on account
of sin*, i.e., in his sins, yet *the spirit lives* because it is joined to God who
is life; and this takes place *on account of justification*, i.e., the remission
of sins that is from the Holy Spirit. *the body is dead.* He does not say the
body is mortal, for even before sin the animal body was mortal, i.e., able
to die though it did not have to die. But now the body is dead *on account
of sin*, i.e., it has to die. Or *on account of sin*, i.e., for the sake of avoiding
sin this weakness is retained, so that he should thus fear to sin further.

> **if Christ is in you**—the Spirit of Christ, for Christ is one with
> the Spirit
> **then**—although
> **the body is dead on account of sin**—is dead in sin, or because
> of original sin
> **the spirit lives**—because it is joined to God who is life
> **justification**—which is from the Holy Spirit

**8:11 And if the Spirit of him who raised Jesus from the dead dwells in
you, then he who raised Jesus Christ from the dead will also give life to
your mortal bodies on account of his Spirit dwelling in you.**

And if the Spirit of him. Augustine: Notice that the Holy Spirit is called
here both the Spirit of the Father, where it reads, *And if the Spirit of him
who raised Christ*, and the Spirit of the Son, where it reads, *and if anyone
does not have the Spirit of Christ* (Rom. 8:9). This is because the Holy Spirit
proceeds from both. But what is said of the Son's generation is just as true
of the Spirit's procession: *Who will be able to explain it* (Isa. 53:8)?[154] *will
also give life.* Augustine: Behold four conditions: in the first condition,
before the law, there is no struggle with the pleasures of the world; in
the second, under the law, there is a struggle, but we are defeated; in the

third we struggle and win; in the fourth there is no struggle, but eternal peace, because our lower nature is subject to us. Thus it was not subject to us before because we had forsaken God, who is superior to us.[155] *to your mortal bodies*. <u>Augustine</u>: It does not say your dead bodies because in the resurrection, *when this mortal body will put on immortality* (1 Cor. 15:54), not only will the necessity of dying not remain, which it now has on account of sin, but neither will mortality remain, which the animal body had before sin.[156] *on account of his Spirit dwelling in you*. It is seen most clearly that on account of sin a person merited not only the death of the spirit but also the death of the body, and that both are liberated by Christ through the Holy Spirit.

> *And if the Spirit*—He already said to you, *But if.* Now see
> further the good works of the Holy Spirit.
> *of him who raised Jesus*—of God the Father
> *who raised Jesus*—this is the cause by which he will raise
> others: that Christ has been raised; and who was able to
> do this, just as he said
> *will also give life to your mortal bodies*—he will make them
> immortal and impassible; he does not say your dead
> bodies, since they are already dead (Rom. 8:10)
> *on account of his Spirit*—not because of your worthiness,
> not because of your merits, but because of his gifts

8:12 Therefore, brothers, we are not debtors to the flesh, that we should live according to the flesh;

> *Therefore*—because of these blessings from the Spirit, and
> because nothing but death comes from the flesh
> *we are not debtors*—rather we should serve and obey the Holy
> Spirit out of debt
> *not debtors to the flesh*—but to the reason
> *that we should live according to the flesh*—according to the
> pleasures of the flesh, even if we must provide necessities
> for the flesh

8:13 for if you live according to the flesh you will die. But if by the Spirit you put to death the deeds of the flesh you will live.

But if by the Spirit. Or by our spirit, which nevertheless is not able to do this except by agency of the Holy Spirit.

> *if you live according to the flesh you will die*—because sins arise
>   from the senses, which are considered to be of the flesh
> *by the Spirit*—by the Holy Spirit, which he soon makes clear
>   when he says *by the Spirit of God* (Rom. 8:14)
> *But if . . . you put to death the deeds of the flesh*—if you
>   completely reject what the flesh demands
> *you will live*—because the Son of God lives, in this life
>   you will live in justice and in the world to come you will
>   live in glory

8:14 For those who are led by the Spirit of God are children of God.

are led. It is better for a person to be led, as though barely doing anything, than to be ruled, as though already doing something and thus ruled so that he may act rightly. They, however, are led: not that they do nothing of themselves, but barely anything, so that they might be moved to do something by the impulse of grace.

> *For*—by this they can mortify the flesh, because *those who
>   are led*, etc.
> *those who are led*—are ruled
> *by the Spirit of God*—not by their own spirit or by the law
> *are children of God*—serving him out of love

8:15 For you have not received the Spirit of bondage again in fear, but you have received the Spirit of adoption of the children of God, in whom we cry out, Abba Father.

you have not received. You should be children, not slaves, because *you have not received the Spirit of bondage* that makes the unwilling serve out of fear of punishment, *but you have received*, etc. *Spirit of bondage . . . Spirit of adoption.* This is the same Spirit, but named differently because of different works: He was a spirit of wrath to the Egyptians, whom the water destroyed when it was divided by the Spirit. To the children of Israel, whom he helped, he was not a spirit of wrath. He was a spirit of fear to those who, being convicted by the law concerning sins and their own weakness, did not understand the grace of the Spirit. He was a spirit of freedom to those who by his grace received regeneration to eternal life and faith that works through love. Therefore there is one Spirit who causes two kinds of fears and who makes two kinds of slaves. There is the slave, who is also a son, who fears his master and honors his father. Thus Malachi: *If I am a master, where is my honor? If I am a father where is my love?* (Mal. 1:6) There is also a slave that fears punishment but does not love justice.[157] It should also be noted that, besides the natural fear that is in everyone, there are four kinds of fear: a worldly fear that is evil and not from God; a servile fear that is good and from God, but insufficient; an initial fear that is good and sufficient; and a chaste fear that is good and brings perfection. The chaste fear is spoken of here, for it begets us as children of God.

in whom we cry out. This again is a gift of the Spirit, which makes us cry out, *Abba Father*: Abba in Hebrew, Father in Latin. In the sacrament of the Church, in the Passion, Christ said, *Abba Father* (Mark 14:36), because the Church is made up of both Jews and Gentiles. Suffering in himself, he showed that his children, namely, his martyrs, should not despair if sadness creeps in from human weakness at the time of their passion.

> *again in fear*—because it is the same Spirit as was formerly in the law
> *the Spirit of adoption*—the giver of good works that are from his mercy
> *in whom*—through whom there are children from both peoples
> *we cry out*—intently, not ungrateful for justice
> *Abba Father*—Jews cry out *Abba*, Gentiles *Father*

8:16 For the Spirit himself bears testimony to our spirit that we are children of God.

that we are children of God. The Holy Spirit causes us to recognize this when forgiveness of sins takes place in the Church. Although the whole Trinity does this, it is nevertheless understood to pertain to the Holy Spirit because he is the communion of Father and Son, the union of both. By this comes the fellowship and unity by which we are made one body of the only Son of God. For unity joins us together, and love causes unity, and there is no love except by the Holy Spirit. These things are said so that we may love unity and fear division.

the Spirit himself—certainly the Spirit of the Son
bears testimony—the Holy Spirit causes our spirit to
    recognize this
to our spirit—when we are living uprightly
that we are children of God—which is not a little thing

8:17 But if children, heirs as well, heirs indeed of God and coheirs of Christ, if however we suffer together so that we may also be glorified together.

heirs. Even though God does not accede to heirs, as is said in human law, or even though he will accede in the sense that he will no longer be seen *through a mirror dimly*, as now, *but face to face* (1 Cor. 13:12), it can also be said that Christ, our head, acceded to the passion and left to us the possession of ecclesiastical peace, as he himself says: *My peace I give to you, my peace I leave with you* (John 14:27). Christ is the inheritance of his people and they are his inheritance, and thus it says: *I will give you nations*, etc. (Ps. 2:8); and again: *The Lord is my portion of inheritance*, etc. (Ps. 15:5). *if however we suffer together*. No one is able to mortify the deeds of the flesh, from which shall come life, without difficulty that requires patience.

heirs—sharers in his glory
of God—because we will enjoy his beatitude
coheirs—hence we will be like him
of Christ—in whom and with whom
if however we suffer together—by which merit we are heirs
    according to his likeness. Notice what was said above: *if
    by the Spirit you put to death the deeds of the flesh* (Rom. 8:13).
so that—for this purpose
we may also be glorified together—notice again the gifts of the
    Holy Spirit

8:18 For I consider that the sufferings of this time are not worthy of the future glory that will be revealed in us.

I consider—i.e., I know there must also be suffering in order
    to obtain glory
the sufferings of this time—all the temporal and momentary
    sufferings together

> *are not worthy of the future glory*—not worthy to merit future
> glory, if it were strictly transacted with us. But the Spirit
> does what our merits cannot do.
>
> *that will be revealed*—although hidden now, *which eye has not*
> *seen nor ear heard*, etc. (1 Cor. 2:9)
>
> *in us*—revealed to all the good and the evil; yet not revealed to
> be in the evil but only in us who are good

8:19 For the anticipation of the creation awaits the revelation of the children of God.

the anticipation of the creation. The creation means the good people who remain in God's creation, or it means the causes of all things. Corruption is the vanity to which creation has been subjected, for all things that arise are weak and corruptible and thus vain because they cannot maintain their state. *the creation* means whatever is now in us that grieves when we mortify the flesh through fasting and hardships, and now it *awaits* what will be, namely *the revelation of the children of God.* Consequently, when he says: *the creation awaits the revelation of the children of God*, the distinction between creature and children is not one of nature, but one of quality.

> *the anticipation of the creation*—it will be revealed as it truly is,
> which he proves by the authority of those who anticipate it
>
> *awaits*—it is constantly in a state of expectation; groaning de-
> notes constancy because what will be or what it is going to
> be does not yet appear
>
> *the revelation*—when what it is going to be like shall appear
>
> *of the children of God*—therefore all things should be endured

8:20 For the creation was subjected to vanity, not willingly but because of him who subjected it in hope,

not willingly. It sinned willingly, however, it does not willing bear the penalty of being subject to vanity, but bears this because of the justice and mercy of him who both punishes sin and intends to heal it.

> *the creation*—humanity, or good people
>
> *was subjected to vanity*—it must wait because it has been
> subjected to vanity, and it is able to wait because it does

not love the vanities, which are all worldly things, as is
said: *Vanity of vanities, all is vanity* (Eccles. 1:2)
not willingly—not loving these fallen things
but because of him who subjected it—yet patiently enduring,
knowing that God has subjected it in order to preserve
humility
in hope—but not without the comfort of hope that it shall also
be set free just as Christ its head

**8:21 because also the creation itself will be freed from the slavery of
corruption unto the freedom of the glory of the children of God.**

because also the creation itself. Now it is only a creature, when the form of
children has not been perfected, but it will itself also be freed just as we
are, who are already children of God, even if we do not appear as such.
Because he does not say simply *the creation itself* but <u>*also*</u> *the creation itself*,
he would have us understand that we should not despair of those who
have not yet believed. For they too will come to believe and be freed, they
who are not yet called children of God but only creatures, since they have
not yet received the grace of adoption. For after humanity lost the seal of
God's image, it remained only a creature. *will be freed.* It will be revealed;
it awaits the revelation. It was subjected, it will be freed. All these things
come through the Spirit.

from the slavery—from the concern of seeking food and other
things to which our mortality is subservient
of corruption—or "of death"
unto the freedom of the glory of the children of God—unto the
glorious freedom to come which the children of God
shall possess

8:22 For we know that all creation groans and is in labor until now.

all creation, etc. This means humanity in its full nature: corporeal nature
that is extended through space, animal nature that gives life to the corporeal, and spiritual nature that rules the animal. For all these are in a
person since by his spirit he understands like the angels, his soul senses,
and he is in a local body. But the entire creation is not in him because
besides him there are angels and other things. By analogy, the whole
person sees the sun, but not all of the person since it is only the eyes that

see it. Under this universal expression he does not include individuals of all genera, but genera of all individuals.

all creation groans and is in labor. <u>Augustine</u>: Some say that even the highest angels grieve before we are completely freed. But even if they help us, they do it without grief. And it is irreverent to say of them that they are subject to vanity and will be freed from corruption. But all in a person grieves and all in a person is freed, although not in all people.[158] ***all creation***. <u>Ambrose</u>: With labor all the elements fulfill their duties, which they do for our sake. Hence they will rest when we are adopted, and therefore we should diligently prepare ourselves.[159] ***groans***. There is always something new in this, as is indicated by the inchoative verb,[160] and it groans out of desire for the heavenly homeland. ***is in labor***. <u>Augustine</u>: To be in labor is to grieve.[161] ***until now***. Because even if some are in the bosom of Abraham, "all" still includes those who have not yet been freed.

> ***For we know***—as if to say: Believe what has been
>   experienced
> ***all creation***—i.e., humanity, which has communion with every
>   creature, even the worthier creature, but not with the
>   entire creation[162]
> ***groans***—not willingly; because of its despair
> ***is in labor***—when it is engaged in labor
> ***until now***—i.e., until death; or all our forefathers groaned in
>   this way up to the present; now it is just as it was before

8:23 And not only this but also we ourselves who have the first fruits of the Spirit, we also groan within ourselves, awaiting the adoption of the children of God, the redemption of our body.

not only this. That is, in a person not only do body and soul and spirit grieve from the difficulties of the body but also we grieve in ourselves on account of the body. ***the adoption***. So that even the body receives the benefit of adoption, that they may be children of God in every part. ***the first fruits of the Spirit***. That is, those who now belong to the Spirit, as if they were offered to God in sacrifice and set aflame by the divine fire of love.

> ***this***—creation
> ***we ourselves***—the apostles, who are greater because they have
>   the first fruits

> *the first fruits*—first in time and more abundant than the rest
> *the Spirit*—the Holy Spirit
> *we also groan*—we have troubles as others do
> *within ourselves*—or in ourselves; we groan from this and not
>   only for others
> *awaiting*—not disheartened by delay or adversities
> *the adoption*—the complete adoption
> *the redemption of our body*—redeemed namely from mortality,
>   having been redeemed from sin before; he explains what
>   this adoption is

8:24 For we were saved in hope. But hope that is seen is not hope, for why does anyone hope for what he sees?

For we were saved in hope. He says this so that the merit of hope may appear greater and thus it ought to save us.

> *we were saved in hope*—we wait because we are certain, as if
>   we were already saved, for our hope is not in ourselves
> *hope*—that which is hoped for
> *is not hope*—i.e., is not considered hope, for hope concerns
>   future things; it is not under the virtue of hope, which
>   only concerns things that are not present
> *why*—or how
> *does anyone hope*—is anyone said to hope

8:25 But if we hope for what we do not see, we wait in patience.

> *But if we hope for what we do not see*—in other words, what
>   is seen is not hoped for, but what is unseen; and if this is
>   true then the merit of hope grows
> *we wait*—for what we do not see; as long as we dwell in
>   vain things
> *in patience*—enduring adversities; therefore we groan

8:26 And likewise the Spirit also helps the weakness of our action, for we do not know for what we should pray as we ought; but the Spirit himself asks for us with unspeakable groans.

the Spirit also helps the weakness. Because we groan and beg to be freed, the Spirit helps us lest we ask before the proper time or in a wrong way. That prayer obtains the gift of God is clear, but even the ability to pray is from grace. He says how he helps our weakness: *the Spirit himself asks*. Before he dwells in them, the Spirit helps them to become faithful; dwelling in them now, he helps the faithful to pray.

but the Spirit himself asks. When the apostle says here that the Spirit asks with groans, he is using the same figure of speech the Lord used when he said to his apostles, *the Spirit speaks in you* (Matt. 10:20). For the Holy Spirit does not ask or groan as though he were in need or suffered distress. Thus it means that he causes us to ask and inspires within us a feeling of intercession and groaning. Here, therefore, is expressed the help of the Holy Spirit. It is love, which is caused by the Holy Spirit, that groans in us, that prays in us. And he that gave it is unable to close his ears against love. So too *the Holy Spirit asks for the saints* (Rom. 8:27) because he causes the saints to ask. The apostle expresses the same thing elsewhere: *But now that you know God, rather that you are known by God* (Gal. 4:9). This was said so that we may understand that God caused his own knowledge to be in us. For what is it that he says? *You are known by God*, i.e., he has made you to be those that know him. For God causes us to know him and hence we are said to be known by him.

with unspeakable groans. For how could it be speakable when we desire what is not known? Yet it is not completely unknown, for if it were not known at all then it would not be desired. And again, if it were seen then it would not be sought with groans.

> *likewise the Spirit*—not only does the Spirit help us in the
>   ways already mentioned but likewise, i.e., through his grace
> *helps*—teaching and causing us to pray
> *the weakness of our action*—or our weakness of action
> *action*—prayer
> *we do not know*—see here the weakness
> *as we ought*—as it is proper to pray
> *the Spirit himself asks*—he causes us to ask
> *for us*—not against us
> *unspeakable*—of something that cannot be uttered

groans—i.e., he makes us groan for more than can be spoken, both because of this exile and because of the desire for our homeland

8:27 And he that searches hearts knows what the Spirit desires, because he asks according to God for the saints.

he that searches hearts. Not as though he were seeking what he does not know, for nothing is hidden from him.

> *And he*—who causes us to ask and to obtain
> *that searches hearts*—that he may understand even unspeakable groans
> *knows*—approves and fulfills
> *what the Spirit desires*—what he causes us to desire
> *according to God*—as God wills
> *for the saints*—i.e., he makes the saints to ask; or he asks on behalf of the saints

8:28 But we know that all things work together for good for those who love God, for those who are called saints according to his purpose.

But we know, etc. In other words, not only does the Holy Spirit cause this but he also causes all things to turn out well for those who love God, whether there be prosperity or adversity, for God consoles them in prosperity and trains them in adversity. For evils are beneficial when the faithful bear them devoutly so that sins are corrected or removed, righteousness is trained and proved, or the misery of this life is demonstrated. For while death of the flesh comes originally from the sin of the first man, good use of it makes most glorious martyrs. And so not only this evil but all evils of the world had to remain after sins were forgiven so that humanity might have that against which to fight for truth and so that from them the virtue of the faithful might be exercised.[163]

called saints according to his purpose. In other words, the fact that they are called is not from anything other than the predestination of God. And it is from this, not from merit, that all things work together for good. For God has predestined, i.e., through appointed grace he has prepared this: that by the word of preaching those should believe whom he foreknew, i.e., whom long before he foreknew would become conformed to the

Son, who is the image of the Father and in every way equal with the Father. Hence it is said: *He who sees me, sees also the Father* (John 12:45). And notice that predestination is understood improperly concerning the present, namely, when it is taken for the assigning of the grace by which they are prepared to receive the word; but predestination is properly the foreknowledge and preparation of God's blessings by which they are most certainly freed, whoever are freed.[164]

> *But we know*—In other words, we do not know how we ought to pray, but we know, etc. The "we" are those who are greater and more learned, by whose authority it should be believed.
> *all things work together*—or turn out; through the Spirit, or the Holy Spirit works together with us
> *for good*—for true good
> *for those who love God*—by keeping the commandments
> *for those*—i.e., for those who do not retreat but persevere to the end
> *who are called*—through predestination, or who are called interiorly
> *saints*—called to holiness
> *according to his purpose*—not according to their merit but according to the purpose of God, i.e., according to his foreknowledge and predestination

8:29 For those whom he foreknew he also predestined to become conformed to the image of his Son, so that he might be firstborn among many brothers.

he also predestined. Predestination, then, is the preparation of grace which cannot be without foreknowledge.[165] But God foreknew also what he was not going to make, i.e., evils. Because while there are certain things that are sins in such a way that they may also be punishments of sin, according to the words: *God handed them over*, etc. (Rom. 1:24, 26), nevertheless this is not God's sin but his judgment. Grace is the effect of this predestination.[166] But it should be known that God has also prepared eternal fire for the wicked. Yet surely he did not prepare for the predestined to perform sins whose punishments he justly prepared to take away. For God has prepared what divine justice would render, not what human injustice would commit. For he has not prepared saints for receiving justice in the same way as he has prepared the wicked for losing justice, because he was never a preparer of depravity.[167] This rule, then, must be commonly held: sinners were foreknown, not prepared, to be in sin, but their punishment was prepared according to which they were known before.

conformed to the image. So that they may bear the image of heavenly humanity just as they bore the image of earthly humanity. *that he might be firstborn*. Because he was not made but born, before every creature. He was also born first without sin and was first to rise impassible, whereby he has brothers. For he does not have brothers because he is the only-begotten. But because he is firstborn he was considered worthy to call brothers all who are born again in God's grace through his primacy.

> *For*—to foreknow and predestine, etc., all things for good
> *those whom he foreknew*—that is, according to his purpose
> *he also predestined*—In the foreknowledge within himself
> from all eternity he predestined. He chose them to be
> called unto his promised rewards.
> *to become conformed*—in purity of life here and afterward in
> beatitude
> *so that*—conformed in such a way that
> *firstborn*—obtaining by right the inheritance of the Father,
> and distributing to others what belongs to those who
> are firstborn

8:30 And those whom he predestined he also called; and those whom he called he also justified; and those whom he justified he also glorified.

he also called. External calling takes place through preachers and is common to the good and the evil, while internal calling is only of the elect. Concerning the external calling it is said: *Many are called but few are chosen* (Matt. 20:16). Predestination is fulfilled in calling. To call is to assist the understanding of faith or to convict him who is able to hear, which only happens to the elect.[168] *he also glorified*. This concerns only the foreknown and not others who, even if they appear so for a time, are not glorified because they do not continue. *He ... glorified*. That is, he will glorify. The sense is future, although it is expressed in the past, because it means that he will accomplish what he has ordained to do from eternity, as is said by Isaiah: *Who did things that are to come.*[169] To such people all things are for good, even to those who go astray, so that they may become more careful and not trust in themselves.

Four things are mentioned here: predestination, calling, justification, and glorification. The first is in God, the other three in us. For our predestination is not in us but hidden with him in his foreknowledge, while the three others are in us.

> *whom he predestined*—which took place before we existed
> *he also called*—however estranged they were before; called
>   through preachers, because they had been prepared in
>   foreknowledge
> *those*—the estranged
> *whom he called*—according to his purpose, because they
>   are called, not elected, externally
> *he also justified*—by the forgiveness of sins and good works
> *whom he justified*—while they were sinners
> *he also glorified*—with every kind of virtue; or with eternal
>   reward, that they may be like God, and this is future

8:31 What, then, shall we say to these things? If God is for us, who is against us?

God is for us. He predestines things that do not exist by calling the estranged, justifying sinners, and glorifying mortals.

> *What, then, shall we say to these things?*—against these things,
>   or in regard to these things, or being aware of the bless-
>   ings of God, since all these things are for those that
>   are foreknown
> *If God is for us*—as was just said
> *who is against us?*—a person can do us no harm at all but only
>   cooperates with God for our good

8:32 He who did not spare even his own Son but delivered him up for us all, how has he not also given us all things with him?

delivered him up. <u>Augustine</u>: It is said that the Father delivered up the Son, but the maker of this cup is also the one who drinks it. Hence the apostle says: *Christ loved us and delivered himself up for us* (Eph. 5:2)

Therefore when the Father delivered up the Son, the Son also delivered up himself. And Judas, what did he do? The Father did well in delivering up his Son; the Son did well in delivering up himself; but Judas did wrong in delivering up his teacher out of greed. For what was given[170] to us from Christ's passion will not be considered evil; Judas will have the reward of evil and Christ the praise of grace.[171]

all things. It is less to give us all things than to deliver him up to death for our sake. This means 1) all higher things, namely, to see or enjoy God, the Trinity; 2) all equal things, namely, angels, to whom we will be equal when we live together in the future, although we are inferior now; and 3) all lower things, which are also ours to have dominion over. And likewise certain higher things, like sublime angels and their universal heavenly ministries, are also ours, not by ownership but by use, just as the property of a master belongs to his servants for food, clothing, and other things of this sort.

> *who did not spare even his own Son*—God is for us and above other things he gave his consubstantial Son for us; no one can bring harm against us because he has given us all things
> *but delivered him up for us all*—for us sinners; for our restoration
> *how has he not also given us all things with him?*—If he gave us his Son, which is the greater deed, how can he refuse to give us all things with him, which is the lesser deed? Higher things, lower things, and equal things; justice in the present and eternal life hereafter.

8:33 Who shall bring an accusation against God's elect? God who justifies?

Who shall bring an accusation. The pressure of the devil is called an accusation.

> *Who shall bring an accusation*—since what he just said is true, no one's accusation does any harm
> *against*—so that it might prevail, that it might do harm
> *God's elect*—whom he foreknew
> *God who justifies?*—no one else is able, and God is not willing to bring an accusation because it is he that justifies

8:34 Who is it that shall condemn? Christ Jesus who died, or rather who also rose again, who is at the right hand of God, who also intercedes for us?

at the right hand of God. At the place of honor, whose intercession God cannot despise. *who also intercedes.* When he daily offers to the paternal countenance the human nature he assumed and the awful manner of death which he endured for us.

> *Who is it*—since no one accuses
> *that shall condemn*—Who can inflict death? None who wish to inflict it will be able to, for only Christ is able, but he is unwilling.
> *Christ Jesus*—is it not Christ Jesus?
> *who died*—does he wish to condemn those for whom he died?
> *or rather*—who died, I said, or rather:
> *who also rose again*—which is greater; so that we too may rise again
> *who*—and what is greatest
> *is at the right hand*—in a more powerful state
> *of God*—the Father
> *who*—as mediator between God and people
> *intercedes for us*—with human representation, not with voice but with compassion

8:35 Who, then, shall separate us from the love of Christ? Shall tribulation, or distress, or persecution, or hunger, or nakedness, or danger, or sword?

> *Who, then*—and since these things are true
> *shall separate us*—shall these adversities separate us?
> *tribulation*—bodily affliction
> *distress*—anxiety of mind
> *persecution*—from place to place
> *hunger*—lack of food
> *nakedness*—lack of clothing
> *danger*—instruments of death
> *sword*—death itself

8:36 As it is written: Because for your sake we are put to death all day, we are regarded as sheep for slaughter.

As it is written. As though someone were asking: Why do you mention these things? Are these evil things for us? He answers: Indeed these evils things are for us, as it is written: *Because for your sake*, etc. *for your sake*. He indicates the cause without which a martyr's crown is not rendered. For the cause, not pain, makes a martyr,[172] because he suffered for us that we too might suffer for him: *But in all things we overcome* (Rom. 8:37).

> *Because for your sake*—because we cling to you inseparably
> *we are put to death*—by various torments
> *all day*—our whole life
> *we are regarded*—without any consideration of mercy
> *as sheep for slaughter*—which are only good for killing

8:37 But in them all we overcome because of him who loved us.

> *in them all*—in the mentioned tribulations and torments
> *we overcome*—we are made victorious
> *because of him*—not because of ourselves
> *who loved us*—whose kindness overcomes these adversities

8:38 For I am certain that neither death, nor life, nor angels, nor principalities, nor powers, nor things present, nor things to come, nor strength,

nor angels, nor principalities, nor powers. These are understood as orders of evil angels and, if it may be inferred, of good angels.

> *For I am certain*—we overcome, I say, for I am certain from his
>   promise, when he says: *I will not desert you nor forsake you*
>   (Heb. 13:5; Deut. 31:6, 8; Josh. 1:5)
> *death*—which their enemies threaten
> *life*—promised life
> *angels*—the lower order
> *principalities*—the middle order
> *powers*—the higher order that performs wonders
> *things present*—present things whether good or evil

things to come—whether good or evil
strength—the violence of anyone

8:39 nor height, nor depth, nor any creature will be able to separate us from the love of God which is in Christ Jesus our Lord.

nor height, nor depth. Ambrose: That is, neither prosperity nor adversity, as Solomon says: *Give me neither riches nor poverty* (Prov. 30:8) lest, being full, I become false or, being poor, I steal and perjure the name of God.[173] Many people sin from elevation, many from necessity. On the other hand Ahaz is put forward in Isaiah, who did not want to seek a sign either in the heights or in the depths (Isa. 7:11–12). The remedy comes from Christ, who was neither puffed up in power, in which he is equal to the Father, nor disturbed in the debasement of death. And he is the sign in the heights and in the depths, so that he was neither lifted up by royal power nor disturbed by distress, as Ahaz was at that time because of war with the Assyrians.

> *height*—of human power, or the elevation of Satan
> *depth*—the wisdom of anyone; or, if the devil, it indicates hell; or a threatening precipice
> *any creature*—other than those mentioned; or a new creature, like the two-legged horse Jannes and Mambres made, if this could be done[174]
> *the love of God*—whereby we love him; because God is better than all things
> *which is*—for us, not from us
> *in Christ*—God showed his love for us in Christ whom he delivered up for us

9:1 I speak the truth in Christ Jesus, I do not lie, my conscience bearing me witness in the Holy Spirit,

I speak the truth. Now nothing can separate me; but once I was separated, for which I grieve, and in this way evil is now turned to good. *I speak the truth.* <u>Ambrose</u>: Because he seemed to speak against the Jews, he expresses his feelings towards them, which he confirms by an oath. He grieves that his own nation is deprived of the benefit of Christ.[175]

> *in Christ*—established in Christ
> *I do not lie*—in any way
> *my conscience bearing me witness*—even if you do not believe
> *in the Holy Spirit*—my conscience is rooted and founded in
> the Holy Spirit; and the Spirit is a witness concerning
> this, *that I have*, etc.

9:2 that I have great sadness and continual sorrow in my heart.

> *great sadness*—numbness of heart
> *continual*—not for an hour
> *sorrow*—of compunction
> *in my heart*—not in appearance

9:3 For I myself used to desire to be anathema from Christ for my brothers who are my kinsmen according to the flesh,

I myself used to desire, he says, not *I desire*, because he knows that, such as he is, he cannot be separated from Christ. Nevertheless he expresses his affection for those who are separated. And he enumerates their many praises to produce sorrow in everyone for them, who are so much the worse than the Gentiles because they lost the privilege of the fathers and of the promise. For it is a worse evil to lose dignity than not to have had it. But this, he says, is what God said would come, so that *the seed of Abraham are not children of the flesh* (Rom. 9:7–8) but those who have faith. Through faith was born Isaac, and Isaac is a type of Christ. Jacob and Esau are of two peoples. (Job was from the sons of Esau, of the fifth generation from Abraham; he was a grandson of Esau.) *for my brothers.* Or for drawing back those who are now my brothers in the faith, who are also my kinsmen; thus I used to sin more grievously.[176]

> *For I myself*—who am now an apostle
> *used to desire*—and I rightly grieve for this
> *to be anathema*—a separation of others
> *for my brothers*—for Jews who were brothers in the law, whose
> > law I used to defend, who were straying from it because of
> > Christ
> *my kinsmen*—and thus who should be supported more
> *according to the flesh*—from the tribe of Benjamin

9:4 who are Israelites, whose is the adoption of children, the glory, the testament, the legislation, the worship, and the promises,

> *Israelites*—true Israelites as far as they are good, or Israelites
> > by race
> *whose*—to whom belong
> *adoption of children*—which means:
> *the glory*—because they are a peculiar people, or because of
> > what they now do through miracles
> *the testament*—the New Testament.
> *the legislation*—which the Old Testament presented through
> > figures
> *the worship*—of one God
> *the promises*—to whom the promises were made

9:5 whose are the fathers, from whom is Christ according to the flesh, who is over all things, God blessed for ever. Amen.

> *whose are the fathers*—praise from earlier things
> *from whom is Christ*—praise from later things

according to the flesh—because he was born human in the flesh
who is—even though he was born from the fathers according
   to the flesh
over all things—hence: *And the Most High founded her*
   (Ps. 87:5).[177]
God blessed for ever. Amen—it is true that he is God; as if to
   say: I who used to speak against this truth, now confirm it

9:6 But the word of God has not failed, for they are not all Israelites who are of the circumcision of Israel;

But the word of God has not failed. The apostle comforts himself in his sorrow with the fact that God never decreed to save them; having foreknowledge, he is not a respecter of persons. For he condemns no one before he sins and crowns no one before he is victorious. But foreknowledge is limited to how someone's will is going to be, by which he is condemned or crowned.[178] Because he was grieving for the Jews, he consoles himself, finding it written that not all would be saved but only those like Isaac. In these words he shows that God's grace alone will make children of God. *But the word of God has not failed.* He said that the promise of eternal inheritance was made to the Jews; but since they in large part did not believe, it appeared that the word of God was not fulfilled. To this he responds: Even if the promise is not fulfilled in certain Jews, it is fulfilled in others, namely, in the Gentiles who believe, who are now true children of Abraham. *But the word of God has not failed.* As if to say: Even if I have labored so hard and not all believe, *the word of God has not failed* (or: it is not that it will have failed). The word of God is said to fail when his promises are not fulfilled.

> *But the word of God has not failed*—Or, it is not that the word of God will have failed;[179] rather it is true. Even if I have labored so hard and if not all believe, yet *the word of God has not failed*; the promise is not empty even if not all are saved, because *they are not all*, etc.
>
> *Israelites*—those truly belonging to Israel
> *of the circumcision*—according to the flesh

9:7 nor are all children of Abraham who are the seed of Abraham, but in Isaac shall the seed be called yours.

in Isaac. That is, in Christ: they are gathered together as he calls them by grace. They were prefigured in the promise, not those who are just in themselves but those whom God made just. These are *the children of the free Jerusalem, which is above, which is our mother* (Gal. 4:26). The children of the flesh are of the earthly Jerusalem, *which is in bondage with her children* (Gal. 4:25). Just as Isaac did not merit the promise to be born, so too these heirs did not merit, but the promised adoption of children was given to them by grace alone.

> *children*—i.e., heirs
> *the seed of Abraham*—according to the flesh
> *but in Isaac*—but those who are like Isaac, for Scripture
>   speaks thus
> *shall the seed be called yours*—because a person is Abraham's
>   seed from the call of God

9:8 That is, those who are children of the flesh are not the children of God, but those who are children of the promise are accounted in the seed.

> *That is*—he explains the text
> *are not the children of God*—they are not children of God
>   through human effort
> *children of the promise*—this means the same thing as *children
>   of Abraham*; i.e., those who, like Isaac, are generated by
>   God's promise alone
> *in the seed*—in the spiritual seed

9:9 For this is the word of the promise: At this time I shall come to you and Sarah shall have a son.

> *For*—because indeed
> *this is the word*—namely in Genesis (Gen. 18:10)
> *of the promise*—or, concerning the promise of Isaac
> *At this time*—on this day in the following year
> *I shall come to you*—O Abraham, and I shall do this
> *Sarah shall have a son*—either conceived or born, for he does
>   not determine which

9:10 And not only she but also Rebecca, who by one intercourse conceived of Isaac our father.

And not only she. Sarah had the promise, but Rebecca also had the promise, namely, conceiving two sons of Isaac our father *by one intercourse.* by one intercourse, he says, lest there seem to be different merits of the parents at the time of generation, but *of Isaac our father,* i.e., of our founder whom we should imitate if we wish to be children of God. The promise made to Sarah shows that no one is saved on account of race; the promise made to Rebecca shows that no one is chosen on account of any merit of his own or of his parents, but by grace alone.

> *not only she*—i.e., not only Sarah had the promise
> *conceived*—two sons

9:11 For when they had not yet been born or done anything good or evil, so that the purpose of God according to election might stand,

For when they had not yet been born, Rebecca had this promise: *The elder shall serve the younger* (Gen. 25:23), i.e., Jacob shall advance while Esau trails behind.

> *For when they had not yet been born*—lest someone should
>   think the difference is due to their merits
> *or done anything good or evil*—since it could be that even by
>   struggling in the womb a person may seem to have
>   merited something
> *so that the purpose of God*—Therefore, then, so *that the purpose,*
>   i.e., foreknowledge of God, *might stand,* i.e. might be
>   fulfilled, *according to election,* i.e. grace by which he chose
>   as he foresaw, not according to the debt of merits, because
>   he makes them to be chosen and does not find them so.

9:12 not from works but from him who calls, it was said to her: The elder shall serve the younger.

not from works. Not from future works, which were not going to be good or evil except by grace being applied or taken away. *The elder shall serve the younger.* This is literal, because it is said of the Edomites, who came from Esau and Edom: They were subject to the children of Israel (Ps.

60:8).[180] But more is intended in this prophecy: that the people of the Jews, who are elder, i.e., earlier in the worship of one God, are going to serve the younger, the later Christian people.

> *from him who calls*—from the grace of God who calls
> *to her*—to the mother
> *The elder shall serve the younger*—he says these things from
> foreknowledge

9:13 As it is written: Jacob I loved, but Esau I hated.

Jacob I loved, but Esau I hated. He found nothing to be loved in Jacob except the gift of his own mercy; he hated nothing in Esau except original sin. But how does God love and hate rightly when they had done nothing? Because this is so amazing, he brings up the objection to himself: *What, then, shall we say?* From mercy comes the ability to will and to run, which is seen in some who are of the same lump that deserves perdition, for Scripture says it.

> *As it is written*—i.e., the words are about grace, just as Malachi
> spoke concerning things now past: that Jacob was chosen
> by grace, not merit, while Esau was reprobated when grace
> was taken away
> *Jacob I loved, but Esau I hated*—this again concerns judgment

9:14 What, then, shall we say? Is their injustice with God? May it never be!

What, then, shall we say? Because without merit God chose one and reprobated another, shall we say that God is unjust? No, because he chose one through mercy and reprobated the other through justice. There is no injustice in doing either. He chose one through mercy, as Moses says; he reprobated the other through justice, as Scripture says, citing words that God spoke to Pharaoh. *May it never be!* It is certain that no one is freed except by gratuitous mercy and no one is condemned except by most equitable justice. But why is one freed rather than another? He that can may search into so deep a judgment, but let him beware of the precipice.

> *What, then, shall we say?*—in regard to what has been said,
> that without merit he chooses one and reprobates another

> ***Is their injustice with God?***—i.e., shall God be called
> unjust? No.

9:15 For it was said to Moses: I will be merciful to whom I am merciful and I will show mercy to whom I will be merciful.

I will be merciful to whom I am merciful. That is, to whom I foreknew was going to be pitied, knowing that an individual was going to be converted and remain in me. This is to give to him for whom it was given, and not to give to him for whom it was not given. Thus he calls him that he knows will obey, like David, who persevered so well after receiving forgiveness. Saul, when he was not heard in prayer, did not persevere but turned to idols, and so it is seen that he was justly reprobated by foreknowledge.

> *For it was said to Moses*—God said, having been prompted
> by Moses
> *I will be merciful*—by calling inwardly
> *to whom I am merciful*—by predestining
> *I will show mercy*—by giving eternal life and perseverance;
> notice that no merits precede in justification
> *to whom I will be merciful*—by calling

9:16 Therefore it is not of him that wills nor of him that runs but of God who shows mercy.

it is not of him that wills, etc. It does not depend on both God and humanity, as though he were saying that human will alone is not enough without also God's mercy. This would mean, on the other hand, that God's mercy is not enough without also human will. And thus if the one statement is correct, then why would its corollary not be correct as well, namely: It is not of God who shows mercy but of the person who wills? Therefore it is clear that the verse should be understood in such a way that all credit is given to God, who both prepares a person's good will to be helped and helps after it has been prepared, going before the one who wills that he might will and following after the one who wills that he might not will in vain.[181]

Augustine: Who is really so impiously foolish that he says God cannot change the evil wills of people to good however and whenever he wills?[182] For nothing resists his will. But it is through mercy that he does it, when he does it; and it is through judgment that he does not do it, when he does not do it. He shows mercy, indeed, according to grace that is given freely; but he hardens according to judgment that is rendered for merits.[183] Hence we may understand it thus: When there is hardening from God, this means that he is not willing to show mercy, so that God imposes nothing which makes a person worse, but only dispenses with what makes a person better. Therefore it is not said how it is not of him that wills, nor why, but that it is of God who shows mercy. So too it is not said why it is not of him that wills but of God who hardens, since he does not harden by imparting evil but by not granting good. And this he does out of his justice, just as he gives grace out of his mercy.[184]

> *Therefore*—because out of mercy he prepares those whom he
>   wills and calls
> *not of him that wills*—it is not to will the good
> *nor of him that runs*—it is not to run, i.e., to work
> *of God who shows mercy*—notice that God does not choose
>   on account of future works that he foresees

9:17 For Scripture says to Pharaoh: I have stirred you up for this very thing, that I may show my power in you and that my name may be proclaimed in all the earth.

I have stirred you up, or raised you up, or preserved you. <u>Ambrose</u>: For this very thing I have preserved you, when you were not worthy to live. Or it says, I have raised you up, because after Pharaoh was dead in God's eyes he received a short time of life in order that all the Gentiles might learn of God's power in him.[185] *I have stirred you up*. You were evil, but like someone asleep, and when I showed you signs I stirred you up to the same wickedness, so that you might become worse. And this is just, so that *he who is in filth may be filthy still* (Rev. 22:11). Nor is it useless, for when you are hardened I will show my power in the signs of Egypt.

> *For Scripture says to Pharaoh*—good deeds follow when grace
>   is added because evil deeds follow when grace is sub-
>   tracted, which is surely through justice
> *I have stirred you up*—another reading has: I have raised you
>   up; and another: I have preserved you

> *for this very thing*—to this same wickedness, so that you may
> become worse, because *he who is in filth, let him be filthy
> still* (Rev. 22:11)
> *my power*—God makes good use even of the wicked, with
> signs and wonders
> *in*—i.e., through, or against
> *you*—when you are hardened
> *my name*—the example of Pharaoh pertains to Esau, who was
> reprobated (just as Jacob was elected) by the just, though
> secret, judgment of God
> *may be proclaimed*—through manifest power

**9:18 Therefore he has mercy on whom he will and hardens whom he
will.**

Therefore he has mercy on whom he will. There is no meriting of mercy,
but the sin of the whole condemned lump merits hardening. Nor does
God harden by imparting evil, but by not imparting mercy which they
do not deserve. He does this by a hidden justice that is beyond human
understanding; and the apostle does not explain it but simply marvels: *O
the depths of the riches of wisdom* (Rom. 11:22)! *and hardens whom he will.*
Not as though he forces anyone to sin, but only that he does not impart
the mercy of his justification to some who are sinners, and he is said to
harden them because he does not have mercy on them, not because he
compels them to sin. But by a most hidden justice that is far beyond human understanding, he determines that grace is not to be offered to those
on whom he does not have mercy.

> *Therefore*—since I have loved Jacob and hated Esau
> *he has mercy*—gratuitously
> *hardens*—in just judgment
> *whom*—as Esau and Pharaoh

**9:19 Surely you will say to me: Why is it still asked? For who resists
his will?**

Why is it still asked? After it is established that it is a matter of God's
will, then why is it asked whence one person is good and another evil? Is
it not necessary that a person will be the way God wills him to be? And
so he unjustly condemns one and saves another. Or, *Why is it asked,* i.e.,

Why does anyone strive to do good when he can do nothing if God does not will it? Or, Why does God find fault with the sins of people when they are not able to avoid what he himself wills? In such a way are carnal people, living in pleasures, accustomed to murmur against God and to suppose that they are evil because of God's will rather than their own corruption.

> *Surely you will say to me*—Since it is according to God's own desire, then why is it asked about?
> *Why is it still asked?*—Why is it asked if we offend God?
> Or, Why is it asked of anyone to act rightly?
> *his will*—the will of him who hardens us

9:20 O human, who are you to answer back to God? Does a thing that is made say to him who made it, Why have you made me thus?

O human. He says this not out of need to restore reason, but he is recalling humanity to itself. The apostle rebukes them for such presumption: *O human*, you who are flesh and not spirit, O pitiful one, *who are you?* What capacity do you have *to answer back to God*, i.e., to understand what God does, namely, why he shows mercy to this one and hardens you? As if to say to you: You are not able to answer, i.e., to understand, because of your carnality; nor can your own wisdom or own powers help you in this. Or, as in another reading, *what would you answer to God*, i.e., on what grounds would we argue against God that he unjustly elects and reprobates?

> *O human*—the apostle checks this impudence; see the difference between you and God
> *who are you*—you are human and he is God; you are flesh and he is spirit; yet it displeases you that God finds fault
> *Does a thing that is made*—he takes this from Isaiah (Isa. 29:16); and in the same way you too are made
> *to him*—by whom it has been made
> *who made it*—who owes it nothing
> *Why have you made me thus?*—a work cannot complain against its maker

9:21 Or has not the potter power to make from the same lump one vessel for honor, another for dishonor?

from the same lump. Thus the whole lump of humanity is justly corrupt and full of clay. It is mercy if a vessel for honor is made out of it; it is just if a vessel for dishonor is made out of it, since this is what it was by nature. Behold the justice in those who do not have the opportunity to work; but of those who have time, he adds: *What if* (9:22), i.e., what would you answer to God if, etc.? *another for dishonor.* A vessel not for honor but for dishonor. If it is contemptible, this comes not from the potter but from the clay itself.

> *Or*—truly a person cannot ask why he was made such, because *has not the potter*, etc.
> *potter*—he that works in clay
> *power*—the right

9:22 What if God, willing to show wrath and to make known his power, endured with much patience the vessels of wrath fit for destruction,

What if God. As if to say: It has now been shown that God is not unjust even if he gives nothing to the good. But what will you say if he has also given good things to some when they were fit for destruction? He *endured with much patience*, and, in the meantime, while he waited, he used many signs, punishing them at times or punishing others in their sight, to show that they should beware of the wrath to come. And by enduring and showing them his wrath he was making known his power, that he cleanses the good through the wicked. You might say that he justly takes away grace and condemns those who, having been waited for, were unwilling to repent and abused this grace. *endured with much patience.* God endures the wicked, that he might destroy them at the appointed time; and he uses them as instruments for the salvation of the good. For God did not create beings he foreknew would be evil, whether angels or humans, unless he knew at the same time how he would adapt them for the benefit of the good.

> *What*—namely, what would you answer to God?
> *God*—some manuscripts omit
> *to show wrath*—upon the lost. When they suppose he is not going to punish, because he is concealing his purpose, he will appear mighty when he punishes.
> *to make known his power*—in those to be saved

endured with much patience—for a long time they have been
waited for, and so they are without excuse; and thus God
waited for them although he knew they were not going
to believe

9:23 that he might show the riches of his glory in the vessels of mercy which he prepared for glory,

that he might show. In other words, for this reason he endured the wicked
and showed wrath in earlier days and drew them toward knowledge of
himself: *that he might show the riches of his glory*, i.e., how rich and how
great and how glorious is his mercy, *in the vessels of mercy*, i.e., in those
elected by mercy. That is why he gives so many good things to the wicked,
so that he might convince them that they are justly condemned, and so
that the faithful, for whom he keeps this grace, might love him more.

Notice that God does not grant grace to some while to others he applies
it as if they were compelled. Thus <u>Ambrose</u> says concerning foreknowledge: He allowed Pharaoh to be damned, knowing that he was not going
to reform himself. He chose the apostle Paul, on the other hand, knowing with certainty beforehand that he was going to be faithful. But grace
was given for use to some, like Saul, Judas, and others, to whom he said:
Behold your names are written in heaven, although they later turned
back. Of them Ambrose says: But this was on account of the justice they
deserved.[186] It is just that God respond to the merit of each person, even
if he had said: Now you are worthy of eternal life. For they were good
and their names had been written in heaven on account of the justice
they were deserving at the time, but they were among the number of the
wicked according to foreknowledge. For God judges by justice and not by
foreknowledge. Hence he tells Moses: *If anyone sins before me I shall delete
him from the book of life* (Exod. 32:33), so that according to the judgment
of a judge he seems to be deleted when he sins; but according to foreknowledge he was never in the book. As John says: *They went out from us
but they were not of us* (1 John :19). However at the time, such a one seems
to be enrolled when he ceases to be evil, who never was enrolled according to foreknowledge. Therefore God's riches and glorious goodness are
shown when out of gratuitous mercy he assigns grace to whom he will
and frees whom he will.

that—so that
he might show—in the age to come; he shows how much he
   has done for them when the others receive a punishment
   that all equally deserved
the riches of his glory—either through the fire of his glory or in
   comparison to his glory
which he prepared—by waiting in the same way
for glory—for future glory.

9:24 and whom he called, not only from the Jews but also from the Gentiles.

and whom—and in all the vessels whom
he called—through preachers, interiorly; out of the single
   lump of Adam

9:25 As he says in Hosea: those not my people I shall call my people, and those not my beloved, my beloved, and those who have not found mercy, those who have found mercy;

As he says in Hosea. After showing that they are children by grace alone, he begins to prove through the Prophets that they come from both peoples.

As he says in Hosea—Not Hosea himself speaking, but God
   in him
those not my people—the nations that have not known me
my people—so that they may know me
those not my beloved—namely the heathen
my beloved—so that they may serve me out of love
and—and I shall call
those who have found mercy—so that they may attain eternal life

9:26 and it shall be in the place where it was said to them: You are not my people, there they shall be called children of the living God.

and it shall be—this which I speak shall be
in—namely that in
the place—the whole world, or among the Jews who were saying to the Gentiles: You are not the people of God

where it was said to them—by the same Jews
there—i.e., in the whole world
children of the living God—thus far Hosea (Hosea 2:23)

9:27 And Isaiah cries out before Israel: If the number of the children of Israel be like the sand of the sea, the remnant shall be saved.

If the number, etc. Behold he is speaking of the salvation of the Jews in such a way that the greater part is understood to have been blinded.

> *cries out*—speaking openly
> *before Israel*—before the Jews
> *If the number*—whether they be innumerable or sterile, the
> root of the patriarchs has not therefore perished
> *like the sand of the sea*—on account of sterility
> *the remnant*—i.e., those whom I have left when I rejected
> others; or those who were left behind by others because
> they were insignificant or few

9:28 For he is completing the word and cutting it short in justice, because the Lord will make a short word over the earth.

For he is completing the word. The prophet adds how they were saved so that the glory of works is excluded. The word of the gospel brings to completion all the laws in the one Christ. Yet he shortens the justice from the prior law, meaning that nothing is lacking to justice from all that was prefigured there, or that the gospel retains all that is just, such as the moral laws, while it cuts out all that it is proper to remove, such as the figures. *and cutting it short in justice.* So that he saves by grace in the weighing of faith and not by innumerable observances.

> *the word*—i.e., the gospel
> *cutting it short*—the shortened word is love, on which the Law
> and the Prophets depend (Matt. 22:40)
> *because*—let no one doubt this, because the prophet confirms
> it by repetition
> *a short word*—as opposed to the ancient word, which it is
> certain that God also made

9:29 And as Isaiah foretold: Unless the Lord of Hosts had left us a seed, we would have become as Sodom and would have been like Gomorrah.

Unless the Lord of Hosts. The Lord made the word, and it was so necessary that *unless* there were *a seed*, i.e., the word, etc. Or the remnant shall be saved, and except for them the nation would have perished. And in this way it would read: *Unless the Lord of Hosts,* when he blinded others, *had left us,* i.e., for our advantage, *a seed,* i.e., the apostles who made the crops of Christ grow. *as* and *like.* He used both terms to note the similitude of guilt and punishment. In other words, we would have been equal in punishment because we would have been alike in guilt.

> *Lord of Hosts*—Lord of armies
> *a seed*—or Christ
> *Sodom*—mute to confess
> *like*—as though equal in punishment because alike in guilt
> *Gomorrah*—harsh, without grace, covered with thorns of sins

9:30 What then shall we say? That the Gentiles, who were not pursuing justice, attained justice, but the justice that is from faith,

> *What then shall we say*—having cited Hosea and Isaiah, he
>> asks about the meaning of the prophets so that the Jews
>> might not twist it differently
> *who were not pursuing justice*—through works of the law
> *attained*—suddenly and firmly
> *but*—not just any justice, but
> *that is from faith*—through grace

9:31 while Israel, pursuing justice, did not come to the law of justice.

while Israel. Israel followed the law backwards, as it were, because they never reached a spiritual understanding. *pursuing justice.* The law of Moses is a law of justice if it is rightly understood. Or they were pursuing justice out of fear of punishment rather than from love of justice.

> *while Israel*—i.e., the Gentiles obtained justice, while Israel
>> was pursuing it

> *pursuing justice*—through works of the law; other manuscripts
>   have: pursuing *the law* of justice
> *the law of justice*—i.e., purity and the rest that the law truly
>   teaches

9:32 Why? Because it was not from faith, but as from works. For they stumbled against the stone of stumbling.

not from faith. They did not obtain justice from faith because they did not seek it from God. They did not believe in him who justifies the ungodly; they did not believe that God works in the person that is justified. *they stumbled.* Like a small stone that is not guarded against, Christ was able to cause stumbling, lying hidden in humility.

> *Why?*—as if to say: Listen carefully!
> *it was not from faith, but as from works*—they were seeking
>   to be justified, but from works of the law as if these could
>   justify them
> *For they stumbled*—Why do they not have faith? Because they
>   stumbled, i.e., they suffered blindness in Christ.

9:33 As it is written: Behold I lay in Zion a stone of stumbling and a rock of offense, and everyone that believes in him shall not be ashamed.

Isaiah attests to this: *Behold I lay* in view, i.e., I will cause to be born, *in Zion*, i.e., among the Jews, *a stone of stumbling*, i.e., Christ, who, being small, is not guarded against, *and a rock of offense*, i.e., that crushes them completely, that brings sorrow in the future (Isa 28:16, 8:14). Christ is called a stone of stumbling according to the condition in which he appeared to the wicked in this life; he is called a rock of offense according to what he will do to the wicked in the life to come. The *rock* before polishing is Christ before the passion, at which time the Jews were scandalized, raging and indignant because he claimed to be the Son of God. The *stone* through polishing is Christ in his passion, when they especially stumbled and were blinded.

> *Behold I lay*—openly and in plain view
> *in Zion*—among the Jews

a stone of stumbling—Christ, like a small pebble against whom
they were not on guard

rock of offense—the same Christ as he completely crushes the
wicked in the future

everyone that believes—whether Jew or Gentile

shall not be ashamed—when Christ comes in the future he will
not only be an offense to the wicked but also salvation to
the good

Chapter 10

10:1 Brothers, indeed, it is the desire of my heart, and a prayer to God is made for them unto salvation.

Brothers. Lest he seem to speak out of hatred, or lest the Gentiles totally reject them, he adds: *Brothers*, they are *the desire*, etc. *and a prayer to God.* For God must help the will through grace if it is to be moved to believe the truth. Hence: *No one comes to me unless it is given him by my Father* (John 6:66).

> *desire of my heart*—unfeigned desire
> *and a prayer to God*—here he indicates that it is given by grace
> *is made*—by me
> *for them*—for those who are stumbling
> *unto salvation*—that God may give them faith by which they
>   may be saved

10:2 For I bear them witness that they have devotion to God, but not according to knowledge.

I bear them witness. <u>Ambrose</u>: He is speaking of those who have not received Christ out of misunderstanding, not envy. They are those to whom Peter says: *I know that you did this through ignorance* (Acts 3:17).[187] *not according to knowledge.* For it is foolish to honor the law and persecute the God of the law.

> *I bear them witness*—it is right that I pray, because *they have devotion for God*; and it is necessary because I myself was once like them, having a zeal *not according to knowledge*

155

> *devotion to God*—zeal for God; they believe that they are
>   acting out of love of God
> *knowledge*—of how to love

10:3 For being ignorant of God's justice and seeking to establish their own, they did not submit to the justice of God.

being ignorant of God's justice. Not the justice by which God is just, but the justice that comes to a person from God. *they did not submit to the justice of God.* This is God's justice, which was not established in the commandment of the law that instills fear, but in the assistance of the grace of Christ.

> *For being ignorant*—here is the meaning of *not according to knowledge*
> *God's justice*—which is through faith in Christ, which comes from God
> *seeking*—or *wishing*
> *to establish*—like the proud
> *their own*—which is through observances of the flesh
> *they did not submit to the justice of God*—by which God justifies those who believe

10:4 For the end of the law is Christ for justice to everyone that believes.

the end of the law. Not the end as of destruction but of completion; therefore he completes justice through faith without works of the law. *Christ for justice.* Justice comes from Christ because if it were through the written law or the natural law and not by faith in Christ, then Christ died in vain. *for justice.* Not human but divine justice. For there is both a human justice and a divine justice. He speaks of human justice at *But Moses said* (Rom. 10:5), of divine justice at *But the justice that is of faith* (Rom. 10:6).

> *the end of the law*—they are ignorant of God's justice because they are ignorant of Christ, who is the giver of justice, who fulfilled what the law foretold
> *Christ for justice*—Christ who indeed avails for justice

10:5 For Moses said that the person who performs the justice which is from the law shall live in it.

For Moses said. In Numbers and Leviticus, where it is expressed in this way: *He that does these things shall live in them* (Lev. 18:5). *shall live in it.* He has this reward, that he will not be punished with death. For it is no great justice to fear, nor does it have merit before God.

> *Moses*—Christ alone is justice unto salvation, because the justice of the law is only profitable for the present life
> *said*—another reading has: *wrote*
> *the person who performs*—i.e., without assisting grace
> *which is from the law*—which is out of fear, not love
> *shall live in it*—he shall not be punished with the penalties of the law

10:6 But the justice that is from faith speaks thus: Do not say in your heart, who shall ascend into heaven?—that is, to bring Christ down;

Do not say. Justice is of faith. Let him not doubt concerning the hope of God that is in Christ; let him not doubt that Christ despoiled hell and ascended to heaven with souls, for the believer is made just from this. *Do not say in your heart*, i.e., do not even think, *Who shall ascend*, i.e., no one will ascend because he who thinks this denies that Christ ascended.

> *But the justice that is from faith speaks thus*—Moses speaks of the justice of the law in that way, but of the justice of faith in this way; or justice itself speaks thus in the human heart, that when it is observed it leads to heaven, and when it is not observed it leads to the abyss
> *that is*—these begin the words of the apostle by which he explains the meaning of the cited words of Moses
> *to bring Christ down*—because that is to ponder how to bring Christ down, insofar as you can

10:7 or, who will descend into the abyss?—that is, to call Christ back from the dead.

or, who will descend into the abyss? In other words, do not think that no one will descend who has not observed the law. To think this is *to call*

Christ back from the dead, i.e., to believe that Christ did not descend into hell. For if those who do not observe justice do not descend, then much less did Abraham and the ancient fathers descend. But if they did not descend, then neither did Christ, who descended only to liberate them.

Or it may be understood in this way: When you hear that Christ was preached to have ascended into heaven after his resurrection, *do not say in your heart*, It is untrue, for *who will ascend?* Because such disbelief *brings Christ down* from heaven to earth, in so far as you can. Likewise, when you also hear it preached that Christ descended into hell, do not say: It is untrue, for *who has descended into the abyss?* Therefore do not say this, because to say it is **to call Christ back from the dead**, insofar as you can, i.e., to deny that Christ has ascended.

    that is—here begin the words of the apostle

10:8 But what does Scripture say? The word is near, in your mouth and in your heart. This is the word of faith which we preach.

The word is near. In other words, it is effective; or it is not something unsuitable; or to speak and to believe this is near and not far from the nature of our souls, since when reason speaks it says to us that we should believe. *This is the word*. Of this word the Lord says: For *you are clean on account of the word that I spoke to you* (John 15:3). He does not say this is through baptism. Why not, except that it is the word in the water that cleanses? Take away the word and what is the water besides water? Add the word to the element and it becomes a sacrament. Whence comes this power of water, so great that in touching the body it cleanses the heart? Is it not the word that accomplishes this, not because it is spoken but because it is believed? For in this word, the transitory sound is one thing and the remaining power another.

> **But what does Scripture say?**—do not say that, but rather believe in this word that Scripture utters in Deuteronomy (Deut. 30:14)
> **The word**—Christ who is the Word in the beginning with the Father; or the preaching of Christ
> **is near**—is effective because it justifies and saves
> **in your mouth**—to confess it
> **in your heart**—to believe it

This is—he explains the text of Moses
the word of faith—by which indeed baptism is consecrated

10:9 Because if you confess the Lord Jesus with your mouth and believe in your heart that God raised him from the dead, you shall be saved.

Because if you confess, etc. Behold the glory of faith and its reward. Faith's glory: if you believe that the Lord is Jesus, i.e., Savior, and that he has risen. And its reward: eternal salvation.

Because—it should be near, because
if you confess—when anyone attacks
the Lord Jesus—not the works of the law; confessing that he
    has risen, or that he is Lord and Jesus, i.e., Savior
raised him—or lifted him up

10:10 For it is believed in the heart unto justice, and confession is made in the mouth unto salvation.

it is believed in the heart. A person can do other things unwillingly, but to believe cannot be done except willingly. *confession.* To confess means to say what is in the heart; otherwise it is speaking but not confessing. That which is in the heart ought to be in the mouth because the mouth is in the face, i.e., in the seat of shame. Not without reason do we make the sign of the cross: it is so that a Christian may not be ashamed of disgraces Christ suffered. It was Peter's sin to deny by his mouth what he believed in his heart. For why did he wash away with tears the sin of having denied with his mouth if it were enough for salvation that he held it in his heart?[188] For truth must both be believed and spoken.

For it is believed in the heart unto justice—believing gives
    salvation because it gives justice, which is the cause of
    salvation; in other words, a person is justified through
    the faith of his heart, i.e., from being ungodly he be-
    comes godly
confession—which is added to faith, as in the martyrs
in the mouth—after faith of the heart; otherwise it is of no
    benefit
unto salvation—not only unto justice

10:11 For Scripture says: Everyone that believes in him shall not be put to shame.

> *For Scripture says*—through Isaiah (Isa. 28:16)[189], regarding
> believing in the heart unto justice
> *Everyone*—not only Jews but also Gentiles
> *shall not be put to shame*—will not be ashamed in the future
> even if they seem ashamed here

10:12 For there is no distinction between Jew and Greek: the same is Lord of all, rich towards all who invoke him.

who invoke him. He that prays, invokes; but he cannot invoke unless he first believes. Therefore those who invoke not only believe but also pray. Thus, after the mind believes, it will not cease to ask for what God has promised to those who keep vigilant with their whole heart, because believing gives remission of sins and invoking obtains the promises of God.

> *For there is no distinction*—everyone, he says, because *there is
> no distinction*, but *in every nation, he that fears God is
> acceptable to him* (Acts 10:35)
> *the same*—the same Creator
> *rich*—sufficing to enrich all
> *towards all who invoke him*—who invoke him by faith and
> works; he is not rich towards others

10:13 For whosoever invokes the name of the Lord will be saved.

> *For*—he proves what he had said with a text from Isaiah
> (Joel 2:32; Acts 2:21)
> *whosoever*—whether Jew or Gentile
> *invokes*—by rightly subjecting himself
> *will be saved*—in eternal beatitude

10:14 How, then, will they invoke him in whom they have not believed? Or how will they believe in him of whom they have not heard? And how will they hear without a preacher?

How, then, will they invoke, etc. Having proved that individuals are taken from both peoples, he shows how they are taken, namely, through forgiveness achieved for both peoples. And he that does not receive this forgiveness is without excuse. Invocation saves. Therefore it is necessary to believe, because *how will they invoke*, etc. Believing comes from hearing; hearing from preaching; preaching from sending by God. And thus all comes down from the fountain of grace. Preaching comes from sending because God truly sends even false messengers, knowing how to use evil for good. Sometimes out of wrath he also sends wicked messengers to the wicked so that they may perish in turn through themselves, as is just.

> *How, then, will they invoke him*—or, but how, etc. A person
>   who is turned away from God cannot do this.
> *in whom they have not believed*—i.e., they will not invoke him
>   unless they believe
> *how will they believe in him*—he is not believed in when they
>   refuse to obey him
> *of whom they have not heard*—nor has anyone ever believed
>   who did not hear in some way; they will not believe unless
>   they hear
> *how will they hear without a preacher*—they will not hear
>   unless it is preached to them; he that resists a preacher
>   does not receive the sender

10:15 But how will they preach unless they are sent? As it is written: How beautiful are the feet of those who evangelize peace, of those who evangelize good things.

But how will they preach unless they are sent? Behold it is clear that preachers were also sent to the Gentiles, and thus the apostle refutes those who supposed that the Gospel should only be preached to the Jews. *How beautiful are the feet*, because they enlighten the world. In this it is clear that they were sent by God, since otherwise they could not have done it. *peace*. Reconciliation between people and people, when the wall of legal ritual among the Jews was destroyed as well as the wall of idolatry among the Gentiles. Also reconciliation between God, who justifies the ungodly through faith, and people who believe in him. *who evangelize good things*. The peace above peace, since the kingdom of God is also peace.

> *how will they preach*—they will not preach unless they are
>   sent; they are not true apostles if they are not sent

As it is written—but they were sent, because it is written in
   Isaiah (Isa. 52:7) and in the prophet Nahum (Nah. 1:15)
feet—the apostles who enlighten the world
who evangelize peace—who proclaim reconciliation
who evangelize—he proclaims well who fulfills in works what
   he preaches with his mouth
good things—good things to come

**10:16 But not all obey the Gospel, for Isaiah says: Lord, who has be-
lieved our report?**

for Isaiah says. Having foreknowledge, God foretold the faithlessness of
the Jews, but he did not cause it. Nor would he have foreknown their evils
unless they were going to have them. In the same way God blinds, not
by causing but by abandoning, which their will merited. If it is said that
the Jews are unable to believe because Isaiah foretold this (Isa. 53:1), I
say that they are unable because they are unwilling, which God foreknew
and foretold, but did not cause. They are unable to believe as long as they
are proud and attribute everything to their own powers, thus denying
that they need divine aid for doing good.

> *But not all obey the Gospel*—i.e., not all who have heard it
>   through the apostles; for while hearing comes from grace,
>   there is also another grace necessary to move the heart
> *for Isaiah says*—that some and not all obey
> *who*—i.e., it was believed by some, not all
> *has believed*—the things they hear from us; or the things we
>   hear from you

**10:17 Therefore faith comes from hearing, and hearing by the word of
God.**

faith comes from hearing. While God teaches inwardly, the preacher proclaims outwardly. *by the word of God.* That is, through the grace of Christ,
who sends us teachers of the evangelical word. For unless something is
spoken, it cannot be heard or believed.

> *Therefore*—since everyone believes from hearing, though not
>   all believe

faith comes from hearing—at some time, though not everywhere
by the word—not by our merits
of God—another reading has *of Christ*

10:18 But I say: Have they not heard? Indeed they have. Their sound has gone forth to the whole world and their words to the ends of the earth.

Indeed they have, or surely, i.e., certainly, and thus they are without excuse, as David shows in the Psalms, saying: *Their sound has gone forth*, etc. (Ps. 18:5). *to the whole world.* This was not fulfilled in the apostles' time, but he sees, by revelation of the Holy Spirit, that this will be fulfilled in their successors. Therefore he spoke in the past tense because of the certitude of prophesy, and by "their" he wished to be understood not only the apostles but also their successors. In the same way is understood the verse: *You will be my witnesses to the ends of the earth* (Acts 1:8).

> *Have they not heard?*—They believed from hearing, but those
>   who did not believe, *have they not heard?* As if to say:
>   They have heard and thus are without excuse.
> *sound*—reputation
> *to the whole world*—i.e., not only to nearby lands but even to
>   far off lands.
> *their words*—their very words
> *to the ends of the earth*—on every side

10:19 But I say: Has Israel not known? First Moses says: I will make you jealous by those who are not a people; by a foolish people I will provoke you to anger.

But I say: Has Israel not known? Because it was possible for them to hear but not to know, he affirms that they indeed knew. Israel knew because they were unable to deny it through reason or authority, yet they did not truly know in such a way that it remained in their minds. *I will make you jealous.* The Jews are envious when the Gentiles say that the God of the Jews is their own God and that the promises in the Law and the Prophets pertain to themselves. *by those who are not a people.* The Gentiles were not called a holy people before; or now they are not a people because they are not born such. *by a foolish people.* That is, in comparison to a foolish people, i.e., the Gentiles who had not known the true God.

> *But I say*—All have heard; but concerning the Jews in parti-
> cular I say: *Has Israel not known?*
> *not known*—of course they have known from Moses, who is
>   *first*, i.e., greatest, and from the other prophets who came
>   after him
> *I will make you*—I will allow you to become
> *jealous*—envious at the conversion of the Gentiles
> *those who are not a people*—i.e., Gentiles, who were not a
>   people before, or who are not a people now
> *a foolish people*—which had not known God
> *I will provoke you to anger*—I will allow you to become angry
>   and to persecute; and when they see this happen, let them
>   consider what has come

**10:20 And Isaiah dares to say: I was found by those who were not seek-
ing me; I appeared openly to those who did not ask for me.**

> *And Isaiah dares*—even though he could foresee that punish-
>   ment was coming, nevertheless he dares; not only Moses
>   says this but also Isaiah (Isa. 65:1–2)
> *to say*—in the person of Christ
> *I was found*—I freely offered myself
> *by those who were not seeking me*—not seeking of themselves;
>   and the Jew's envy came from this
> *I appeared openly*—manifestly
> *who did not ask for me*—who did not ask others about me

**10:21 But to Israel he says: All day I stretched out my hands to a people
that did not believe and even spoke against me.**

All day I stretched out my hands. During the whole time I dwelt with
them and gave light to the world; or I stretched out my hands on the
cross; or I enlarged works and compassion, i.e., I revealed more to the
Jews seeing that I denied them no blessing: I raised their dead, I healed
their various illnesses. For he is said to stretch out his hands who lavishly
gives blessings to those who ask for them. *my hands.* This may be understood of the works he showed to that people, or it may be understood
of his hands extended on the cross, so that the whole crucifixion is ex-

pressed in the part. Thus, *All day*, i.e., for part of the whole day, *I stretched out my hands* on the cross *to a people that does not believe* but, even worse, that *speaks against me* (Isa. 65:2).

> ***But to Israel***—in the verse before he addressed the Gentiles
> ***my hands***—works and compassion
> ***and even spoke against me***—which is worse

Chapter 11

11:1 Therefore I say: Has God rejected his people? By no means! For I too am an Israelite of the seed of Abraham, from the tribe of Benjamin.

Therefore I say. Because he has countered the Jews with so many Scriptures, the Gentiles where able to insult them, saying that the Jews have been completely rejected. So now he begins to oppose these Gentiles.

> *Therefore I say*—I seem to be saying that God has rejected his people, but did I really say this?
> *rejected*—completely
> *his people*—or his inheritance; or his nation, the Jews, for whom he did so much
> *By no means!*—when I say the Jews are unfaithful I do not mean all the Jews
> *For I too*—because he has not rejected me and other Jews that have been predestined
> *an Israelite*—a Jew, not a proselyte but of the seed of Abraham through the line of Benjamin
> *from the tribe of Benjamin*—lest he be thought to come from Ishmael

11:2 God has not rejected his people whom he foreknew. Or do you not know what Scripture says in Elijah, how he interceded with God for Israel?

he foreknew. He uses this in place of "he predestined." That it should be understood in this way is clear from what follows. But he said *he foreknew* lest the Jews become proud again when he says they were not rejected but people of God. *Or do you not know.* In other words, do you not know that

166

the remnant in this time is comparable to when it seemed to Elijah that he was the only one left? And if Elijah was unaware that others besides himself were also preserved, it is no wonder if those today are unaware of this.

> *God has not rejected his people*—just as he has not rejected me
> *whom he foreknew*—whom he predestined
> *Scripture*—the Books of Kings (1 Kings 19:14, 18)
> *in Elijah*—where it speaks of Elijah
> *how*—namely
> *he interceded*—between himself and them
> *with God*—the judge
> *for*—or against

11:3 Lord, they have killed your prophets, they have dug under your altars, and I alone am left; and they seek my life.

> *Lord*—saying, Lord
> *they have killed your prophets*—this took place under Jezebel
> *dug under*—they toppled them from their foundations

11:4 But what does Scripture say was the divine answer to him? I have left to me seven thousand people who have not bowed their knees before Baal.

seven thousand people. By *seven* the whole is designated, by *thousand*, perfection.

> *But what does Scripture say*—He thought he was alone,
>   but what does Scripture say?
> *I have left to me*—I have preserved by grace
> *seven thousand people*—all the good people
> *Baal*—the god of Ahab and Jezebel

11:5 So too at this time a remnant shall be saved according to the election of God's grace.

So too. In other words, since there were many at that time, even if Elijah did not know it, *so too*, i.e., today, there are some hidden in the same way or saved through the same grace.

at this time—at this time of grace, when it is easier
shall be saved—or are saved
according to the election—through grace by which they were
    chosen; not by merits; hence: *You have not chosen me, but
    I have chosen you* (John 15:16)

11:6 But if by grace, then it is no longer from works; otherwise grace is no longer grace.

But if—I said that they are saved by grace, *but if*
by grace—i.e., they are saved by grace
works—of the law
otherwise—i.e., if they are saved by works of the law
grace—and it is certain that there is grace
is no longer grace—but something owed

11:7 What then? Israel did not obtain that which it was seeking, but election obtained it while the rest were blinded.

What then? At hearing that a remnant was saved by grace, not works, what then should be said? *but election obtained it*. Election is from grace, not merits, but blindness is from merits. They were blinded because they were unwilling to believe, just as the others believed because they were willing. Therefore mercy and justice are brought about by God in their wills: by assigning grace through mercy in his elect while allowing others to be blinded through judgment. Whoever was unwilling to believe, although he understood, is obliged to follow what he wills so that he is unable to believe otherwise. Thus they were aided in their will not to understand what is true, because they knew the truth but were saying it was false. The envy of an evil will merits this. But this is not true for those who act in ignorance.

What then?—what then should be said? This, namely, that
    Israel did not
that which it was seeking—justice from works
election obtained it—by grace the elect received justice
    through faith
while the rest were blinded—not only did they not obtain it
    but *the rest were blinded*

11:8 As it is written: God gave them a spirit of compunction until today, eyes to see not and ears to hear not.

God gave them. He is speaking of evil compunction, because it often happens that even something good is an annoyance to a person, as the teaching of Christ was to the Pharisees. And so he calls the envious mind, whereby it envied the teaching of Christ, *a spirit of compunction.* *until today.* As long as the day can be called today, i.e., up to the present day, including all the days to which this Scripture will reach.

> *As it is written*—in Isaiah (Isa 6:9–10; 29:10), although in
>   different words
> *God gave them a spirit of compunction*—he allowed them to
>   have evil compunction
> *eyes to see not*—reason that can see by itself, but they have
>   reason that sees not
> *ears to hear not*—reason that understands another's teaching,
>   but they have reason that hears not

11:9 And David says: Let their table become a snare and a trap before them, a scandal and a retribution to them.

their table. That is, the Scripture first bestowed on them and placed *before them*, which became *a trap* because they delighted in its carnal observances. Or *before them* because they could have understood it if they had wished to pay attention to reason. Or *before them* because they understood iniquity and yet were preeminent in it. *a snare.* As they offered me vinegar, so it became for them. *a snare*, etc. Let Scripture, which is bread for the mind, trap them when they misunderstand it and reject Christ's preaching because of it. This was also the cause of their captivity when they killed Christ out of zeal for Scripture. And this captivity was the cause of *scandal* and shame, and later of eternal damnation, which is specifically called *retribution*.

> *says*—adding
> *their table*—the malice they maintained towards me
> *a snare*—so that their very iniquity hinders them
> *a trap*—to hold them
> *a scandal*—to cause them shame
> *a retribution*—eternal damnation

11:10 Let their eyes be darkened, so that they do not see, and their back be always bent.

Let their eyes be darkened. Because without cause they saw not, let them be unable to see. These words (Ps. 68:23–24) were not spoken in the desire of prayer but in the prophetic office.

> *eyes*—reason which sees
> *so that they do not see*—that they are sinful
> *back*—free choice which ought to be straight
> *bent*—aggravated by sins

11:11 Therefore I say: Did they stumble so that they fell? May it never be! But in their sin is salvation for the Gentiles, so that they may be jealous of them.

Therefore I say. Because I say, from the authority of the prophets, that they have been blinded, do you think it is incurable and without benefit? Rather their fall is beneficial and they can be restored. Therefore, let no one despise them. *salvation for the Gentiles.* When the Jews were scattered throughout the world as a testimony that the prophecies of Christ were true. *that they may be jealous of them.* This has often happened, and it will happen more fully at the end of the age, when the Jews will imitate Christians by having faith in Christ. Then the hand of Moses will be called back to his bosom (Exod. 4:7); then our Moses will return to his mother and brothers (Exod. 2:9–11). It can also be understood thus: that the Gentiles may be jealous of the Jews, i.e., that they might believe as the Jews used to believe, or that they might be moved with jealousy for God on account of the evil works of the Jews.

> *I say*—I seem to say
> *so that they fell*—so that they simply fell, without recovery
> or benefit
> *May it never be*—that their fall was useless; rather it was
> beneficial
> *their sin is salvation for the Gentiles*—hence: *Since you have
> rejected the word of God, behold we turn to the Gentiles*
> (Acts 13:46).
> *so that*—so that in this way

they may be jealous—that the Jews, having zeal for the law and
　　the fathers, might be envious and hate them
of them—of the others

**11:12 But if their sin entails riches for the world and their decline
riches for the Gentiles, then how much more their fullness?**

But if their sin. He said that the Jews' sin is beneficial; but if this is true,
then their conversion will be more so. *how much more*, etc. That is, if God
turned their evil into good, i.e., into riches for the world, then how much
more will their good, when their fullness is converted at the end, enrich
the Gentiles by teaching and example. For it shows that their fall was
neither unprofitable nor incurable.

　　their sin—that they killed God, or that they rejected his word
　　entails riches for the world—if the world was enriched by
　　　　their sin
　　their decline—i.e., their being cast off, for few of them were
　　　　converted
　　riches for the Gentiles—few Jews were converted, while the
　　　　apostles enriched the Gentiles
　　their fullness—when a great number of them will be converted
　　　　at the end of the world

**11:13 Indeed I say to you, Gentiles, as long as I am apostle of the Gen-
tiles I will honor my ministry,**

as long as. Although *I am apostle of the Gentiles, I will honor my ministry*
by going beyond what I owe, so that, as I also try to labor for the Jews, if
one approach is unsuccessful, I will undertake another, which I would not
do if I despaired of their salvation.

　　Indeed I say to you—as if someone had asked whether the
　　　　Jews can be converted, he says they certainly can
　　Gentiles—who are particularly mine
　　as long as I am apostle—which is always
　　of the Gentiles—not of the Jews, because I was sent to the
　　　　Gentiles

11:14 if by any means I may provoke my flesh to jealousy and save some of them.

> *by any means*—with either prosperity or adversity
> *I may provoke*—I may be able to provoke
> *my flesh*—the Jews
> *to jealousy*—i.e., to imitate me
> *and*—or, that I may thus
> *save*—with the help of God's grace
> *some of them*—at least some of them

11:15 For if the loss of them is the reconciliation of the world, what is their acceptance if not life from the dead?

> *For if*—and if, as is true; and so I labor for them because
> their acceptance will be beneficial for the instruction
> of the Gentiles
> *the loss of them*—their unfaithfulness
> *what is*—what will be
> *their acceptance*—the acceptance of the remnant
> *life from the dead*—life for the Gentiles, who before were dead

11:16 Now if a portion is holy, so too the lump; and if the root is holy, so too the branches.

Now if a portion. I said that the acceptance of them will be very beneficial; nor should you say this cannot happen, as if the entire people must be repudiated. For *if a portion*, i.e., if a few of them have been accepted, as the apostles and other disciples, *is holy*, then *so too the lump*, i.e., the people can be made holy. Ambrose: A portion is a small taking of something, such as food or drink, for the testing of the whole amount.[190] *and if the root*, i.e., the patriarchs from whom they derive the disposition of holy faith, *so too the branches*, those who grew out of the race that was founded in them.

> *so too the lump*—can be made holy

11:17 But if some of the branches were broken off and you, although you were a wild olive plant, were grafted into them and became a companion of the root and of the richness of the olive tree,

a companion. One who shares in the hope of the promise. This is against common practice, for a good tree is usually grafted into an inferior tree; but here an inferior tree is grafted into a good tree.

> *But if*—he argues that the Jews are still able to be accepted
>   so that he may restrain the Gentiles
> *the branches*—the natural branches
> *broken off*—cut off from the promise
> *and you*—O Gentile
> *a wild olive plant*—which is naturally barren and bitter
> *were engrafted*—conjoined by an another's action
> *into them*—in the place of those broken off
> *a companion*—a partaker
> *of the root*—of the patriarchs and prophets
> *of the richness*—of the apostles who, above all others, possess
>   the spirit of the root
> *of the olive tree*—of the fruit-bearing Jewish people before
>   the advent of Christ

11:18 do not boast against the branches. But if you boast, you are not supporting the root, but the root you.

> *do not boast*—If, I say, this is true, then do not boast; for
>   although the olive tree was pruned, it was not cut down.
>   Do not gloat over the other's misfortune.
> *the branches*—the broken-off branches
> *if you boast*—O Gentile
> *you are not supporting the root*—this is said to you because
>   the Jewish people have received nothing from you, but
>   you have faith from them

11:19 You say, then: The branches were broken off so that I might be grafted in.

You say, then, etc. You say, as it were, that it is not right to boast against the Jews who are standing, but is right to boast against those who were removed for the sake of my engrafting.

> *You say, then*—O Gentile

11:20 Indeed, they were broken off on account of unbelief. But you stand in faith. Be not high-minded, but afraid.

The apostle refutes what they were saying in this way: *Indeed* you are right, since it is true that *they were broken off on account of unbelief.* However, *you stand in faith*, i.e., not by your own merit but by the grace of God. And so do not boast lest you also be broken off through pride, as the Jews were broken off through unbelief. You undermine your own stability if you destroy them by whom you stand. He is easily deceived who rejoices in another's misfortune. *you stand in faith.* It is because of God's blessing, not your own merit, that you stand. *but afraid,* lest in the end you lose the blessing of grace and fall into punishment—for chaste fear is when a soul takes care lest God abandon it after he has been abandoned.

> *Indeed*—what you say is right, however
> *on account of unbelief*—i.e., by their own fault; thus your
>   opportunity of salvation was not on account of you
> *Be not*—And therefore be not
> *high-minded*—proud
> *afraid*—of stumbling, with chaste fear

11:21 For if God did not spare the natural branches, perhaps he will not spare you either.

For if God. God did not spare the Jews, who traced their origin from the holy fathers, from whose race he also took flesh. How much less, then, will he spare you if you depart from the faith or swell up with pride?

> *For if God*—be afraid, which is proper, for *if God*, etc.
> *did not spare the natural branches*—with the prerogative
>   of the fathers to whom the promise was made
> *perhaps*—be careful, then, lest this happen which surely
>   can happen
> *he will not spare you either*—for the sake of another

11:22 See, then, the goodness and the severity of God: severity indeed to them who fell, but God's goodness to you if you remain in goodness. Otherwise you too will be cut off.

See, then—because you stand in faith
the goodness and the severity of God—he encourages by his
  goodness and frightens by his severity; learn to be
  humble through both
severity—i.e., strict judgment, because they were broken off
  through unbelief
God's goodness to you—whereby he has blessed you
if you remain—if, however, you remain
in goodness—so that you attribute all to God
Otherwise—if you do not remain in it
you too—just as the Jews
will be cut off—from the holy root and experience the
  severity of God

11:23 But they also will be engrafted if they do not remain in unbelief. For God is able to graft them in again.

But—i.e., not only will you fall if you do not remain in goodness
they also will be engrafted—therefore they should not be
  despised
if they do not remain in unbelief—which surely can happen
to graft them in again—to himself, since he was even born
  from them

11:24 For if you were cut from a natural wild olive tree and against nature were grafted into a good olive tree, how much more will they, who are according to nature, be grafted into their own olive tree?

against nature. It is said that it goes against the custom of nature for a graft to bear the fruit of the root. Yet God does nothing against nature because his action constitutes nature. God's work is the highest nature, and nothing happens against this, but only against what we are accustomed to. *olive tree*. The faith of the fathers is understood here.

For—For God is able to engraft them. For they will be
  engrafted; this is an argument from the lesser to the greater.
you were cut—by God's power
natural—because you were born in it
wild olive tree—the rites of the sterile Gentiles

against nature—because idolatry and such sins were natural,
    as it were, to the Gentiles from practice
were grafted into a good olive tree—were united by faith to
    the patriarchs and apostles who possessed the richness
    of the Holy Spirit
how much more—if this is true, how much more, etc.
who are according to nature—who were taught in the law
    how to worship God
grafted into their own olive tree—they will be united to
    their own people

**11:25 For I would not have you ignorant, brothers, of this mystery,
so you may not be wise in yourselves, that partial blindness has come
upon Israel until the fullness of the Gentiles should enter.**

I would not have you ignorant—the Jews will be grafted in,
    some surely in the interim and then a fullness in the end,
    and I want you to know this
this mystery—the hidden judgment of God
so you may not be wise in yourselves—a mystery, I say, lest
    you think you can examine it by your own powers
partial blindness—not all have been blinded
has come upon Israel—not from nature but from guilt
until—so that or till when; that the cause and the end may
    be indicated

**11:26 And thus all Israel might be saved. As it is written: Out of Zion
shall come he that can rescue and turn away ungodliness from Jacob.**

ungodliness. Worship in legal observance. The worship of the Jews is ungodliness since the coming of Christ.

And thus—after they have entered
all Israel might be saved—through the preaching of Elijah
    and Enoch; by emulating the Gentiles
As it is written—in Isaiah (Isa. 59:20)
Out of Zion—from the Jews
shall come—according to the flesh
rescue—since in the interim hardly any are converted

turn away—by their own volition; at the end when this is
   easily done
ungodliness—unfaithfulness
from Jacob—from the Jews

11:27 And this a testament from me to them, when I take away their sins.

when I take away. This will be at the end when the Jews shall be converted by the preaching of Elijah and Enoch. Thus Malachi: *I will send you Elijah the Tishbite, who shall turn the hearts of fathers to their children and the hearts of children to their fathers* (Mal. 4:5–6; Luke 1:17), so that the children might understand like their fathers, i.e., as the prophets understood.

And this—and this will be
a testament—or testimony; the promise shall be fulfilled
from me—because I myself shall do what I promised
I take away—I will forgive

11:28 According to the gospel, indeed, they are enemies for your sake, but according to election they are most dear for the sake of the fathers.

According to the gospel, etc. <u>Augustine</u>: In other words, at that time they will be converted, but now they are indeed enemies of Christ and certainly our enemies. They will be reconverted from themselves, i.e., from their own sin.[191] But this is *according to the gospel* and *for your sake*, i.e., for the advantage of the gospel and for your advantage. *enemies for your sake*. He shows that this comes about by God's arrangement. For of themselves they can only be enemies, which benefits the gospel—God using the wicked for a good end. Thus when they act against God's will, the will of God is fulfilled, which disposes everything wisely. *for the sake of the fathers*. The beloved are chosen for the sake of their fathers, to whom these things were promised. For they are not called by the calling whereby many nonetheless perished, not being foreknown. About this calling it is said: *Many are called but few chosen* (Matt. 20:16, 22:14). Rather they are called by that calling whereby they are chosen, which is without change, because he that hears from the Father comes to the Son, who does not lose any of all who are given to him (John 6:39). But when someone perishes it is not because the Son has lost him. Hence: *they went out from us but they were not of us* (1 John 2:19).

> *According to the gospel*—in regard to the gospel. Then they will be converted, but now they are enemies; behold the reason why part was blinded and part enlightened.
>
> *for your sake*—for your benefit; that you might have a place to enter by faith
>
> *but according to election they are most dear*—in other words, some are enemies according to the gospel, and this is for your sake; but some are most dear or beloved according to election, not according to merits
>
> *for the sake of the fathers*—i.e., for the sake of the promises made to their fathers

11:29 But without repentance are the gifts and calling of God.

without repentance. They are going to be saved *according to election and for the sake of the fathers*, because *the gifts*, i.e., the promises, *and calling*, i.e., election from eternity, are *without repentance*, i.e., without change in God's counsel. Or it may be understood in this way: I say *according to election* because God inspires faith in them without their preceding repentance. *without repentance.*[192] God's grace in baptism does not require sighs or lamentation or any work, but faith alone, and it freely pardons all sins. He says this, then, lest they suppose that those whom they do not see grieving cannot receive mercy.

> *without repentance*—without change
>
> *the gifts*—remission of sins in baptism; the promises
>
> *calling of God*—the election from eternity; or the interior and gratuitous calling unto faith, which no one's merit precedes

11:30 For just as you also at one time did not believe in God, but now you have found mercy because of their unbelief,

For just as, i.e., for which reason God once allowed you not to believe, namely, that you would not have cause to boast after being converted.

> *For just as*—thus was it necessary that some were enemies and others elect

at one time—for a longer time than they

did not believe in God—which had this significance: that now, being humble, you may believe

now—recently

you have found mercy—proof that nature is insufficient, i.e., that you were unable to be helped through free will

because of their unbelief—which is a cause of your mercy

11:31 so they also now have not believed unto your mercy that they too might find mercy.

that they too. When they have come to know that salvation is not through the law but through grace, so that they too might find mercy through humility.

they—the Jews

have not believed—lest they have reason to boast after being converted

unto your mercy—when you came into mercy; i.e., they did not have the grace of faith through God's mercy as you had

they—having been made humble

mercy—the grace of faith

11:32 For God closed up all in unbelief that he might have mercy on all.

God closed up. That is, he allowed all to be closed up. He seems in some way to explain the mystery here: for God closed up all in unbelief so that, having been put to shame by repenting for the bitterness of their unbelief, they might remain more humble when they are converted by believing in the sweetness of God's mercy. In this way too the grace of his gift might be most gracious so that they cry out, *How great is the abundance of your sweetness*, O Lord (Ps. 30:20).

on all, i.e., Jews and Gentiles. Not that none will be condemned, as some falsely imagined. For their understanding is too narrow to examine the justice of God's judgments or consider the gratuitous grace rendered for no proceeding merits. Nor does it disturb us as much that grace is offered to the unworthy as that it is denied to others who are just as unworthy. <u>Augustine</u>: I know that just as nothing is impossible with God, so there is no injustice with God. And I know that he resists the proud and gives grace to the humble. But it is unclear why he gives it to some that are unworthy and denies it to others. This, then, is something in the hidden depths of God's judgments. Nor is it clear why he should save Jews and Gentiles in this way, allowing them first to be closed up in unbelief.[193]

> *For God closed up all*—this happened therefore to both Jews and Gentiles
> *in unbelief*—since otherwise they would come to ruin from pride

11:33 O the depths of the riches of the wisdom and knowledge of God! How incomprehensible are his judgments and unsearchable his ways!

O the depths. If anyone asks why they are saved in this way when there are many ways of salvation, the apostle, full of wonder, states that he does not know.

Take note of the following: since we perceive that creatures have come into being, we should not doubt at all the existence of God the Father from whom all things have their origin. Further, if he were without reason then reality would appear meaningless. Therefore we know without a doubt that he has such reason, which proceeds from him and not he from reason. That is, he has a Son through whom we discern that all things are rationally disposed. And we believe in faith that he proceeded from the Father, and we recognize that God the Father rejoices that he has such a reason and this reason rejoices that it proceeded from such a Father; therefore we have no doubt that the joy and goodness proceeding from both is the Spirit in whom they have established all things. Nor do we doubt at all that this Spirit comes to creatures. And thus the Spirit is said to proceed, i.e., to be given, not so much to the Father and Son but to people. For if we see any good in anyone we believe it has been given to him by the Father and the Son through the Spirit. It should be noticed that to say that reason proceeds from the Father, while goodness and joy proceed from both, as Augustine says, is nothing else than to say that the Father generates the Son; but that the Spirit is said to proceed from the Father and the Son means he is sent and also given by them.[194] *his ways,* that is, the carrying out of his determinations; for what he has disposed cannot be known from its outworking.

O the depths—and why? That you may not think he can be
    comprehended.
the riches—because he knows the deepest things
wisdom—regarding spiritual matters
knowledge—regarding mundane matters
How incomprehensible—just as his wisdom and knowledge
    are incomprehensible, so too his judgments, for which
    he drew upon his wisdom and knowledge[195]
his judgments—i.e., the arrangement of all things

11:34 For who has known the mind of the Lord? Or who has been his counselor?

his counselor. His only begotten Son, who is also called an angel of great counsel,[196] is his counselor. But no human or angel has been his counselor.

    For who—since his wisdom and knowledge are so high; Isaiah
        says this (Isa. 40:13)
    the mind—in wisdom and knowledge
    who has been his counselor?—In the arrangement and outwork-
        ing of things, who was there whose counsel he followed?
        Or who has known his counsel?

11:35 Or who has first given to him and he will be repaid?

Or who has first given, etc., since we are unable to know his judgments; or he is asserting that God gives by grace alone.

    given—faith and good works
    he will be repaid—a reward from God because he first gave
        God his faith

11:36 Because from him and through him and in him are all things. To him be honor and glory forever. Amen.

Because from him, etc. "From," "through," and "in" indicate distinction of persons and the repeated pronoun indicates identity of substance. *Because.* Because such glory belongs to God and not to those who are just. *from him.* Not *of* him, for heaven and earth are *from* him since he made them, but not *of* him since they are not of his substance. *in him are*

all things which he established; yet those who sin do not defile him, of whose wisdom it is said: It extends to all things because of its purity and no defilement can touch it.[197]

Augustine: It is right that we understand the Trinity, perceiving the creator with our mind through things that have been made. And traces of the Trinity appear in creatures, for in the Trinity is the highest origin of all things and the most perfect sweetness and most blessed love. And so these three are seen to be determined by one another; and in themselves they are also infinite, and thus each are in each, and all are in each, and each are in all, and all are one. Therefore it should not be understood in a confusing way when the apostle says: *From him and through him and in him.* He says "from him" for the Father, "through him" for the Son, and "in him" for the Holy Spirit. And when he says *from him*, he does not want you to understand that all things are only from the Father and deny that all things are from the Son or from the Holy Spirit. It can be correctly said that from the Father and through the Father and in the Father are all things. And the same can be asserted of the Son and the Holy Spirit. But when it is said that *from him and through him and in him are all things* then certainly the equality of Father, Son, and Holy Spirit is shown. And because he had not mentioned the Father or Son or Holy Spirit by name before, but only God and Lord, which can also be used for the Trinity itself, he wished that each of these three be indicated separately.[198]

all things. Things that exist naturally, not sins that corrupt nature and arise from the will of sinners. Traces of the Trinity appear in creatures. In the Trinity is the highest origin of all things and the perfect sweetness and the most blessed love.

> **Because**—no one (answering the question), indeed *because from him*, etc.
> **from him**—the Father from whom is the Son
> **through him**—the Son through whom are all things
> **in him**—the Holy Spirit, because God has created and conserves all things in his love alone

Chapter 12

12:1 And so I beseech you, brothers, by the mercy of God, to present your bodies as a living sacrifice, holy, pleasing to God, your rational service.

From here on is found moral admonition, which comes after the treatise on the law and faith and on the nature of the Jewish people and the Gentiles. *I beseech you.* Up till now he has humbled each of them sufficiently and brought to naught the boast in their earlier condition. Now, having brought the matter to a close, as it were, he finally comes to morality. *I beseech you.* Until now his aim was that one side might not boast over against the other; from now on it is that one might work for the benefit of the other. *by the mercy of God,* i.e., by the apostolate mercifully entrusted to me by God; or by the mercy granted to you by God. *as a living sacrifice.* Augustine: Formerly a sacrifice was killed so that people might be shown that they were subject to death on account of sin; now, because we are free from sin, a living sacrifice is offered for a sign of eternal life. [199]

And so—since all things are in him
brothers—fraternity requires me to seek this
to present—to offer
your bodies—not only your minds; although your flesh resists
as a living sacrifice—in mortification of carnal desires
living—through good works
holy—steadfast in good works
pleasing to God—that you ask with good intention
rational—with discretion, lest you go too far
service—all that has been mentioned should be your service

12:2 And do not be conformed to this world, but be refashioned in the newness of your mind, that you may prove what is the will of God: good, acceptable, and perfect.

do not be conformed. Augustine: Here the soul becomes a sacrifice to God when, inflamed with the fire of love, it loses the form of worldly concupiscence and, bringing itself back to God, is refashioned and subjected, so to speak, to that unchangeable form.[200] *do not be conformed* is a general prohibition and *be refashioned* is a general command. The one pertains to continence, the other to justice; the one to not desiring, the other to loving; the one to departing from evil, the other to doing good. For by not desiring we are stripped of oldness and by loving we are clothed with newness.[201] *be refashioned.* Because the image of God has been partly lost, the soul should begin to be refashioned by him who fashioned it— for it is not able to refashion itself as it was able to deform itself.[202]

what is the will of God, etc. The will of God is either the will itself that is in God whereby he wills or it is that which he wills. Here it is understood as God's will whereby he wills, which is always fulfilled. Sometimes it is called the good pleasure or disposition of God, and of this the prophet says: *He has done all things, whatsoever he willed* (Ps. 113:11); and the apostle: *Who shall resist his will* (Rom. 9:19)? Therefore God is the author of all good things and wills them to happen. However he does not will evil things to happen, but neither does he will them not to happen. For if he willed them not to happen and they happened, then something would have resisted his will; yet he foreknows only things that happen. Further, the will of God is called his operation or his permission. Hence Augustine says: Nothing takes place which the almighty does not will to be done either by allowing it to be done or by doing it himself.[203] Again, sometimes God's will is called his counsel or his approval.

> *And do not*—for it is within your power
> *do not be conformed to this world*—do not receive the form of worldly concupiscence
> *be refashioned*—having been deformed in Adam; or be refashioned again and again and, as it were, day by day
> *in the newness*—to the conduct of the new person
> *of your mind*—or, of your understanding; over which sin has no dominion

that you may prove—in testing what God wills
good—because whatever God wills is good
acceptable—to those who rightly understand and have
    been tested
perfect—in all commandments; in all goodness, so that
    nothing is better

12:3 For I say, through the grace that has been given me, to all who are among you, not to be wiser than you ought but to be wise according to sobriety and as God has divided a measure of faith to each.

For I say. This is the sacrifice of Christians, the many who are one body in Christ (Rom. 12:5). For in the sacrament of the altar this is shown to the faithful in the prayer of the Church, which is signified in the reality that she offers. For just as bread is made up of many grains, the holy Church consists of many members of the faithful, who rejoice together by participation in their creator, by whose gift they are holy. And this is also shown in what follows, where he says: *We who are many are one body in Christ* (Rom. 12:5), which cannot happen unless they are *wise according to sobriety*, which he commands here.

to be wise according to sobriety. Such wisdom does not go beyond the limits of justice, which is only useful to us without being harmful to anyone.[204] *to each.* Just as he admonished them not to be proud of their earlier condition, so they should not be proud of the blessings they have received in faith. *to each.* To the greater and to the lesser, according to the purpose whereby God has granted gifts measured out separately, as faith merits them. God did this, then, so that the Church might not be in need and that there might be occasion for serving, in order to foster mutual love. Hence he adds: *For just as . . . in one body*, etc. (Rom.12:4). *to each.* Since it lacks its own strength, an infant grows only if it is continually nourished; otherwise it dies.

a measure of faith. God also divides faith by measure, without which there are no good works. The Spirit was not given to Christ according to measure, but to all others it is given according to measure. Hence John says about Christ: For God gives the Spirit not according to measure (John 3:34). To others it is divided: not the Spirit, of course, but the gifts of the Spirit.

> *I say*—the former I besought but this I forbid
> *the grace*—of his apostleship
> *who are among you*—because not all are doing this
> *to be wiser*—to inquire into divine mysteries
> *according to sobriety*—without presumption
> *a measure*—in terms of quantity or quality
> *of faith*—because God also divides faith to each by measure;
> > this is faith that works through love

12:4 For just as we have many members in one body, and not all members have the same task,

> *For just as we have many members*, etc.—He distributed gifts
> by measure because many people are one body, and so all
> necessary things should not be given to one.

12:5 so we who are many are one body in Christ and individually members of one another,

individually members. Having various gifts; or we are individually members and therefore it results in different gifts.

> *many*—through different gifts
> *one body*—serving one another
> *individually*—no one is excluded, greater or lesser
> *of one another*—serving some, needing others

12:6 having gifts, moreover, that differ according to the grace which has been given to us: whether prophecy, according to the order of faith;

whether prophecy. We who have the gift of prophecy, let us be members of others so that we may prophesy to them. Having prophecy, I say, *according to the order of faith*: insofar as their own faith demands, or the faith of the hearers to whom the prophecy is given. *whether prophecy.* He begins with prophecy because believers will prophesy when they have received the Spirit.

> *moreover*—or, *therefore*
> *according to the grace which has been given to us*—i.e., we are
> > members one of another

prophecy—of future or hidden things
the order of faith—which is the measure mentioned above

12:7 or ministry, in ministering; or he who teaches, in teaching;

> *ministry*—those who have ecclesiastical ministry, such as priests
> *in ministering*—diligently, since we are members of others
> *he who teaches*—who has the grace of teaching
> *in teaching*—let him be another's member in the exposition
> of doctrine

12:8 he who exhorts, in exhortation; he who shares, in simplicity; he who rules, in solicitude; he who shows mercy, in cheerfulness;

he who shows mercy. Daily medicine for daily wounds; and there will be judgment without mercy for him who does not show mercy even for lesser wounds. Whoever thinks he can face judgment without mercy, as though he were altogether just and secure, provokes wrath against himself. This mercy is multiple: forgiving sin, helping the oppressed, etc. And therefore he adds (although stated previously): *he who shares, in simplicity.* Simplicity excludes hypocrisy. *cheerfulness* shows joy that rests on the hope of future joy.

> *he who exhorts*—who has the grace of exhorting
> *in exhortation*—let him be another's member
> *he who shares*—alms
> *in simplicity*—let him be another's member, not in duplicity
> for present or future glory
> *he who rules*—such as a prince
> *in solicitude*—that he may lead prudently, let him be another's
> member
> *he who shows mercy*—he who has the grace of helping or
> showing compassion to the oppressed
> *in cheerfulness*—let him help with a joyful spirit

12:9 love without insincerity, hating evil, clinging to good;

> *love*—this is the love in which various good works are united
> *without insincerity*—and so one member will belong to another

hating evil—so that love of a friend may not cause us to
   love evil
clinging to good—so that hatred of evil may not cause us to
   neglect good

**12:10 loving one another with fraternal love, preferring one another
in honor;**

fraternal love—namely the love of brothers among themselves,
   or wishing to be loved by brothers in return
preferring one another—it is not fraternal love unless they
   prefer each other with mutual deference
in honor—in all reverence

12:11 not sluggish in solicitude; burning in spirit; serving the Lord;

not sluggish. Cursed is he who does the works of God negligently. The
sluggard is without hope. And therefore, in order to banish frigid slug-
gishness, he says: You should be *burning in spirit.* That by which love
burns is a fire of the spirit, and thus the Lord says: I have come to cast
fire on the earth, and what do I wish but that it be kindled (Luke 12:49)?
serving the Lord, or, *serving the time.* Although fervent, you should not
pour out the words of God haphazardly and inopportunely but *serving
the time,* i.e., the opportunity.

not sluggish—at work
in solicitude—you should be solicitous in your heart
burning—and therefore burning in the flame of love; even
   if you are unable to carry out what you desire
serving the Lord—believe that you are devoting to the Lord,
   what you devote to your neighbor
the Lord—or, *the time*

12:12 rejoicing in hope; patient in tribulation; urgent in prayer;

rejoicing in hope. They rejoice who are certain of future things, and so
they are patient in tribulation.

rejoicing in hope—and there is no rejoicing in these unless you
   hope in eternal things

patient in tribulation—even if bad things occur along with
　　these blessings
urgent—because up to this time the reality is postponed
in prayer—that you may be able to be patient

12:13 participating in the necessities of the saints; pursuing hospitality.

participating, etc.—suffer and unite your sufferings to the
　　saints who have suffered[205]
pursuing hospitality—and welcome the saints in lodging,
　　following the example of Abraham and Lot

12:14 Bless those who persecute you; bless and do not curse;

Bless those who persecute you—pray that they receive good
　　things; this takes you far from the usual custom
bless—again and again
and do not curse—i.e., bless without a mixture of bitterness

12:15 to rejoice with those who rejoice; to weep with those who weep;

to rejoice—and you ought to rejoice
with those who rejoice—from their success
to weep with those who weep—over something that should
　　be wept over

12:16 mutually thinking the same thing; not thinking high thoughts but concurring with the humble. Do not be wise to yourselves,

concurring with the humble. This is not done with the mouth alone, for
true humility is not only on the tongue. Otherwise, presuming on themselves, they do not grieve with others but reproach them.

mutually thinking the same thing—with joy or weeping
not thinking high thoughts—not even in your heart
concurring with the humble—being imitators of the humble
Do not be wise to yourselves—i.e., do not keep your wisdom to
　　yourselves but rather extend it to your neighbors, even if
　　one of them offends you

12:17 repaying no one evil for evil; being careful in good things, not only before God but also before all people,

> *being careful in good things*—he warns them not to cause
> scandal in doing lawful things
> *before God*—in the hiddenness of the heart
> *before all people*—so as not to give scandal, but good example,
> because that ought to be done which neither displeases
> God nor gives scandal to a brother

12:18 if at all possible, so far as it depends on you, keeping peace with all people;

> *if at all possible, so far as it depends on you*—so that they may
> be in agreement, and if not, at least do as much as you can;
> or, *if at all possible*, because it is difficult, yet *so far as it
> depends on you*, i.e., as is in your power
> *keeping peace with all people*—and thus: *With them that hated
> peace I was peaceable* (Ps. 119:7).

12:19 not defending yourselves, beloved, but giving place to anger. For it is written: Vengeance is mine and I will repay, says the Lord.

giving place to anger. He gives place to anger who allows an adversary to do what he will. *giving place to anger.* He is not teaching that they should be unwilling to be avenged by God. The saints cry out for this (Rev. 6:10), not indeed to satisfy their hatred, but the just person will rejoice when he sees God's vengeance. He teaches, however, that they should not avenge themselves but give place to God's anger, who says: *Vengeance is mine and I will repay* (Deut. 32:35). Then if a good person wants God to punish his enemy, is not this to return evil for evil? For in this way he is not loving and doing good to an enemy. But a good person desires his enemy to be corrected more than to be punished. Even when God punishes, a good person does not delight in the punishment, since he does not hate his enemy, but he delights in the justice of God, because he loves God. And God, whom he imitates in this, sends rain on the just and the unjust (Matt. 5:45), correcting with adversities in this age and only condemning the stubborn in the end.

not defending yourselves—not striking back at adversaries
giving place to anger—giving place to God's judgment, or
  giving up their own anger
it is written—in Proverbs (Prov. 20:22; Deut. 32:35)
Vengeance is mine—leave vengeance to me; and so he that
  does otherwise is despising God
I will repay—I will avenge

12:20 But if your enemy is hungry, feed him; if he is thirsty, give him drink. For in doing this you heap coals of fire on his head.

But if your enemy is hungry. Notice the affectedness, but an affectedness of friendship. For it should be pursued as if the friendship between you has not lapsed.

> *But if your enemy*—not only should you not defend yourself
> *coals of fire*—the fervor of love or of the Holy Spirit, or the
>   burning of repentance
> *on his head*—upon his mind

12:21 Do not be overcome by evil, but in good overcome evil.

in good overcome evil. Strive against him with goodness, and this is a wholesome battle, so that there are not two evil people.

> *Do not be overcome by evil*—even if he does not repent, be-
>   cause if you strike back, then you will become evil like him
> *in good overcome evil*—by enduring evil

Chapter 13

13:1 Let every soul be subject to the higher authorities, for there is no authority except from God, and those that are from God have been ordained.

every soul. Even if there are some so perfect in the body of Christ, nevertheless every soul, i.e., every person (the whole expressed through the part). In other words, you should be obedient not only in body but also in will. For it seemed that unfaithful lords should not rule over the faithful, while if the lords were faithful, they should be equals. The apostle also removes this kind of pride. *there is no authority.* Authority is from God. But *those that are from God have been ordained.* Therefore authority has been ordained. Hence *he that resists authority resists God's ordination* (Rom. 13:2). Concerning a good authority, it is clear that God has appointed it. It can be seen that he has also reasonably appointed evil authority, since the good are themselves purified by it and the evil condemned, while the authority itself sinks lower. And you should know that the word authority sometimes means the authority which is given to someone by God and sometimes it means the person himself who has the authority, which the diligent reader should be able to distinguish.

Human malice has in itself the desire to harm. But if God does not give authority, then it has no power to harm.[206] Thus the devil, before he could take anything from Job, had to say to the Lord: *Put forth your hand* (Job 2:5), i.e., give me authority.[207] For even the power of harming does not exist except from God, as Wisdom says of herself: *Through me kings reign* and through me tyrants hold the earth (Prov. 8:15).[208] Hence Job also says of the Lord: *Who makes a hypocrite to reign because of the corruption of the people* (Job 34:30). And the Lord says of the people Israel: I have given them a king in my anger (1 Sam. 8:7-8). The power of harming is given to wicked and unworthy rulers so that the patience of the good may be proved and the iniquity of the evil may be punished. For through power given to the devil Job was proved that he might appear just; and Peter was tempted that he might not rely on himself; and Paul was buffeted that he might not glorify himself; and Judas was condemned that he might hang himself.[209]

and those that are from God have been ordained. That is, they have been reasonably disposed by God. Job says that *God does not reject the mighty since he himself is also mighty* (Job 36:5). Gregory: God surely desires to be imitated. He directs the heights of power, being attentive to the benefit of others and not his own praise. He desires to be useful to other rulers, not to rule over them. For the swelling of pride is to be blamed, not the order of authority. God distributes authority while the malice of our heart engenders the pride of authority. Therefore, let us remove what we have brought from ourselves and let us hold onto the things that are from God's generosity. For just authority is in no way condemned, but only its depraved action.[210]

> ***higher***—higher because they are elevated in worldly things; or the cause is noted here, i.e., because they are higher authorities, let every soul be subject
> ***authorities***—good or evil secular authorities
> ***for there is no authority***—and therefore he ought to be subject. Hence: *You would have no authority over me unless it had been given you from above* (John 19:11).
> ***ordained***—reasonably ordered

13:2 Therefore he that resists authority resists God's ordination. And those who resist gain condemnation for themselves.

And those who resist. Augustine: What if an authority commands what is not lawful? Then rightly disregard authority by respecting a greater authority. Therefore if the emperor commands one thing and God another, the emperor must be disregarded and God obeyed.[211]

> ***he that resists***—by force or deceit
> ***authority***—in those matters which pertain to authority, in taxes and such
> ***resists God's ordination***—i.e., resists one who has authority through the ordination of God

> *And those who resist*—which is very serious
> *gain condemnation for themselves*—and therefore a person
> should not resist, but be subject

13:3 Because rulers exist not for fear of good work, but of evil. Do you not want to fear authority? Then do good and you will have praise from it.

rulers. He calls rulers those who are created to correct behavior and forbid what is harmful. They possess the image of God, so that others may be under one ruler. *exist not for fear of good work.* If he is a good ruler, he does not punish someone that does good but esteems him. If he is an evil ruler, he does not harm the good person but purifies him. Only the evil person should fear, because rulers have been established to punish wickedness. *you will have praise*, either when the authority praises you, if it is itself just, or when it offers you an occasion for praise, if it is unjust.

> *Because*—they deserve to gain condemnation because, etc.
> *rulers*—whether good or bad
> *not for fear of good work*—not to bring fear on those who do
> good
> *Do you not want to fear*—in other words, rulers exist to bring
> fear on those who work evil, so *if you do not want to fear*, etc.
> *authority*—whatever authority may exist
> *Then do good*—and you will have nothing to fear
> *you will have praise from it*—even if it is an evil authority,
> since you have occasion for a greater crown

13:4 For he is God's minister to you for good. But if you do evil, then be afraid, for not without cause does he bear the sword. For he is God's minister, an avenger for wrath on him that does evil.

For he is God's minister. Rulers were given for this reason, lest evils should flourish. *an avenger for wrath*, i.e., to execute God's wrath or to reveal God's wrath, because this punishment shows that those who persist in evil will be punished more severely.

> *For he is God's minister*—you will surely have praise from that
> authority because *he is God's minister to you*, carrying out
> good whether he is good or evil

But if you do evil, then be afraid—a good person has nothing
   to fear
not without cause—but that he might punish the wicked
bear the sword—He should be feared because he holds the
   sword of judicial power. And this is so because *he is God's
   minister*, avenging in the place of God.
for wrath—i.e., unto injury

**13:5 Therefore, by necessity, be subject; not only because of wrath but
also for the sake of conscience.**

Therefore—because he is God's minister
by necessity—necessarily, by decree, as if out of necessity
not only because of wrath—not only to avoid the wrath of a
   ruler or of God
for the sake of conscience—that your mind may be clean by
   loving a superior

**13:6 Therefore you should also pay taxes, because the authorities are
God's ministers, serving this very purpose.**

Therefore you should also pay taxes. You ought to be subject, and *therefore
you should also,* i.e., to manifest your subjection, *pay taxes,* as if for things
to be repaid to you. For the authorities repay you when they fight for the
country and when they render judgments. You should pay those who
serve God, since by giving taxes to them you are serving God, because
they are God's ministers. Or you should pay taxes because they are God's
ministers, so that the good may be praised and the wicked punished.
They are serving you in this regard, I say, when they defend the country.

Therefore you should also pay taxes—this is the proof of
   subjection
serving this very purpose—because with this very taxation
   they are able to serve you in defense of the country

**13:7 Therefore render to all their dues: to whom tax, tax; to whom tar-
iff, tariff; to whom honor, honor; to whom fear, fear.**

tax . . . tariff. Perhaps tax is what is paid at home, tariff what is carried to
the house of a lord.

Therefore—because they are God's ministers
render to all their dues—so that, namely, evangelical discipline
  may be praised
to whom tax—to whom you owe tax
tax—render tax; tax is what districts pay
to whom tariff—to whom you owe tariff
tariff—render tariff; tariff is the tribute that is given to lords
  when they travel through the country
to whom honor—to whom you owe honor
honor—render honor, such as rising in respect
fear—that we may fear their dominion and venerate their
  persons

13:8 Owe no one anything, but to love one another, for he that loves his neighbor has fulfilled the law.

Owe no one anything, etc. Maintain peace toward all and love between brothers, for otherwise they are not truly brothers. *but to love.* Mention of love is made here because it achieves humility. It is only love which, even when granted, always keeps the granter in debt. For it is granted when it is paid, but it is still owed after it is granted since there is never a time when it should not be paid. Nor is love lost when it is granted, but rather multiplied in the very granting of it. For love is granted by possessing it, not by relinquishing it, as with the granting of money. Love cannot be granted unless it is possessed, nor possessed unless it is granted. Indeed when love is granted by someone, it grows in him, and more is acquired as it is granted to more people.[212]

he that loves his neighbor. Although there are two commandments of love, one commandment is often stated in the place of these two, since God is not loved nor can be loved without a neighbor nor a neighbor without God. Love of neighbor appears in deeds; love of God is more hidden. The former, then, is stated with more particularity, of which the Lord says: *A new commandment I give to you, that you love one another* (John 13:34), where the greater commandment of the love of God seems to be missing. But to those who understand it correctly, each commandment is found in the other, because he that loves God cannot ignore the one whom God has commanded to be loved; and he that loves his neighbor in a holy and spiritual way, what does he love in him if not God?[213]

By *neighbor* should be understood everyone, because there is no one to whom evil should be done. Therefore he that loves others should love them either because they are just or because they are unjust. For in the same way he should also love himself, either because he is just or so that he might be just. For he that loves himself in another way, loves himself unjustly, since he loves himself in order to be unjust. When, therefore, his aim is to be evil, then he no longer loves himself, for *he that loves iniquity hates his own soul* (Ps. 10:6).[214]

> *Owe no one anything*—pay off others so that you do not owe
>   anything
> *but to love one another*—pay off love so that you always owe love
> *for he that loves his neighbor has fulfilled the law*—and he goes
>   on to show this in detail

13:9 For you shall not commit adultery, you shall not kill, you shall not steal, you shall not bear false witness, you shall not covet, and if there is any other commandment, it is repeated in this word: You shall love your neighbor as yourself.

> *any other commandment*—through Moses
> *repeated*—contained, fulfilled
> *this word*—which Moses established in Leviticus (Lev. 19:18)
> *You shall love your neighbor as yourself*—to good purpose, for
>   *he that loves iniquity hates his own soul* (Ps. 10:6)

13:10 Love of neighbor works no evil. Love, therefore, is the fulfillment of the law.

> *Love of neighbor works no evil*—he that loves does good
>   because he does no evil, and therefore love is the fulfill-
>   ment of the law
> *the fulfillment of the law*—he that loves completely fulfills
>   the law

13:11 And knowing this time, that it is already the hour for us to rise from sleep, for now our salvation is nearer than when we believed.

And knowing this. Here is another commendation of love, for love does not perform evil and it prepares the opportunity of doing good. *And knowing this*, namely, *that it is already the hour*, or as some books have: *knowing this time*, namely, this time of grace. *it is already*, from the time we have possessed love, *the hour*, i.e., the opportunity, but a brief one, *to rise from sleep*: sleep is negligence or ignorance. *for now*. Reasons are given for why we should rise. *nearer*. The one who does good is near to eternal life. For baptism brings forgiveness and good life a crown. Or *nearer* means that we are closer to death.

> *And knowing this*—we know this, that love does not work evil
> *to rise*—by doing good
> *from sleep*—from sloth
> *for now*—we should rise
> *our salvation*—eternal salvation that is promised to us
> *is nearer*—more owed through good works[215]
> *when*—at that time
> *we believed*—when we only believed; because we have believed and have worked, it is more disgraceful if we do not rise up.

13:12 Night has passed and the day is at hand: therefore let us cast off the works of darkness and put on the armor of light,

Night has passed. It is shown again why we should rise, because the *Night* of unbelief and ignorance *has passed*, i.e., it was but no longer is, and the memory of it warns you to be careful. *the day* of eternal beatitude *is at hand*, when sins are forgiven, when Christians are just by grace. *Night* is the old nature which passed away in baptism; *day* is the sun of justice by whose light they learn truth so that they may know what should be done. *works of darkness*. Evil deeds that have come out of the darkness of ignorance; or works that love darkness and lead to darkness.

> *therefore let us cast off*—because of the mentioned reasons
> *put on*—as an ornament
> *the armor*—virtues
> *of light*—which light, i.e., faith, requires

13:13 so that we may walk decently in the day, not in reveling and drunkenness, not in beds and impurities, not in contention and rivalry;

not in reveling, etc. Notice that the Romans are affected by these and so they have no right to boast. Now the mother of these vices is pride and the eagerness for human praise, which also often generates hypocrisy. And nothing resists this unless fear and love are instilled by the numerous testimonies of the divine books.

> *so that we may walk decently in the day*—having received the virtues, let us exercise ourselves in carrying them out as befits the day of faith
> *not in*—the works of darkness follow
> *reveling and drunkenness*—lascivious carousing
> *beds*—the sleep of laziness
> *impurities*—lust that arises from too much food and drink
> *contention and rivalry*—as they were accustomed to have by considering themselves above one another, whereby the lesser would envy the greater

13:14 but put on the Lord Jesus Christ and make no provision for the flesh in its desires.

> *but put on*—i.e., do not do the things mentioned
> *the Lord Jesus Christ*—i.e., the form of Christ
> *make no provision for the flesh*—having put on Christ, do not think about serving the flesh
> *in its desires*—in its illicit desires, not in desires that are necessary for sustenance

Chapter 14

14:1 And receive the weak in faith, not in arguments over thoughts,

the weak in faith. It belongs to perfect faith not to distinguish between foods nor to consider any food unclean, since *to the pure all things are pure* (Titus 1:15). But some weak people were supposing that they should abstain from certain foods, and so there was contention among the Romans. Hence he teaches them to receive and not to reject such weak ones, and by patient example and word to build up their faith, and, if the matter is hidden, not to argue about what someone thinks in his heart. *not in arguments*. He should not be condemned whose thought is not disclosed and whose future we do not know.[216]

> *And*—thus you should act honorably among yourselves, as was said
> *receive*—as Christ received the sick, in order to heal them
> *the weak*—he that does not yet believe as perfectly as he should
> *not in arguments*—so that you judge him guilty of secret faults

14:2 For one person believes he may eat everything, but let the weak person eat vegetables.

the weak person. The one who distinguishes between foods, thinking that some are clean and others unclean because the Jews were forbidden to eat them. He says that such a person should be left to his own judgment so that he does not eat against his conscience. Or, although his faith is perfect and he may eat everything, nevertheless the weak person, who fears falling and is easily overwhelmed by an impulse of lust, let him eat vegetables, i.e., simple and dry foods that are not an inducement to vice, and let him abstain from those foods by which lust is aroused. For plump meats and luxurious meals provoke the body to lust.

one person—such a one can receive others
everything—all things given for human consumption
the weak person—he needs to be received and allowed to eat
    only vegetables about which there is no question

14:3 He that eats, let him not despise the one that eats not; and he that does not eat, let him not judge the one that eats, for God has received him.

He that eats. Above he taught them not to argue about the thoughts of others; here he teaches them not to despise others. *let him not judge.* Manifest acts should be judged, not hidden thoughts. But things that cannot be done with a good heart are manifest, such as fornication, blasphemy, stealing, and the like. We are permitted to judge concerning such things. But concerning those things about which it is doubtful whether they are done in the heart, we should give others the benefit of the doubt, as is the case with foods, because all human foods can be consumed indifferently with a good and simple heart without the sin of concupiscence.

    He that eats—and since these things are so, then *he that eats*
        all things indifferently, etc.
    let him not despise—because it is voluntary whether to eat or
        not to eat
    the one that eats not—who abstains
    he that does not eat—everything
    let him not judge him that eats—let him not think that the one
        who eats sins, since he does not know what is in his heart
    for—neither should judge the other, for each is a servant of God
    God has received—unto faith
    him—either the one who eats or the one who does not eat

14:4 Who are you to judge another's servant? It concerns his own master whether he stands or falls. But he will stand, for God is able to make him stand.

It concerns his own master. You do not have the power to judge the unknown heart of another's servant. The ability to correct or judge belongs to his own master, for whose honor he stands when he stands and to whom pertains the fall when he falls. *whether he stands or falls.* He says this because it is in doubt: perhaps he is standing who is thought to be falling. By these words he shows that a person does not know how someone may henceforth conduct himself in doubtful cases. *But he will stand.* Here he suggests that we should assume the better side of things that are in doubt—preferring the salvation rather than the death of the guilty, and hoping for good in the future, even if it is otherwise at present. *But he will stand*, because he is not guilty whether he eats or does not eat as long as he does either with devotion.

> *Who are you*—and since this is true, by whose power do you judge?
> *to judge another's servant*—you are asserting that he should be condemned, which you should not do since he is the servant of another
> *It concerns his own master whether he stands or falls*—by his own conscience he eats or not; God is the judge of his own servant
> *he will stand*—this is said of the predestined; he will be enabled to stand by his master
> *God is able*—of which no one has any doubt
> *to make him stand*—that he may not presume to stand by himself

14:5 For one judges between day and day, another judges every day. Let each one abound in his own understanding.

For one judges. Above, discussing kinds of foods, he said that some eat everything and others do not eat everything; here he says that some abstain always while others abstain at a certain time; and he says both can be practiced rightly. *in his own understanding.* That is, leave him to his own counsel lest, taking offense, he withdraws from love, the mother of all virtues.

> *For one judges*—he will stand, I say, and it can be believed that he will stand, because what he does he does from judgment
> *one judges between day and day, another judges every day*—one judges that a set day should be chosen for abstinence; i.e. some think abstinence should be on certain days, others think there should be abstinence every day
> *another judges every day*—he judges that every day should be chosen for abstinence

Let each one—so that he who eats, eats with thanksgiving,
   and he who abstains, does so for God
abound—for the better
in his own understanding—according to his own conscience

14:6 He that regards a day regards it to the Lord; and he that eats, eats to the Lord, for he gives thanks to God; and he that does not eat, does not eat to the Lord and gives thanks to God.

He that regards. When he *abounds in his understanding*, I say, *he that regards a day*, either *every day* or *between day and day*, *regards it to the Lord; and he that eats, eats to the Lord*, i.e., to the honor of the Lord, believing that all things he has created are clean and that he will be able to serve him because he is sustained by them.

   regards it to the Lord—i.e., acts for the honor and praise of
      the Lord and thinks that he is pleasing God
   he that eats—everything
   eats to the Lord—to the praise of the Lord
   for—the effect shows that he eats to the Lord
   he gives thanks to God—for good creatures by which he is
      sustained and fed
   he that does not eat—i.e., he that abstains
   does not eat to the Lord—to the honor of the Lord; which
      the effect shows, because he gives thanks
   and gives thanks to God—for the abstinence granted

14:7 Indeed none of us lives for himself and no one dies for himself;

Indeed none of us lives for himself. For he that is restrained by the law lives not for himself but for God who gave the law. Were there no law, each person would live for himself. *for himself.* Rather he lives for the Lord, by whose judgment he is damned or crowned. Or *none of us lives for himself*, i.e., for his own praise, but for the praise of God. For as there is no end to his greatness, so there will be no end to our praise. When we shall have died in this flesh we will not cease praising God. According to this interpretation, the words apply only to the faithful. Or *none of us lives for himself*, i.e., none will be judged by himself, but by the Lord. According to this interpretation, the words are understood of both good and evil people.

> **Indeed none**—and we should eat or not eat to the Lord,
> because *none of us*, etc.
> **of us**—of the faithful
> **lives**—through the virtues, i.e., spiritually; or also temporally
> in the union of soul and body
> **for himself**—but for the Lord
> **dies**—in sins

14:8 for either we live and live to the Lord, or we die and die to the Lord. Thus whether we live or die we are the Lord's.

> *for*—and surely no one lives or dies for himself but for the
> Lord, because *either we live*, etc.
> **we live**—by a life of virtues
> **live to the Lord**—to be judged by him; or that we may
> please him
> **we die**—spiritually through vices and sins or temporally
> through the dissolution of body and soul
> **die to the Lord**—i.e., in the likeness of Christ into whose death
> we have been baptized, so that as Christ died once and
> lives forever, so we too, having died once for sin in
> baptism, should always live for God, to be judged by him
> **Thus**—And since both are done for the Lord, we are therefore
> his and will be judged by him. Why, then, does one person
> judge another?
> **we are the Lord's**—because he bought us with the price of his
> blood; nor shall death hold him for whom he died; he is a
> free person among the dead[217]

14:9 For to this end Christ died and rose again, that he might be Lord of both the living and the dead.

Christ died . . . that he might be Lord of both the living and the dead and that he might judge both. And the apostle understands the living and the dead literally, so that it should not be supposed that Christ only judges the dead, as though judgment were entrusted to people while they live and to God after death. For the perverse teaching of the foolish handed this down, but it is better to say that Christ rules and judges both the living and the dead. Similarly those whom he granted to become children of God also reign with Christ both now and after death. But his saints reign with him in one way now and will reign in another way then: now they reign because they know and seek the things that are above; in the end they will reign with him when they are in his kingdom and are themselves his kingdom. For the souls of the pious dead are not separated from the Church, which is also now a kingdom of Christ, because she now reigns with Christ in the living and the dead.

Or *Christ died* to free the dead from their sins, for while he lived he showed the way of salvation to the living, *and rose again* to cause the justified to live with him.

> *that he might be Lord*—it should be understood that he is Lord
> *of both the living and the dead*—and that he judges both

14:10 But you, why do you judge your brother? Or you, why do you despise your brother? For we shall all stand before the tribunal of Christ.

the tribunal. A figure is used here, for a tribunal is the seat of judges that is set up high so that a judge may be seen by all and may himself be able to look down at all from a prominent place. In the same way Christ will sit as though on a tribunal, since he will be seen by all and will himself view the consciences of all and decide their cases.

> *But*—Christ ought to rule and judge, but you, etc.
> *you*—who eat all things
> *your brother*—who does not eat
> *Or you*—who do not eat
> *your brother*—who eats
> *For*—you should not do this, *for*, etc.
> *we shall all stand*—to be judged
> *before the tribunal*—before God who sits as judge

14:11 For it is written: I live, says the Lord, because every knee shall bow to me and every tongue shall confess to God.

> *it is written*—in Isaiah (Isa. 49:18)
> *I live*—i.e., I who once was dead am now alive in power, which
>   is clear from this: that *every knee shall bow to me*, i.e., I am
>   going to judge all

every knee—even of enemies
shall bow—at judgment
every tongue—every conscience will acknowledge that I
    am God
shall confess—what it has done
to God—to me

14:12 And so let each one of us render[218] an account of himself to God.

And so—and because the Scripture says this
each one of us—that will be judged by God
render an account of himself—he will not escape through
    evasion

14:13 Therefore let us no longer judge one another but judge this instead: that you not place a stumbling block or offense in your brother's way.

let us no longer judge one another. Let us not usurp for ourselves what does not belong to us. Let us not reprove things that we do not know, since they take place in the heart; or even if it is proper, let us not reprove in such a way that we despair of another's well being. In these two cases it is rash judgment, and there is either pride or envy. Wherefore it is said: *Judge not and you will not be judged* (Matt. 7:1).

Therefore—and since each one will render an account of himself
let us no longer judge one another—by opinion, as we have done
    up till now
but judge—discern what is profitable to be observed
this instead—namely:
that you not place a stumbling block—so that he perishes from
    your example when he does the same thing
offense—affliction, which is less serious

14:14 I know and I trust in the Lord Jesus that nothing is common through him. But to him who considers something to be common, it is common to him.

I know and I trust. I am saying that you should not give offense to your brothers, but I am not saying that the offense or scandal occurs because the food is unclean. For I know that our trust is in Jesus who, after he came, freed us from the law. *common*. He uses this word for unclean, taking the meaning from vessels that were common to all uses; after they had been dedicated for sacrifices they were no longer called common, but holy. Or the Jews themselves were properly called the people of God before, while all others were called common and unclean.

> *I know and I trust*—I know this because *I trust in the Lord Jesus*
> *common*—unclean
> *through him*—after his advent, or by his creation
> *who considers something to be common*—hence: *What enters the mouth does not defile a person, but what comes out* from it (Matt. 15:11)
> *it is common*—because of his conscience
> *to him*—this is the weak person of whom it was said above: *but let him that is weak eat vegetables* (Rom. 14:2)

14:15 For if your brother is disturbed because of food, then you are no longer walking according to love. Do not destroy by your food someone for whom Christ died.

> *For if your brother*—and therefore do not give offense or scandal to your brother
> *is disturbed*—I do not say he is scandalized, but something less strong
> *then*—from this alone it is clear that *you are no longer walking according to love*
> *you are no longer walking according to love*—you are sinning in this, because you are not walking according to love
> *Do not destroy*—therefore take care not to disturb him with your food, but take more care not to destroy him; because you should strengthen him, not make holy things into stumbling blocks[219]
> *Christ died*—what he did was so great that by his death we recognize how important the salvation of a brother is

14:16 Therefore do not let our good be reproached.

do not let our good be reproached. Because he that has good works, if he is criticized in the smallest matter, his good is obscured and begins to be reproached as evil. Hence Ezekiel says that the justice of a just person does not profit him if he makes a mistake (Ezek. 33:12). ***Therefore do not let our good be reproached.*** A good meal in itself may be reproached when it harms others. And because it does harm, abstain from it, because food is not a principle of God's kingdom.

> ***Therefore***—seeing that a brother is disturbed or lost, *therefore do not let*, etc.
>
> ***our good***—which, if it were good, you would forego for the sake of not giving offense to anyone
>
> ***be reproached***—then at least other good things would not be obscured

14:17 For the kingdom of God is not food and drink but justice and peace and joy in the Holy Spirit.

For the kingdom of God is not food and drink. The use of foods is not to be restrained, but concupiscence. It does not matter what kinds of foods or how much someone consumes, as long as they are suitable to humans in general and to the person himself in particular, and are necessary for maintaining his health. What matters is how easily and cheerfully he goes without them when it is either right or necessary to go without them.[220] ***joy.*** Not joy in meals, as is often true for many people, but joy in the Holy Spirit. This joy arises from fraternal peace, just as anger arises from fraternal argument, where there is no Spirit since he is only in peaceful places. And by his grace these three things are in a person: justice, peace, and joy.

> ***justice***—so that you do to a brother what you would have him do to you
>
> ***peace***—i.e., concord, which is an effect of justice
>
> ***in the Holy Spirit***—i.e., not boasting of the gifts of the Spirit, which were not in you before, but receiving them humbly and thankfully

14:18 For he that serves Christ in this way pleases God and is approved by people.

pleases God. By this he has joy in the Holy Spirit. He is *approved by people* according to justice and also peace.

> *For*—truly justice and peace are causes of the kingdom, *for*, etc.
> *in this way*—in justice, peace, and joy
> *pleases God*—he that gives offense to no one pleases God who commands this

14:19 Therefore, let us pursue the ways of peace, and let us guard things that bring edification to one another.

Because argumentation causes discord, *therefore*, having put aside rash judgments, *let us pursue the ways of peace*, not discord, and *things that bring edification*, so that others may be built up or that those already built up may be preserved. *to one another*. The Jew toward the Gentile and the Gentile toward the Jew.

> *Therefore*—because argument causes discord
> *things that bring edification*—by instructing with peace

14:20 Do not destroy the work of God for the sake of food. Indeed all things are clean, but it is wrong for a person to eat by offense.

> *Do not destroy the work of God*—let us pursue these things, but let us not destroy the work of God; therefore, in addition, you should not eat when it causes offense to a brother, because you would destroy God's work, i.e., his faith, virtues, and other good things that God has accomplished in him
> *Indeed all things are clean*—now I am not saying this because the food is actually unclean, because *indeed*, etc. Hence: *And God saw all the things that he had made and they were very good* (Gen. 1:31)
> *to eat by offense*—by offending others. How much worse it is to eat by offending God, as when Adam ate the fruit, Esau the lentils, and the Jews meat in the desert.

14:21 It is good not to eat meat and not to drink wine, nor anything by which your brother is offended or scandalized or weakened.

offended. He is confused, not knowing what obliges him. He is **offended** who departs from the true faith; he is **weakened** who does not depart but begins to doubt.[221]

> *It is good not to eat meat*—you should abstain from things that cause offense because it is also good to abstain from all meat
> *nor anything*—nor to do anything
> *offended*—by something which, for him, is a cause of condemnation
> *scandalized*—disturbed
> *weakened*—so that he doubts, even if he is not offended

14:22 The faith that you have within yourself, have before God. Blessed is he that does not judge himself in what he approves.

The faith, by which you believe that all things are clean and able to be eaten, *have before God,* so that you keep peace with your brother, which is beneficial before God. *Blessed.* He calls blessed someone that does nothing else than what he approves as beneficial. But he thinks a person should be condemned by his own judgment who does not do what he says he ought to do.

> *The faith that you have*—you are well able to do this because you are losing nothing of your own good
> *within yourself*—in the heart, which no one may take away
> *have before God*—keep before God alone, not before the one who abstains, lest you do him harm
> *Blessed*—because *blessed is he,* etc.
> *that does not judge himself*—that does not make himself liable to damnation by harming others by his own good
> *in what he approves*—in what he considers good

14:23 But he that discerns is condemned if he eats because it is not of faith. All that is not of faith is sin.

All that is not of faith is sin. Yet all that is with faith is not good, since ignorance that comes from sin does harm. The entire life of the unfaithful is sin, and there is nothing good without the highest good: when it is missing, the acknowledgment of eternal truth is a false virtue, even when accompanied by the best morals.[222] Works that seem commendable without faith are like the tremendous strength and speed of someone running outside the course.[223] *not of faith.* Your faith holds that a person should do what he rightly understands should be done, and sin is doing anything else than what faith has approved.

> **But he**—the former is blessed, *but he that discerns,* etc.
> **discerns**—that some foods are clean and others unclean
> **is condemned if he eats**—if he eats with that kind of conscience
> **it is not of faith**—he does not eat from faith
> **All**—even a good thing
> **that is not of faith is sin**—it is against faith, i.e., against
> conscience, so that it is believed to be evil

Chapter 15

15:1 And we who are stronger ought to bear with the frailties of the weak and not to please ourselves.

not to please ourselves. In other words, we ought not to defend what pleases ourselves but what pleases our brother, because we should show concern for one another.

> *And we who are stronger*—the weak person is condemned
> if he eats, but *we who are stronger*, etc.
> *ought to bear with*—to tolerate, to encourage, and not to
> provoke, not to argue
> *the frailties of the weak*—when they are unable to rise
> to our level
> *not to please ourselves*—not to yield to our own desire

15:2 Let each of you please his neighbor for good unto edification.

> *Let each of you*—making love his concern
> *please*—take care to please
> *for good*—for that which is useful
> *unto edification*—unto what is worthwhile

15:3 For Christ did not please himself, but as it is written: The insults of those who insult you have fallen on me.

For Christ, etc. Hence: *I have not come to do my own will, but the will of him that sent me* (John 6:38). *insults.* In other words, when I did your will, O God, the Jews said I was a sinner against you. Yet by not receiving me, whom you sent, it is they that have sinned against you. They reproached

212

and then killed me. Thus the sins of those sinning against God fell upon Christ, because the innocent one was killed by sinners as a blasphemer.

> *For Christ*—and surely we ought not to please ourselves, *for Christ*, etc.
> *did not please himself*—did not do what was pleasing to the flesh but what was pleasing to God the Father
> *as it is written*—in the Psalms (Ps. 69:10)
> *The insults*—because I threw them out of the temple, which they had made a den of thieves; therefore, *the insults*, etc.
> *have fallen on me*—they were the cause of my oppression

15:4 For whatever things were written were written for our instruction, so that through patience and the comfort of the Scriptures we might have hope.

whatever things were written. Things written in the divine books, whence he said above, *as it is written.*

> *For whatever things*—answering the question: What does this have to do with us?
> *were written*—of Christ, whose life is for the training of our life and morals
> *through patience*—that through patience we may be taught to be compassionate to our neighbors; and in this we may be comforted by the example of Christ, and thus we may hope for the things Christ has received

15:5 But may the God of patience and comfort give you to have the same mind toward one another according to Jesus Christ,

to have the same mind. In other words, if you do not think the same, then you will not be able to honor God.

> *But may*—Scripture is for instruction, but *may the God of patience*, etc.
> *the God of patience and comfort*—God, the giver of patience and comfort

> *to have the same mind toward one another*—to think without
> disagreement, so that one thinks the same as another
> *according to Jesus Christ*—not apart from Christ but in him,
> so that you may be wise according to his teaching

15:6 that with one mind and one mouth you may honor God and the Father of our Lord Jesus Christ.

> *with one mind*—with the same will
> *one mouth*—with the same vocal confession
> *God*—because he is God in essence; because he is the creator
> *and the Father of our Lord Jesus Christ*—and because he is
> benevolent in sending Christ

15:7 Wherefore, receive one another just as Christ received you to the honor of God.

> *Wherefore*—that you may honor God
> *one another*—the weak
> *as Christ received you*—when you were weak
> *to the honor of God*—that he may make you immortal

15:8 For I say that Christ Jesus was a minister of circumcision for the truth of God to confirm the promises of the fathers,

circumcision. This means the Jews to whom he came bodily; hence: *I was not sent except to the lost sheep of the house of Israel* (Matt. 15:24). *for the truth*. He did not reject the Jews to whom the truth belonged, and there was mercy for the Gentiles who had not received the promise. *the promises*. For he had promised Abraham: *In your seed shall all the Gentiles be blessed* (Gen. 22:18, 26:4, 28:14); and David: *From the fruit of your loins I will set on your throne* (Ps. 131:11); and he also said to Jacob: *A star shall arise from Jacob* (Num. 23:17).

> *For I say that Christ Jesus*, etc.—Christ received you because
> he received the Jews, that he might be their minister, i.e.,
> their apostle and preacher. And he did this to be true to
> what was promised and to fulfill the promises that he
> made to the fathers, namely Abraham, Isaac, and Jacob.

15:9 but the Gentiles honor God for mercy. As it is written: Therefore I will confess you among the Gentiles, O Lord, and will sing to your name.

I will confess. Confession is not only of sins but also of praises.

>*but*—I say
>*the Gentiles*—and the Gentiles were received through mercy
>*for mercy*—concerning mercy
>*As it is written*—in the Psalm about the Gentiles (Ps. 56:10;
>   2 Sam. 22:50), about whom it hardly seemed possible
>*Therefore*—textual variant: *propterea* instead of *propter hoc*
>*I will confess you among the Gentiles*—from the Gentiles I
>   will make those who confess you
>*and will sing to your name*—I will sing a new song of joy
>   when they praise you

15:10 And again he says: Rejoice, O Gentiles, with his people.

>*he says*—Isaiah (Isa. 66:10)
>*Rejoice, O Gentiles*—because you have been adopted into
>   one sheepfold .
>*with his people*—the Jews, since you are one with them

15:11 And again: Praise the Lord all you Gentiles, and magnify him all you peoples.

>*And again*—David (Ps. 116:1)
>*all you Gentiles*—because you have been adopted
>*magnify him*—because he has increased the number of his
>   people by adding in the Gentiles
>*all you peoples*—the twelve tribes

15:12 And again Isaiah says: There shall be a root of Jesse and one who shall rise to rule the Gentiles; in him shall the Gentiles hope.

There shall be a root of Jesse. And from this root shall come he who shall rise. Jesse is the root, David the tree that through its branch, i.e., Mary, has produced fruit, i.e., Christ.

> *again Isaiah says*—in the same place (Isa. 11:10)
> *Jesse*—the father of David, who is also called Isai
> *one who*—one from that root who
> *shall rise*—from the dead
> *to rule the Gentiles*—through faith and good works
> *in him*—and therefore in him

15:13 Now may the God of hope fill you with all joy and peace in believing, that you may abound in hope and in the power of the Holy Spirit.

and peace in believing. So that you may rejoice, let all give peace and concord to one another; which will happen if your faith is sound. *that you may abound,* i.e., that by this practice you be more certain of eternal beatitude and abound *in the power of the Holy Spirit,* i.e., in the strength for good works that is given by the Holy Spirit.

> *Now*—I am admonishing you to accept one another
> *may the God of hope*—who gives hope, or in whom we hope
> *all joy*—all spiritual joy, so that none of you may be distressed
>   as you are accustomed to be distressed in your quarreling

15:14 But I myself am assured of you, my brothers, that also you yourselves are full of love, replete with all knowledge, so that you are able to admonish one another.

But I myself am assured of you. This is said lest the apostle seem to understand all of them to be contentious and foolish people needing correction. He therefore pulls back and begins to admonish the more perfect in their correction of the less perfect. Then he gives himself as an example of one who works for others. And they must do this work since he is occupied with other things and is unable to come to them. *replete with all knowledge.* Through this praise he encourages them to greater works, in the manner of one that exhorts. Hence he does not say to teach but to admonish, as with something that is known but evaded by the mind. For something is said to be admonished which, although it is known, is sometimes evaded by the mind or carelessly held.

> *But I myself*—who am saying this

am assured of you—even though I admonish you to accept one
    another, you do not all need this admonition
also you yourselves—not only I
love—by which you may desire the good
with all knowledge—of the old and new law, by which *you are
    able to admonish*, etc.[224]
so that—having been filled with these two laws
you are able—unless your guilt remains
to admonish—I do not say that you are able to teach
one another—in turn

**15:15 But I have written more boldly to you in part, brothers, as
though bringing you back to remembrance, because of the grace that
was given me by God,**

But I have written more boldly, etc., because of my apostolate. In other
words, I was not able to omit this on account of my office. *because of the
grace that was given me.* He does not write rashly, but the apostle of the
Gentiles is bold to write to all peoples by the authority entrusted to him
by grace.

But—but nevertheless
I have written more boldly—even if you are full of love and
    knowledge, nevertheless I have written quite boldly
to you in part—i.e., to the more perfect among you, in part
    of the Church or in part of the epistle
as though bringing you back to remembrance—not as though
    I think you are foolish but as though reminding you about
    what you should do. He is declaring things that are, as it
    were, forgotten and unnoticed.

**15:16 to be a minister of Christ Jesus among the Gentiles, sanctifying
the gospel of God, so that an offering of the Gentiles may be made acceptable, sanctified in the Holy Spirit.**

a minister of Christ Jesus—whom Christ and no other appointed
sanctifying the gospel—showing that it is holy and confirming
    it with good works and miracles

> **so that an offering of the Gentiles**, etc.—so that the Gentiles
>> whom I offer may be accepted by God through their per-
>> fection of faith and sanctified through their good works
> **in the Holy Spirit**—by whose grace there exists faith and
>> good works

15:17 Therefore I have glory in Christ Jesus to God.

Therefore I have glory. And you will too if you labor on behalf of your brothers. He says this, then, to show that he can be considered no less an apostle than the apostles who were with Christ.

> **Therefore**—and since I do this, *therefore I have*, etc.
> **glory**—merit worthy of glory
> **in Christ**—through Christ
> **to God**—to bring glory to God

15:18 For I do not venture to speak of any of the things that Christ has not accomplished through me in the obedience of the Gentiles by word and deeds,

> **I do not venture to speak**, etc.—i.e., I speak only of those things
>> that Christ has accomplished through me, unlike false
>> apostles
> **in the obedience of the Gentiles**—that the Gentiles might obey
>> the gospel
> **by word and deeds**—by my preaching in word, by deeds and
>> good works, and by the power of lesser and greater
>> miracles performed in the power of the Spirit

15:19 by the power of signs and wonders in the power of the Holy Spirit, so that from Jerusalem, through a circuit as far as Illyricum, I replenished the gospel of Christ.

> **the Holy Spirit**—who works such things in me, and I labored
>> in this way as he worked in me
> **through a circuit**—all around
> **Illyricum**—the Illyricum Sea
> **I replenished**—I fully preached
> **of Christ**—or *of God*

15:20 And thus I preached this gospel not where Christ has been named, lest I should build on another's foundation.

not where Christ has been named. Because he was aware that false apostles and others were teaching false things under the name of Christ, which were very difficult to correct afterwards. Therefore he was concerned about coming first to deliver the whole truth where Christ had not yet been proclaimed, which the testimony of the prophet proves.

> *thus*—in such places
> *not where Christ has been named*—by false apostles
> *lest I should build on another's foundation*—That is, lest I should preach to those already converted by others. For were he to preach to them, then he would be building on another's foundation. Not that he would refuse to preach where this had happened.[225]

15:21 But as it is written: They who were not told of him shall see, and they who have not heard shall understand.

and they who have not heard, etc. In order that this message of God's word might prove true, he was anxious to instruct the Gentiles in the truth.

> *as it is written*—I did as it was written in Isaiah (Isa. 52:15) that it would be done
> *who were not told*—who were not told before
> *of him*—of Christ
> *shall see*—shall believe
> *who have not heard*—who have not heard before by anyone's preaching of God
> *shall understand*—that my preaching is true

15:22 For this reason I was hindered many times from coming to you and have been prevented until now.

> *For this reason*—because I have preached so often
> *I was hindered*—from halting the corrupt inventions of the false apostles
> *from coming to you*—as I said at the beginning of this epistle

15:23 But now, having no other place in these regions and having the desire to come to you for these many past years,

> **But**—since he is also eager to claim them first
> **having no other place**—having no reason to stay

15:24 when I begin to travel to Spain I hope to see you as I am passing through, and to be brought there by you if first I will have enjoyed your company in part.

> **when I begin to travel to Spain**—where the journey is difficult
> for false apostles, and therefore I was allowed to tarry
> **I hope to see you**—as if to say, I can do nothing of myself
> **as I am passing through**—because you do not need a long visit;
> but in the meantime you should prepare yourselves so that
> you do not hold me back from visiting others
> **there**—to Spain
> **I will have enjoyed your company**—I will have rejoiced in your
> fruit
> **in part**—in that part of your number which is now conten-
> tious; or in a part of time, i.e., for a period of time

15:25 Therefore I will travel now to Jerusalem to minister to the saints.

to the saints, who placed the proceeds from all their sold possessions at the feet of the apostles, and who suffered afflictions. There was common concern for them among all the apostles.

> **Therefore**—since I have no place here, and since I long to see
> you, *therefore*, etc.
> **I will travel now**—without delay

15:26 For Macedonia and Achaia approved of making a certain collection for the poor of the saints that are in Jerusalem.

approved, etc. He invites the Romans to such works because he that is alive through God's mercy ought to be compassionate toward his brother.
the poor of the saints. These are people that dedicated themselves wholly

to divine service; by having no concern for worldly things they provided the faithful with an example of a good way of life.

> ***approved***—I did not force them
> ***the poor of the saints***—or, *the poor saints*

15:27 For it pleased them, and they are their debtors. For if the Gentiles have come to share in their spiritual works, they are obliged to minister to them in corporeal works.

> ***it pleased them***—they approved of it
> ***their debtors***—he wants them to be merciful in the same way, and so he says that this is owed by anyone who expects mercy
> ***their spiritual works***—of the Jews, who sent them preachers
> ***they are obliged***—then surely they are themselves obliged
> ***to them***—to the Jews

15:28 And when I have completed this and assigned the fruit to them, I will go by way of you to Spain,

> ***And***—because this was pleasing to them, namely, to share with the saints that are in Jerusalem
> ***when I have completed this***—when I have finished this work of charity
> ***assigned***—under the seal of each church
> ***I will go by way of you to Spain***—and so, in the meantime, reform yourselves

15:29 knowing,[226] moreover, that when I come to you I shall come in an abundance of the blessing of Christ.

> ***knowing***—I will cross by you, and yet I am certain of God's grace
> ***when I come to you***—which I have desired for a long time
> ***I shall come***—finally in person
> ***in an abundance***—so that I will be of great profit to you by the blessing of Christ

> *the blessing of Christ*—this is the power of the signs by which
> they were confirmed

15:30 Therefore I beseech you, brothers, by our Lord Jesus Christ and by the love of the Spirit, to help in your prayers for me to the Lord,

to help in your prayers. Those that are very few in number are magnified when they gather together in one mind, and it is impossible for the prayers of many not to achieve their end. Therefore, if they want to see him, let them pray that they may receive him, when he is free, with the joy of love.

> *in your prayers*—by your prayers
> *for me*—that are said for me

15:31 that I may be delivered from the unbelievers that are in Judea and that the offering of my service may be acceptable to the saints in Jerusalem;

may be acceptable, so that they, knowing his love toward them, may give thanks with him to God in one accord. For it is a great encouragement to him when many, who have been made glad by his ministry, give praise to God.

> *that I may be delivered from the unbelievers*—lest they steal
> what I offer
> *my service*—the service enjoined on me
> *may be acceptable*—may be sufficient, in other words, and
> not depleted

15:32 that I may come to you in joy by God's will and may be refreshed with you.

> *that I may come*—pray that it may turn out in this way so *that*,
> with this business accomplished, *I may come*, etc.
> *by God's will*—he says this to show that he does all things with
> God's will
> *and may*—or, *that I may*
> *be refreshed with you*—which will happen to those who have
> found peace

15:33 And may the God of peace be with all of you. Amen.

God of peace. This is Christ, who said: *My peace I give to you, my peace I leave to you* (John 14:27). He is the one who is with his own until the end of the world, and thus he is also with the Romans, just as he said: *I am with you for all days unto the end of the world* (Matt. 28:20).

    And—As if to say: I am hoping to come; but whether I come or not, *may the God of peace*, etc.

Chapter 16

16:1 And I commend to you our sister Phoebe, who is in the ministry of the church in Cenchreae,

I commend to you. Now I am mentioning many people in whom the Romans should place their trust. As if to say: Do as I have said, but imitate these. *our sister Phoebe.* Phoebe was a very wealthy and noble woman who, from her own resources, supported the church in the city of Cenchreae. At that time she would travel to Rome on business, and perhaps Paul sent this epistle by her.

> *I commend*—I declare as commendable
> *our*—or *my*
> *sister*—in the faith

16:2 that you may receive her in the Lord in a way worthy of the saints and assist her in whatever business she may require of you. For she has also assisted many people, including myself.

in a way worthy of, as in some codices, meaning in a way that is very respectful and honorable to.

> *in the Lord*—for the Lord's sake
> *in a way worthy of the saints*—as it is proper for saints to receive, or to be received
> *the saints*—you
> *assist her*—be of use to her

16:3 Greet Prisca and Aquila—my helpers in Christ Jesus,

Aquila. He is the husband of Priscilla. They were fellow workers with Paul and had come to Rome for their confirmation. The same is true with all the others whom he greets.

> *Prisca*—who is also called Priscilla in the Acts of the Apostles
>   (Acts 18:18, 26)
> *in Christ Jesus*—in the preaching of Christ

16:4 who laid down their necks for my soul, and to whom not only I give thanks but also all the churches of the Gentiles—

the churches of the Gentiles. Because they are laboring for the progress of the Gentiles, instructing them in the faith of Christ, and also because they did not shrink from suffering for the Apostle, the Romans ought to be obedient to them.

> *laid down*—before the sword
> *their necks*—by ministering to me
> *for my soul*—i.e., to rescue my life

16:5 and their domestic church. Greet Epaenetus, my beloved, who is the first fruit of the Church of Asia in Christ Jesus.

> *and*—and greet
> *their domestic church*—their family
> *Epaenetus*—who worked very hard to instruct them
> *who is the first fruit*—who was the first there to be reborn in
>   Christ

16:6 Greet Mary, who labored much among you.

> *who labored much among you*—who worked very hard to
>   instruct them, for she reported their discord to the apostle

16:7 Greet Andronicus and Julias,[227] my kinsmen and fellow captives, who are well-known among apostles, and who were before me in Christ Jesus.

my kinsmen—because they are Jews

fellow captives—having suffered imprisonment for their faith.

 Augustine: because *as long as we are in the body we are absent from God* (2 Cor. 5:6) and are thus fellow captives.[228]

among apostles—among preachers

in Christ Jesus—in the faith of Christ

16:8 Greet Ampliatus, beloved[229] to me in the Lord.

Ampliatus—he was the apostle's friend in the Lord and not
 a prisoner

in the Lord—another reading has *in Christ*

**16:9 Greet Urbanus, our helper in Christ Jesus, and Stachys, my be-
loved.**

our helper—a helper to me and others in the instruction of the
 faith; a sharer of the work

Stachys, my beloved—who is my personal friend, even if not a
 coworker, i.e., a sharer of the work

**16:10 Greet Apelles, upright in Christ. Greet those who are of Aristo-
bulus's household.**

Apelles. Through trials he was found faithful in Christ, even if he was
not the apostle's friend or a sharer of his work. *of Aristobulus's household*.
He was in the habit of gathering together brothers in Christ, whom the
apostle greets, thus approving of his work.

upright—approved

**16:11 Greet Herodion, my kinsman. Greet those of Narcissus's house-
hold who are in the Lord.**

of Narcissus's household. Narcissus is said to have been a priest that would
travel about strengthening holy brothers. Because he was not present at
the time, the apostle greets his household; and because he was not aware
of the merits of all of them, he distinguishes, adding *who are in the Lord*,
i.e., those whom you find worthy.

16:12 Greet Tryphaena and Tryphosa, who labor in the Lord. Greet Persis, my dearly beloved, who labored much in the Lord.

who labored much. The labor of which the apostle often speaks of here is the labor of instruction, of ministry to the saints, and of hardship and poverty for the sake of God.

> *who labor in the Lord*—in ministry to the saints and in
>   tribulation
> *who labored*—in ministry to the saints or in tribulation
> *much*—more than those mentioned before

16:13 Greet Rufus, elect in the Lord, and his mother and mine.

his mother and mine. He calls her his mother on account of her holiness, whose son he raised to ecclesiastical office.

> *elect*—because he was promoted to do the Lord's work,
>   namely, to the priesthood
> *his mother*—in the flesh
> *and mine*—in kindness

16:14 Greet Asyncritus, Phlegon, Hermes, Patrobas, Hermas, and the brothers who are with them.

> *Asyncritus*, etc.—he greets at once those whom he knew were
> joined in Christian friendship

16:15 Greet Philologus, Julia, Nereus and his sister, and Olympas, and all the saints who are with them.

and all the saints. All to whom he writes.

> *Philologus*, etc.—and these were all friends together

16:16 Greet one another with a holy kiss. The churches of Christ greet all of you.

with a holy kiss. And he asks those whom he names to greet one another with a holy kiss, i.e., in the peace of Christ. Thus religious kisses are not carnal.

The churches of Christ. Churches that trust in Christ and in nothing else.

> *one another*—everyone
> *with a holy kiss*—in the peace of Christ
> *churches*—of these places

16:17 But I beseech you, brothers, to take note of those who cause dissensions and offenses contrary to the teaching you have learned and avoid them.

to take note. He is referring to the false apostles, whom he warns the Romans to beware of in the entire epistle.

> *But*—greet and imitate the former, but avoid these
> *to take note of*—to discern
> *who cause dissensions*—who cause you to quarrel and offend
>   one another
> *contrary to*—who are contrary to the teaching since they
>   have zeal for the law and force believers to Judaize
> *you have learned*—from genuine apostles
> *and avoid them*—and to avoid them

16:18 For such people do not serve Christ the Lord but their own belly. And with sweet speech and blessings they seduce the hearts of the innocent.

> *the Lord*—our Lord
> *but their own belly*—for they praise some and disparage others
>   so they can fill their own belly
> *with sweet speech*, etc.—for they were commending their own
>   tradition with pleasing words, by which they deceived the
>   hearts of the simple

16:19 Your obedience has become known everywhere, and therefore I rejoice in you; but I would have you be wise in good and simple in evil.

Your obedience. This is why I am warning you to avoid these things, because your faith and obedience are praised everywhere. And since you are in the world's capitol, others may then be corrupted by your bad example. Or I am beseeching you to avoid these things because you are quick to obey, which is good and so I rejoice; but I wish that you were wise in discerning the good and having no part in evil.

> *Your obedience*—your capacity for obedience
> *I would have you*—assuredly
> *wise in good*—in discerning good
> *simple in evil*—having no part in it

16:20 And may the God of peace soon crush[230] Satan under your feet. The grace of our Lord Jesus Christ be with you.

And may the God of peace. You should be wise, but it is God who will *crush Satan,* i.e., the false preachers or anyone, human or devil, that is doing you harm. *under your feet.* So that you may disdain his head, i.e., the first motions of temptation, as was said of Eve in the figure of the church. *grace.* He desires them to have now the grace which he has promised at his arrival.

> *God of peace*—God the giver of peace
> *soon*—namely at my coming
> *under your feet*—so that you cannot be harmed; so that
> > *the grace,* etc.

16:21 Timothy, my brother[231] and assistant, greets you, as well as Lucius, Jason, and Sosipater, my kinsmen.

Timothy . . . greets you. So many important believers rejoice together in your beginning, and so it is meet for you to persevere.

> *Timothy . . . greets you,* etc.—thus they greet you, as though
> > you were in their care
> *assistant*—as if cobishop[232]
> *my kinsmen*—by race or by faith

16:22 I, Tercius, who have transcribed this epistle, greet you in the Lord.

> *Tercius*—the name, not the number (third); the apostle's
> secretary, whom the apostle allowed to greet them
> under his own name

16:23 Caius, my host, and the whole church greet you in the Lord. Erastus, a treasurer of the city, and his brother Quartus greet you.

the whole church. Above he had said *all the churches,* but here he is speaking of the church in another province, where Caius was from.

> *Caius*—he is the one to whom John wrote in his canonical
> epistle (3 John), rejoicing that he was welcoming and
> ministering to brothers
> *a treasurer*—*arcarius* from *archa* [αρχή], and thus a ruler, or
> more likely from fortress (*arx*),[233] and thus a treasurer
> of the city
> *the city*—Athens
> *Quartus*—a proper name

16:24 The grace of our Lord Jesus Christ be with you all. Amen.

> *The grace,* etc.—this is how they greet you; or I myself also
> greet you thus; or this is how those mentioned greet you
> and I myself subscribe in my own hand.

16:25 But to him that is able to strengthen you according to my gospel and the preaching of Jesus Christ, according to the revelation of the mystery kept secret from time eternal,

But to him. Thus I teach you: *But to him that is able to strengthen you* be glory, from whom alone are all things. Here the summation of the epistle is set down. *according to the revelation of the mystery.* He calls the incarnation of Christ, etc., *a mystery* that had been hidden *from time eternal.* For while these things were partly known by the ancient fathers, they were not fully known by anyone until they were revealed in his own time by Christ himself, when he unlocked the writings of the prophets that bear witness to this preaching. *kept secret* from others but known to God alone. For even if it is now revealed to people, it was nevertheless known to God alone, since he alone knows why it was thus made known. Here he restrains questioners who ask why God delayed so long or why he allowed so many people to perish.

> *to him*—to God, the Trinity
> *to strengthen you*—in perfect faith
> *my gospel*—with which the preaching of Christ is not at
> variance
> *and the preaching*—and according to the preaching
> *according to the revelation of the mystery*—which is the gos-
> pel and the preaching; in other words, according to that
> which was revealed to me of God's hidden counsel kept
> secret from eternity; or it is the mystery that reveals itself

16:26 which is now manifest through the writings of the prophets, known according to the commandment of the eternal God unto[234] the obedience of faith among the Gentiles,

now manifest . . . unto the obedience of faith among all the Gentiles, i.e., that they might obey the faith by doing good. *the eternal God.* Only God is properly called eternal because he is without beginning and without end. This is not true of the eternal fire which, although it is without end, still has a beginning. This is therefore the true eternity, that highest incommutability, which God alone possesses and which can in no way be changed. For not to be changed when something is able to be changed is one thing; but not to be able to be changed at all is another. Thus a person is called good, but not as God is good, of whom it is said: *No one is good but God alone* (Mark 10:18). Likewise a person is called an immortal soul, yet not as God is immortal, of whom it is said: *who alone has immortality* (1 Tim. 6:16). Likewise a person is called wise, but not as God is wise, of whom it is said: *to the wise God alone* (Rom. 16:27). In the same way fire is called eternal, but not as God is eternal, to whom alone belongs immortality itself and true eternity.

> *now manifest*—by the Holy Spirit
> *the writings of the prophets*—that have been unlocked

> *known*—the mystery, I say, *known according to the commandment*, etc.
>
> *the obedience of faith*—that they might obey the faith by doing good

16:27 to the wise God alone, through Jesus Christ, to whom be honor and glory forever.

to the wise God alone. Here an error creeps up on some who think that only the Father is meant and that he alone is truly wise, although it does not say to the wise Father alone but *to the wise God alone*, the one God and Trinity. We understand the wise God alone in the same way we understand the powerful God alone, i.e., the Father, Son, and Holy Spirit. This is the one and only God whom alone we are commanded to worship. Yet even if the apostles had said, to the wise Father alone, this would not leave out the Son or the Holy Spirit. For it is read of the Son in the Apocalypse: *He has a name written which no one knows except himself* (Rev. 19:12). Yet it is not asserted from this that the Father, from whom the Son is inseparable, does not know this name. Therefore, just as the Father knows what no one is said to know except the Son, because Father and Son are inseparable, so too, if it should say, to the wise Father alone, both Son and Holy Spirit should be understood at the same time, because they are inseparable from the Father.

to whom be honor. The sentence is complete if you take away "to whom." St. Augustine says it is meant to be there and discusses how it should be understood. Augustine: That "to whom" is added when "to him be glory" was sufficient is an unusual expression in our language, but the meaning is not ambiguous. It is the same as saying, with an unusual word order: to him be glory through Jesus Christ to whom is glory, when the usual order is: to him be glory to whom is glory through Jesus Christ.[235] Through Christ there is glory to the Father, i.e., glorious knowledge with praise, because through him God made known to people the Trinity, which is a mystery.

> *through Jesus Christ*—manifested through Jesus Christ
> *to whom*—to God alone, or to Christ
> *be honor*—from us
> *and glory*—in himself

INTRODUCTION

1. *Biblia latina cum Glossa ordinaria* (Strasbourg: Adolph Rusch, 1480/81), facsimile reprint, Turnhout: Brepols, 1992, with introduction by Kalfried Foehlich and Margaret T. Gibson. My translation is based on this edition, in consultation with a microfilm copy of *Biblia latina cum Glossa ordinaria . . . cum postillis ac moralitatibus Nicolai de Lyra*, ed. Sebastian Brant (Basel: Johann Froben and Johann Petri, 1498). For more information on the history of the Gloss, see B. Smalley, *The Study of the Bible in the Middle Ages*, 3rd ed. (Oxford: Blackwell, 1983); P. Riché and G. Lobrichon, ed., *Le moyen âge et la Bible* (Paris: Beauchesne, 1984); M. T. Gibson, "The Twelfth Century Glossed Bible," in Studia Patristica 23, ed. E.A. Livingstone (Louvaine: Peeters, 1989) and "The Place of the Glossa Ordinaria in Medieval Exegesis," in *Ad litteram: Authoritative Texts and Their Medieval Readers*, ed. K. Emery and M. Jordan (Notre Dame, IN: University of Notre Dame Press, 1992).

2. Smalley, *Study of the Bible*, 46–73; W. Affeldt, "Verzeichnis der Römerbriefkommentare der lateinischen Kirche bis zu Nikolaus von Lyra," *Traditio* 13 (1957): 373–74; M. L. Colish, *Peter Lombard* (Leiden: Brill, 1994), 1:71. K. Froehlich, "Glossa Ordinaria," in *Dictionary of Biblical Interpretation*, ed. John Haralson Hayes (Nashville: Abingdon, 1999) , 1:450. M. Zier, "Peter Lombard and the Glossa ordinaria on the Bible, " in *A Distinct Voice: Medieval Studies in Honor of Leonard E. Boyle, O.P.*, ed. J. Brown and W. Stoneman (Notre Dame, IN: University of Notre Dame Press, 1997.

3. See n. 2 above. On the other side, H. Glunz has argued that Lombard was responsible for the entire Gloss in *History of the Vulgate in England from Alcuin to Roger Bacon* (Cambridge: Cambridge University Press, 1933), 213–45.

4. The marginal gloss on Rom. 4:11 provides an instance of allegorical interpretation: "And circumcision used to be performed on the eighth day with a stone knife because in the eighth age, which will be the age of all the resurrected, the corruption of flesh and spirit will be cut away from the elect by Christ the rock." Another instance is the interlinear gloss to Rom. 2:21–23: "*do you steal?*—do

you steal the understanding of Christ that is in the law?... *do you commit adultery?*—do you take away the truth of Christ from the law and insert a lie?...*by transgression of the law*—when you disregard the Law's meaning concerning the incarnation and divinity of Christ."

5. E. P. Sanders is considered the father of the New Perspective, with his book *Paul and Palestinian Judaism: A Comparison of Patterns of Religion* (Philadelphia: Fortress, 1977). Other important proponents of the New Perspective include James Dunn and N. T. Wright.

✴

Prefatory Material

1. Prefatio sancti Hieronimi in omnes Epistolas sancti Pauli. Pelegius (?), *Prologus in epistulas Pauli a quibusdam Pelagio adscriptus*, in *Novum Testamentum Domini nostri Iesu Christi Latini secundum editionem sancti Hieronymi*, pt. 2/1, *Epistula ad Romanos*, ed. John Wordsworth (Oxford: Clarendon, 1913), 1–5. Rabanus Maurus, *Enarrationum in epistolas beati Pauli libri triginta*, PL 111, col. 1275–78. For discussion of authorship of prologues, see: Samuel Berger, *Les préfaces jointes aux livres de la Bible dans les manuscrits de la Vulgate* (Paris, 1892); Donatien de Bruyne, *Préfaces de la Bible latine* (Namur, 1920); Alexander Souter, *Pelagius's Expositions of Thirteen Epistles of St. Paul*, 3 vols. (Cambridge, 1922–31). Maurice E. Schild, *Abendländische Bibelvorreden bis zur Lutherbibel*, Quellen und Forschungen zur Reformationsgeschichte 39 (Gütersloh, 1970). Bernard Botte, "Prologues et sommaires de la Bible," *Dictionnaire de la Bible*, suppl. vol. 8 (Paris, 1969), 692. Hermann Josef Frede, "Paulus-Prologe," *Vetus Latina: Die Reste der altlateinischen Bibel*, vol. 25.1 (Freiburg, 1975–82), 98–111. Pelagius, *Pelagius's Commentary on St. Paul's Epistle to the Romans*, trans. Theodore de Bruyn (Oxford, 1993).

2. Prologus specialis in Epistola ad Romanos. Pelegius, *Argumentum Pelagii in epistulam ad Romanos*, in Wordsworth, *Novum Testamentum*, 35–38. Rabanus Maurus, *Enarrationum*, PL 111, col. 1277–78.

3. Prothemata in Epistolas Pauli. Friedrich Stegmüller, *Repertorium biblicum Medii Aevi*, #11832 (Madrid: Consejo, superior de investigaciones científicas, Instituto Francisco Suárez, 1977), vol. 9, 531–32).

4. From this point, *Assignatis rationibus* ("Having given reasons"), to the end of the text, the Gloss is taken substantially from Peter Lombard, *In epistolam ad Romanos*, PL 191, col. 1302–1534. In subsequent notes, reference to this work of Lombard will occur only when the Gloss attributes the words to an author but the text can only be found in Lombard's commentary.

5. Peter Lombard, *In epistolam ad Romanos*, PL 191, col. 1302C. Haimo of Auxerre is cited by name 16 times through Rom. 2:5 and none thereafter. This particular citation could not be found in his *Expositio ad Romanos*, PL 117, col. 361–938.

6. *Argumentum in Epistola ad Romanos.* Marcion (?), *Argumentum Marcioniticum in epistulam ad Romanos,* in Wordsworth, *Novum Testamentum,* 41–42.

7. Haimo of Auxerre, *Expositio ad Romanos,* PL 117, col. 364.

8. Origen, *praefatio* to *In epistulam Pauli ad Romanos. Der Römerbriefkommentar des Origenes: kritische Ausgabe der Ubersetzung Rufins,* vol. 1–3, ed. Caroline P. Hammond Bammel (Freiburg im Breisgau: Herder, 1990) 40–41; PG 14, col. 835. Peter Lombard, *praefatio* to *Collectanea in omnes divi Pauli apostoli epistolas,* PL 191, col. 1299. See also Peter Abelard, *Commentaria in epistulam Pauli ad Romanos,* ed. E. M. Buytaert, CCCM 11, prol., lines 175ff.

9. Haimo of Auxerre, *Expositio ad Romanos,* PL 117, col. 361, lines 33–40. Peter Abelard, *Commentaria in epistulam Pauli ad Romanos,* CCCM 11, prol., lines 136ff.

10. Peter Abelard, *Commentaria in epistulam Pauli ad Romanos,* CCCM 11, prol., lines 119ff.

11. Peter Abelard, *Commentaria in epistulam Pauli ad Romanos,* CCCM 11, prol., line 125.

✣

Chapter 1

12. Bede, *Expositio actuum apostolorum,* ed. M. L. W. Laistner, SL 121, cap. 13, line 2.

13. Augustine, *De spiritu et littera,* ed. C. F. Vrba and J. Zycha, CSEL 60, cap. 7, par. 12, p. 163, line 24.

14. Augustine, *Enarrationes in Psalmos,* ed. E. Dekkers and J. Fraipont, SL 39, psalmus 72, par. 4, line 13. Peter Abelard, *Commentaria in epistulam Pauli ad Romanos,* CCCM 11, prol., line 6. Sedulius Scottus, *Collectaneum in Apostolum,* PL 103, prol., p. 109, line 57.

15. Isidore of Seville, *Etymologiarum siue Originum libri XX,* ed. W. M. Lindsay, *Scriptorum classicorum bibliotheca Oxoniensis,* lib. 7, cap. 9, par. 10.

16. Jerome, "Ad Philemonem," *Commentarii in iv epistulas Paulinas,* PL 26, col. 640, line 31. Sedulius Scottus, *Collectaneum in Apostolum,* PL 103, prol., p. 109, line 51.

17. Peter Abelard, *Commentaria in epistulam Pauli ad Romanos,* lib. 1, cap. 1, line 28.

18. Jerome, *Liber interpretationis hebraicorum nominum,* ed. P. de Lagarde, SL 72, p. 74, line 25.

19. Peter Abelard, *Commentaria in epistulam Pauli ad Romanos,* CCCM 11, lib. 1, cap. 1, lines 71–72.

20. Haimo of Auxerre, *Expositio ad Romanos,* PL 117, col. 364, lines 44–56.

21. Augustine, *In Iohannis euangelium tractatus,* ed. R. Willems, SL 36, tract. 7, par. 13, line 6. Isidore of Seville, *Etymologiarum siue Originum libri XX,* ed. W. M. Lindsay, *Scriptorum classicorum bibliotheca Oxoniensis,* lib. 7, cap. 2, par. 6.

Rupert of Deutz, *De gloria et honore filii hominis super Matheum*, ed. R. Haacke, CCCM 29, lib. 1, line 87. Haimo of Auxerre, *Expositio ad Romanos*, PL 117, col. 365, lines 4–8. *Liber Quare*, ed. G. P. Götz, CCCM 60, appendix 2, additio 35, line 28.

22. See Peter Lombard, *In epistolam ad Romanos*, PL 191, col. 1304B; also Peter Lombard, *Sententiae in iv libris distinctae*, ed. I. Brady, Specilegium Bonaventurianum 5, 1971–81, lib. 3, dist. 6, cap. 2, par. 2, line 3. See Augustine, *De trinitate*, ed. W. J. Mountain, SL 50A, lib. 13, cap. 19, line 25.

23. See Peter Lombard, *In Epistolam ad Romanos*, PL 191, col. 1305A.

24. Haimo of Auxerre, *Expositio ad Romanos*, PL 117, col. 366, lines 17ff.

25. These *sacramenta unius Dei* are the spiritual meanings of the history and rituals of Jewish monotheism in the Old Testament.

26. Walter of St. Victor, *Sermones xxi*, ed. J. Châtillon, CCCM 30, sermo 16, line 79. Walter also attributes this to Augustine and explains the phrase, "which is not the case with human nature." "For the union between flesh and soul is not as great as the union between humanity and divinity. Hence a person is not called flesh or soul, nor is the soul called flesh or the flesh soul." ("quod non est in substantiis hominis." "Non enim tanta unio est inter carnem et animam quanta est inter humanitatem et diuinitatem. Vnde homo non dicitur caro, nec anima, nec uicissim anima caro, uel caro anima.")

27. Cassiodorus, *Expositio psalmorum*, ed. M. Adriaen, SL 97, psalmus 56, line 30. Peter Lombard, *Sententiae in iv libris distinctae*, lib. 3, dist. 7, cap. 1, par. 17, line 2.

28. Augustine, *Contra Felicem*, ed. J. Zycha, CSEL 25, lib. 2, par. 9, p. 838, line 8. Isidore of Seville, *De ecclesiasticis officiis*, ed. C. W. Lawson, SL 113, lib. 1, cap. 26, line 18.

29. Peter Lombard, *Sententiae in iv libris distinctae*, lib. 3, dist. 1, cap. 1, par. 4, line 11.

30. Augustine, *De trinitate*, ed. W. J. Mountain, SL 50, lib. 1, cap. 7, lines 35ff. Vincent of Lérins, *Excerpta e sancto Augustino*, ed. R. Demeulenaere, SL 64, cap. 2, lines 32ff.

31. Augustine, *De trinitate*, ed. W. J. Mountain, SL 50, lib. 4, cap. 21, line 40. Augustine, *Epistulae ad Romanos inchoata expositio*, ed. J. Divjak, CSEL 84, par. 4, p. 149, line 21. Peter Lombard, *Sententiae in iv libris distinctae*, lib. 3, dist. 6, cap. 6, par. 4, line 1.

32. Fulgentius of Ruspe, *De fide ad Petrum seu de regula fidei*, ed. J. Fraipont, SL 91A, cap. 21, line 415. Peter Lombard, *Sententiae in iv libris distinctae*, lib. 3, dist. 6, cap. 6, par. 5, line 6.

33. Peter Lombard, *Sententiae in iv libris distinctae*, lib. 3, dist. 7, cap. 1, par. 9, line 5.

34. Pseudo Augustine, *Solutiones diuersarum quaestionum*, ed. B. Schwank, SL 90, solutio 26, line 25. Peter Lombard, *Sententiae in iv libris distinctae*, lib. 3, dist. 7, cap. 1, par. 13, line 3.

35. Ambrose of Milan, *De fide libri V (ad Gratianum Augustum)*, ed. O. Faller, CSEL 78, lib. 3, cap. 5, lines 1–5. Sedulius Scottus, *Collectaneum in Apostolum, In epist. ad Romanos*, PL 103, col. 13, line 35.

36. Peter Lombard, *Sententiae in iv libris distinctae*, lib. 3, dist. 4, cap. 3, par. 1, line 5.

37. Peter Lombard, *Sententiae in iv libris distinctae*, lib. 3, dist. 4, cap. 3, par. 2, line 1 and dist. 11, cap. 1, par. 2, line 4. Augustine, *De trinitate*, SL 50, lib. 1, cap. 6, line 15.

38. Peter Lombard, *Sententiae in iv libris distinctae*, lib. 1, dist. 26, cap. 5, par. 2, line 5.

39. Haimo of Auxerre, *Expositio ad Romanos*, PL 117, col. 366, lines 44–46.

40. See Peter Lombard, *In Epistolam ad Romanos*, PL 191, col. 1314C.

41. Augustine, *De praedestinatione sanctorum*, PL 44, col. 983, line 3. Agobard of Lyons, *Aduersum dogma Felicis*, ed. L. Van Acker, CCCM 52, cap. 25, line 29. Vincent of Lérins, *Excerpta e sancto Augustino*, SL 64, cap. 8, lines 104–8. William of Saint-Thierry, *Expositio super epistulam ad Romanos*, ed. P. Verdeyen, CCCM 86, lib. 1, line 67.

42. Haimo of Auxerre, *Expositio ad Romanos*, PL 117, col. 366–67.

43. Augustine, *De praedestinatione sanctorum*, PL 44, col. 981, lines 54, 59; col. 982, line 12.

44. Augustine, *In Iohannis euangelium tractatus*, ed. R. Willems, SL 36, tract. 105, par. 8, lines 6ff.

45. Peter Lombard, *Sententiae in iv libris distinctae*, lib. 3, dist. 7, cap. 2, par. 2, line 1.

46. See Peter Lombard, *In epistolam ad Romanos*, PL 191, col. 1313D.

47. "Iudei cohabitatione sunt in Gentibus". Or does this cryptic statement mean that Jews and Gentiles are dwelling together in the obedience of faith?

48. Augustine, *Epistulae ad Romanos inchoata expositio*, ed. J. Divjak, CSEL 84, par. 11, p. 159, line 12.

49. Haimo of Auxerre, *Expositio ad Romanos*, PL 117, col. 369, lines 35–37.

50. Ambrosiaster, *In epistolam ad Romanos*, PL 17, col. 51D. Rabanus Maurus, *In epistolam ad Romanos*, PL 111, col. 1288A.

51. Jerome, *In Hieremiam prophetam libri vi*, ed. S. Reiter, SL 74, lib. 1, p. 51, line 23. Agobard of Lyons, *De diuisione imperii*, ed. L. Van Acker, CCCM 52, cap. 7, line 5.

52. See Peter Lombard, *In Epistolam ad Romanos*, PL 191, col. 1319A.

53. *Vel id est ut consolemur vobiscum alia littera.* Paul hopes they will be mutually comforted when he visits or when he receives a letter from them. Both "that I may be comforted" and "that we may be comforted" are allowed by the infinitive *consolari* (συμπαρακληθηναι).

54. Haimo of Auxerre, *Expositio ad Romanos*, PL 117, col. 371, lines 25–26.

55. Haimo of Auxerre, *Expositio ad Romanos*, PL 117, col. 371, lines 32–37.

56. This is Hesychius of Jerusalem (5th century) and likely comes from his

only work available in Latin: *Commentarius in Leviticum*, PG 93, col. 787–1180. Ambrosiaster, *In Epistolam ad Romanos*, PL 17, col. 56A. Rabanus Maurus, *In Epistolam ad Romanos*, PL 111, col. 1294B.

57. Ambrosiaster, *In Epistolam ad Romanos*, PL 17, col. 56A–B. Rabanus Maurus, *In Epistolam ad Romanos*, PL 111, col. 1294C. Hervé de Bourge-Dieu (or Hervé de Déols; Herveus Burgidolensis), *In Epistolam ad Romanos*, PL 181, col. 608B. Hervé died ca. 1150 and likely borrowed from the Gloss or MG, rather than other way around.

58. Hervé de Bourge-Dieu, *In Epistolam ad Romanos*, PL 181, col. 609A.

59. Augustine, *Quaestiones euangeliorum*, ed. A. Mutzenbecher, SL 44B, lib. 2, quaestio 39, lines 2, 12. William of Saint-Thierry, *Expositio super epistulam ad Romanos*, CCCM 86, lib. 1, line 392; Sedulius Scottus, *Collectaneum in Apostolum, In epist. ad Romanos*, PL 103, col. 19, line 23; Peter Lombard, *Sententiae in iv libris distinctae*, lib. 3, dist. 24, cap. 1, par. 3, line 8.

60. See Peter Lombard, *In Epistolam ad Romanos*, PL 191, col. 1324D.

61. Augustine, *Sermones*, PL 38, sermo 141, col. 777, line 26.

62. See Peter Lombard, *In Epistolam ad Romanos*, PL 191, col. 1326C.

63. See Peter Lombard, *In Epistolam ad Romanos*, PL 191, col. 1326C.

64. "A creatura mundi" ("απο κτίσεως κόσμου"). The preposition, *a* (απο), is taken in three different ways: causally in the marginal gloss—knowledge of God coming *from* a perception of the creation, humanity in particular; by personal agency in the interlinear gloss—understanding *by* the creation (i.e., by the human creature, who does the understanding); temporally in another interlinear gloss—understanding *since* creation. This third way is the common interpretation.

65. See Peter Lombard, *In Epistolam ad Romanos*, PL 191, col. 1327A–B.

66. See n. 64.

67. Thus something of the Trinity can be understood from creation, when people perceive *invisible things* (the Father), *his everlasting power* (the Son), and *divinity* (the Holy Spirit).

68. Augustine, *In Iohannis euangelium tractatus*, ed. R. Willems, SL 36, tract. 2, par. 4, line 12. Augustine, *Sermones*, PL 38, sermo 141, col. 777, line 9: "quod curiositate inuenerunt, superbia perdiderunt." Augustine, *In Iohannis euangelium tractatus*, ed. R. Willems, SL 36, tract. 14, par. 3, line 23: "ergo deus quod dederat gratis, tulit ingratis."

69. See Peter Lombard, *In Epistolam ad Romanos*, PL 191, col. 1329C.

70. See Peter Lombard, *In Epistolam ad Romanos*, PL 191, col. 1330C–D.

71. Augustine, *De gratia et libero arbitrio*, PL 44, col. 909, line 10. William of Saint-Thierry, *Expositio super epistulam ad Romanos*, CCCM 86, lib. 1, line 636; Sedulius Scottus, *Collectaneum in Apostolum, In epist. ad Romanos*, PL 103, col. 21, line 8.

72. Gregory the Great, *Moralia in Job* 9.22, PL 76, col. 334B. Peter Lombard, *Sententiae in iv libris distinctae*, lib. 2, dist. 36, cap. 3, par. 2, line 1.

73. Text reads: "Because they defiled" ("Quia contaminaverunt").

74. Ambrosiaster, *In Epistolam ad Romanos*, PL 17, col. 60A. Sedulius Scotus, *In Epistolam ad Romanos*, PL 103, col. 21B.

75. See Augustine, *De unico baptismo*, ed. M. Petschenig, CSEL 53, cap. 4, par. 5, p. 6, line 10.

76. Haimo of Auxerre, *Expositio ad Romanos*, PL 117, col. 376, lines 3–4. Isidore of Seville, *Etymologiarum siue Originum libri XX*, ed. W. M. Lindsay, *Scriptorum classicorum bibliotheca Oxoniensis*, lib. 5, cap. 27, par. 25.

77. Augustine, *De nuptiis et concupiscentia*, ed. C. F. Urba and J. Zycha, CSEL 42, lib. 2, cap. 20, par. 35, p. 289, line 13.

78. Augustine, *Contra aduersarium legis et prophetarum*, ed. K.-D. Daur, SL 49, lib. 1, line 1459. Peter Lombard, *Sententiae in iv libris distinctae*, lib. 2, dist. 36, cap. 3, par. 2, line 9; Sedulius Scottus, *Collectaneum in Apostolum, In epist. ad Romanos*, PL 103, col. 21, line 51.

79. Augustine, *Enarrationes in Psalmos*, SL 39, psalmus 57, par. 18, lines 1, 9–13. Peter Lombard, *Sententiae in iv libris distinctae*, lib. 2, dist. 36, cap. 1, par. 1, lines 6ff.

❧

CHAPTER 2

80. "In quo ostendit se esse quod non est, i.e., iustum."

81. Haimo of Auxerre, *Expositio ad Romanos*, PL 117, col. 379, lines 10–12.

82. See Peter Lombard, *In Epistolam ad Romanos*, PL 191, col. 1338A.

83. See Peter Lombard, *In Epistolam ad Romanos*, PL 191, col. 1338B.

84. Haimo of Auxerre, *Expositio ad Romanos*, PL 117, col. 379C.

85. See Peter Lombard, *In Epistolam ad Romanos*, PL 191, col. 1339C.

86. See Peter Lombard, *In Epistolam ad Romanos*, PL 191, col. 1339D–1340A. Augustine, *Enarrationes in Psalmos*, ed. E. Dekkers and J. Fraipont, SL 39, psalmus 102, par. 16.

87. See Peter Lombard, *In Epistolam ad Romanos*, PL 191, col. 1340A.

88. Augustine, "Sermo 71," *Sermones*, ed. P. Verbraken, *Revue bénédictine* 75 (1965), p. 87, line 460–61. Peter Lombard, *Sententiae in iv libris distinctae*, lib. 2, dist. 43, cap. 1, par. 8, lines 5–8.

89. See Peter Lombard, *In Epistolam ad Romanos*, PL 191, col. 1341A.

90. Sedulius Scottus, *Collectaneum in Apostolum, In epist. ad Romanos*, PL 103, col. 26, line 22.

91. Ambrosiaster, *In Epistolam ad Romanos*, PL 17, col. 67A. Rabanus Maurus, *In Epistolam ad Romanos*, PL 111, col. 1315C.

92. Augustine, *Enarrationes in Psalmos*, SL 40, psalmus 118, sermo 25, par. 2, lines 1–4.

93. Peter Lombard, *Sententiae in iv libris distinctae*, lib. 2, dist. 22, cap. 5, par. 2, line 7.

94. See Peter Lombard, *In Epistolam ad Romanos*, PL 191, col. 1344C. See Ambrosiaster, *In Epistolam ad Romanos*, PL 17, col. 83A.

95. Augustine, *De spiritu et littera*, ed. C. F. Vrba and J. Zycha, CSEL 60, cap. 26, par. 44, p. 198, line 30; par. 45, p. 199, line 23.

96. See Peter Lombard, *In Epistolam ad Romanos*, PL 191, col. 1345D.

97. In which case the phrase would parallel the previous one, reading: *and with their thoughts within them in turn accusing*, etc.

98. See Peter Lombard, *In Epistolam ad Romanos*, PL 191, col. 1348B.

99. See Peter Lombard, *In Epistolam ad Romanos*, PL 191, col. 1349D.

100. See Peter Lombard, *In Epistolam ad Romanos*, PL 191, col. 1349D–1350A.

101. Augustine, *De spiritu et littera*, ed. C. F. Vrba and J. Zycha, CSEL 60, cap. 8, par. 13, p. 165, line 25. William of Saint-Thierry, *Expositio super epistulam ad Romanos*, CCCM 86, lib. 2, line 190.

CHAPTER 3

102. "Homo mendax nec verum esse habens et per peccata defluens."

103. "Quem vicit Deus cum dat promissa." God prevailed against the Jews, showing himself true and them false, when he fulfilled what he had promised, taking *vicit* in the legal sense as found in the following verse. Basel 1498 reads: "quem vicit Deus non dat promissa," which makes little sense, meaning that God prevails against the Jew when he does not fulfill what was promised.

104. An amplified translation of the terse: "declinaverunt quia; adeo quia; quia de illis; preter Christum."

105. Vulgate actually reads: "pax multa diligentibus legem."

106. "Bona opera etiam ante fidem inania sunt ita ut videantur esse magne vires et cursus celerrimus praeter viam." Augustine, *Enarrationes in Psalmos*, SL 38, psalmus 31, enarratio 2, par. 4, line 4. See gloss on Rom. 14:23.

CHAPTER 4

107. "Qui habet tempus operandi." See Bede, *In principium Genesis usque ad natiuitatem Isaac*, ed. C. W. Jones, SL 118A, lib. 4, cap. 15, line 69.

108. "Vel secundum quod Deus legem anteposuit." Literally: "or according to what God laid down earlier as law," which may mean that circumcision suffices for children who do not have opportunity to do works.

109. William of Saint-Thierry, *Expositio super epistulam ad Romanos*, CCCM 86, lib. 2, line 719.

110. "Accepto fert." The gloss is based on a reading that may be rendered: "he brings into acceptance."

111. " . . . in quo sola apparet gratia." The "which" in this phrase refers to God's predestination, as is clear from a comparison to Peter Lombard, *In epistolam ad Romanos*, PL 191, col. 1376A: "Therefore he *calls things that are not as things that are.* In other words, for people who are not, he arranges and prepares from eternity the grace of justification and glorification to be appointed in time *as things that are*, i.e. as it is for those who are already with God through predestination, in which grace alone is manifest." ("Vocat ergo quae non sunt, tanquam quae sint, id est his qui non sunt, disponit et praeparat ab aeterno gratiam justificationis et glorificationis, apponendam in tempore tanquam sint, id est tanquam illis qui jam sunt apud Deum per praedestinationem: in quo sola apparet gratia.")

112. Augustine, *Sermones*, sermo 26, SL 41, lines 93–94. Peter Lombard, *Sententiae in iv libris distinctae*, lib. 1, dist. 36, cap. 1, par. 2, lines 9, 11. William of Saint-Thierry, *Expositio super epistulam ad Romanos*, CCCM 86, lib. 2, line 906.

CHAPTER 5

113. Prov. 5:16-17. Vetus Latina from the Septuagint: "Fons aquae tuae sit tibi proprius et nemo alienus communicet tibi" ("τα υδατα εκ της σης πηγης εστω σοι μονω υπαρχοντα και μηδεις αλλοτριος μετασχετω σοι").

114. Augustine, *Enarrationes in Psalmos*, SL 40, psalmus 148, par. 8, line 29.

115. Augustine, *Enarrationes in Psalmos*, SL 40, psalmus 148, par. 8, lines 55ff.

116. "Et licet iustus melior, causa tamen innocentiae miserabilior quam iusticiae, quia non est huiusmodi iusticia sine severitate." The meaning here is unclear. Perhaps it means that someone will more readily take up the cause of the innocent (children and mentally handicapped) than the cause of the just, who have been hardened by their struggles and are more willing to face death.

117. Augustine, *De trinitate*, SL 50A, lib. 13, cap. 10, line 43: "non ergo ante istam gratiam quoquo modo peccatores, sed in talibus peccatis fuimus ut inimici essemus dei." ("Before this grace we were not sinners in every way, but we were in such sins that made us enemies of God.")

118. Augustine, *Contra Iulianum opus imperfectum*, ed. M. Zelzer, CSEL 85,1; PL 45, lib. 2, par. 49 passim, e.g., p. 198, line 2.

119. Sedulius Scottus, *Collectaneum in Apostolum*, *In epist. ad Romanos*, PL 103, col. 55, line 42.

120. "Regnauit non mors (et sic non legitur etiam) sed . . ." ("Death did not reign [sic: it should say 'Death also reigned'] however. . . .")

121. See Peter Lombard, *In Epistolam ad Romanos*, PL 191, col. 1391D–1392A.

122. Augustine, *De peccatorum meritis et remissione et de baptismo parvulorum*, ed. C. F. Vrba and J. Zycha, CSEL 60, lib. 1, cap. 10, par. 11, p. 12, line 9. Peter Lombard, *Sententiae in iv libris distinctae*, lib. 2, dist. 30, cap. 10, par. 2, lines 3, 12. The words "in whom all have sinned" ("in quo"; "εφ᾽ ω") have proven to be a point of contention in exegesis. Augustine argued that it referred to Adam, in whom all have sinned with original sin. This view held sway in the West until Erasmus, who argues vigorously that it does not mean Adam, but should read "inasmuch as all have sinned" ("quatenus . . ."). Erasmus, *Annotations On Romans*, ed. R. D. Sider, *Collected Works of Erasmus* (Toronto: University of Toronto Press, 1994) 139–61.

123. This gloss follows a variant reading that omits "not."

124. See Peter Lombard, *In Epistolam ad Romanos*, PL 191, col. 1396A–B.

125. See Peter Lombard, *In Epistolam ad Romanos*, PL 191, col. 1399A (which also contains the sentence that follows in the Gloss). Ambrosiaster, *In Epistolam ad Romanos*, PL 17, col. 98C. Rabanus Maurus, *In epistolam ad Romanos*, PL 111, col. 1388A.

126. " . . . gratia Christi etiam his proficit quos diabolus vincere non potuit." It might make more sense to omit the *non*.

127. *Intravit latenter* for *subintravit* in the biblical text.

❧
CHAPTER 6

128. Augustine, *De spiritu et littera*, CSEL 60, cap. 6, par. 9, p. 161, line 15.William of Saint-Thierry, *Expositio super epistulam ad Romanos*, CCCM 86, lib. 3, line 611.

129. Peter Lombard, *In Epistolam ad Romanos*, PL 191, col. 1439D. Second half of 12th century: Hermannus de Runa, *Sermones festiuales*, ed. E. Mikkers, I. Theuws, and R. Demeulenaere, CCCM 64, sermo 28, lines 28–30.

130. Augustine, *Contra Iulianum*, PL 44, lib. 6, col. 825, line 1. Augustine, *Enchiridion de fide, spe et caritate*, ed. E. Evans, SL 46, cap. 13, line 28. William of Saint-Thierry, *Expositio super epistulam ad Romanos*, CCCM 86, lib. 3, line 675.

131. "Hoc quidam qui legem quasi cohaerentem vel coercentem praedicant et tenendam."

132. Peter Lombard, *In Epistolam ad Romanos*, PL 191, col. 1410A.

133. Augustine, *Enarrationes in Psalmos*, SL 38, psalmus 30, enarratio 2, sermo 1, par. 5, line 6; William of Saint-Thierry, *Expositio super epistulam ad Romanos*, lib. 3, line 1032.

134. Augustine, *Contra duas epistulas Pelagianorum*, ed. C. F. Vrba and J. Zycha, CSEL 60, lib. 1, cap. 2, par. 5, p. 426, line 18; Augustine, *Contra Iulianum opus imperfectum*, CSEL 107, lib. 1, par. 94, line 24; William of Saint-Thierry, *Expositio super epistulam ad Romanos*, CCCM 86, lib. 3, line 1040.

CHAPTER 7

135. See Peter Lombard, *In Epistolam ad Romanos*, PL 191, col. 1414C.

136. Augustine, *De diuersis quaestionibus octoginta tribus*, ed. A. Mutzenbecher, SL 44A, quaestio 66, lines 60, 77–78. William of Saint-Thierry, *Expositio super epistulam ad Romanos*, CCCM 86, lib. 4, lines 56, 70–71.

137. Augustine, *Sermones*, PL 38, sermo 153, col. 828, line 57.

138. Augustine, *De diuersis quaestionibus ad Simplicianum*, ed. A. Mutzenbecher, SL 44, lib. 1, quaestio 1, cap. 3, line 48.

139. Augustine, *Exp. quarumdam propositionum ex epistula ad Romanos*, ed. J. Divjak, CSEL 84, par. 29, p. 16, line 14.

140. Text reads "of *God's* consent and action" ("consentus *dei* et operationis").

141. Augustine, *De diuersis quaestionibus ad Simplicianum*, ed. A. Mutzenbecher, SL 44, lib. 1, quaestio 1, cap. 5, lines 80–84. William of Saint-Thierry, *Expositio super epistulam ad Romanos*, CM 86, lib. 4, lines 211–14.

142. Augustine, *Sermones*, PL 38, sermo 153, col. 831, line 35.

143. Augustine, *Sermones*, PL 38, sermo 153, col. 826, line 40.

144. The matter is discussed similarly in Peter Lombard, *Sententiae in iv libris distinctae*, lib. 2, dist. 39, cap. 3, par. 1.

145. Not found: "Augustinus. Semper bonus vult penitus non concupiscere, sed numquam hoc perficit in hac vita."

146. Text reads "like *souls* at the gates" ("quasi ad ianuas *animae*.")

147. See Peter Lombard, *In Epistolam ad Romanos*, PL 191, col. 1425C.

148. Augustine, *De Genesi ad litteram libri duodecim*, ed. J. Zycha, CSEL 28,1, lib. 10, par. 12, p. 311, line 2.

149. Augustine, *Sermones*, PL 38, sermo 154, col. 839, lines 21ff. William of Saint-Thierry, *Expositio super epistulam ad Romanos*, CCCM 86, lib. 4, lines 514ff.

150. Augustine, *Sermones*, PL 38, sermo 154, col. 837, line 13. William of Saint-Thierry, *Expositio super epistulam ad Romanos*, CCCM 86, lib. 4, line 604. Augustine, *Sancti Augustini Sermones post Maurinos reperti*, vol. 1, *Sermones*, éd. G. Morin, Miscellanea Agostiniana, Rome, 1930, sermo 77A, p. 577, line 26.

151. Augustine, *Contra duas epistulas Pelagianorum*, ed. C. F. Vrba and J. Zycha, CSEL 60, lib. 1, cap. 10, par. 22, p. 442, line 21.

CHAPTER 8

152. See Augustine, *De spiritu et littera*, CSEL 60, cap. 28, par. 48, p. 203.

153. Augustine, *Sermones*, PL 38, sermo 69, col. 442, line 37.

154. Augustine, *Contra Maximinum*, PL 42 , lib. 2, col. 771, lines 2–4.

155. Augustine, *De diuersis quaestionibus octoginta tribus*, ed. A. Mutzen-becher, SL 44A, quaestio 66, lines 263–64.

156. Augustine, *De peccatorum meritis et remissione et de baptismo paruulorum*, ed. C. F. Vrba and J. Zycha, CSEL 60, lib.1, cap. 5, par. 5, p. 6, line 20.

157. Hermannus de Runa, *Sermones festiuales*, ed. E. Mikkers, I. Theuws, and R. Demeulenaere, CCCM 64, sermo 33, lines 101ff.

158. See Peter Lombard, *In Epistolam ad Romanos*, PL 191, col. 1445B–C.

159. See Peter Lombard, *In Epistolam ad Romanos*, PL 191, col. 1445C–D.

160. *Ingemiscit* (in comparison to *ingemit*) may be translated: it begins to groan.

161. Ambrosiaster, *In Epistolam ad Romanos*, PL 17, col. 125A.

162. "i.e., homo qui habet communionem cum omni creatura; non tota; etiam dignior."

163. Augustine, *De trinitate*, SL 50A, lib. 13, cap. 16, line 3. William of Saint-Thierry, *Expositio super epistulam ad Romanos*, CCCM 86, lib. 5, line 556.

164. Augustine, *De dono perseuerantiae*, PL 45, col. 1014, line 8. William of Saint-Thierry, *Expositio super epistulam ad Romanos*, CCCM 86, lib. 5, line 591; John Scotus Eriugena, *De diuina praedestinatione liber*, ed. G. Madec, CCCM 50, cap. 14, line 112; Peter Lombard, *Sententiae in iv libris distinctae*, lib. 1, dist. 40, cap. 2, par. 1, line 24.

165. Augustine, *De praedestinatione sanctorum*, PL 44, col. 974, lines 53–56. William of Saint-Thierry, *Expositio super epistulam ad Romanos*, CCCM 86, lib. 5, line 580; Peter Lombard, *Sententiae in iv libris distinctae*, lib. 1, dist. 39, cap. 4, par. 4, line 2.

166. Augustine, *De praedestinatione sanctorum*, PL 44, col. 975, line 6. Peter Lombard, *Sententiae in iv libris distinctae*, lib. 2, dist. 36, cap. 2, par. 4, line 1.

167. Fulgentius of Ruspe, *De ueritate praedestinationis et gratiae dei*, ed. J. Fraipont, SL 91A, lib. 3, cap. 8, line 189. Peter Lombard, *Sententiae in iv libris distinctae*, lib. 1, dist. 40, cap. 2, par. 1, line 17.

168. Sedulius Scottus, *Collectaneum in Apostolum, In epist. ad Romanos*, PL 103. col. 80, line 17.

169. Isa. 45:11. Vetus Latina according to the LXX: "qui fecit quae futura sunt" ("ο ποιησας τα επεϱχομενα").

170. Translation follows Augustine, reading *praestitum* for *praescitum* in the text.

171. Augustinine, *In Iohannis euangelium tractatus*, ed. R. Willems, SL 36, tract. 112, par. 5, lines 2–24. Augustine, *Enarrationes in Psalmos*, SL 39, psalmus 65, par. 7, lines 36–39.

172. Augustine, *Enarrationes in Psalmos*, SL 38, psalmus 34, sermo 2, par. 13, line 10: "itaque martyres non facit poena, sed causa"; Augustine, *Contra Cresco-nium*, ed. M. Petschenig, CSEL 52, lib. 3, cap. 47, par. 51, p. 459, line 13; Augus-tine, *Epistulae*, ed. A. Goldbacher, CSEL 34/2, epist. 108, par. 5, p. 627, line 2; Augustine, *Sermones*, sermo 52A, 94A, 285, 306A, 327, 328, 331, 335C, 335G. Gregory the Great, *Registrum epistularum*, ed. D. Norberg, SL 140, lib. 2, epist. 43, line 8. Peter Abelard, *Commentaria in epistulam Pauli ad Romanos*, CCCM 11, lib. 3, cap. 8, line 288.

173. Ambrose of Milan, *Expositio psalmi cxviii*, ed. M. Petschenig, CSEL 62, littera 8, cap. 38, p. 173, line 4–9.

174. "Vel nova ut equus bipes si fiat ut fecit Iamnes et Mambres." Jannes and Mambres (or Jambres) were two of Pharaoh's magicians that reproduced some of Moses's signs (Ex. 7:11). Their names are mentioned in apocryphal accounts and in 2 Tim. 3:8. I have not found a reference to their making of a two-legged horse.

🌸

CHAPTER 9

175. See Peter Lombard, *In Epistolam ad Romanos*, PL 191, col. 1454B.

176. This alternative understands the "anathema from Christ" as referring to Jewish believers whom Paul used to persecute. That is, as the interlinear gloss explains, Paul now grieves for having once sought to separate his kinsman from Christ.

177. The full verse is: "numquid Sion dicet homo et homo natus est in ea et ipse fundavit eam Altissimus."

178. Sedulius Scottus, *Collectaneum in Apostolum, In epist. ad Romanos*, PL 103, col. 87, line 8.

179. "Vel quod exciderit"; instead of *excidit*.

180. Psalm 60:8: "Moab is the pot of my hope. Into Edom will I stretch out my shoe: to me the foreigners are made subject" ("Moab olla spei meae in Idumeam extendam calciamentum meum mihi alienigenae subditi sunt").

181. Augustine, *Enchiridion de fide, spe et caritate*, ed. E. Evans, SL 46, cap. 9, lines 83–101. Peter Lombard, *Sententiae in iv libris distinctae*, lib. 2, dist. 26, cap. 2, par. 2, line 7. Translation inserts the beginning phrase: "It does not depend on both God and humanity," to clarify the Gloss's abridgment of Augustine here.

182. Augustine, *Enchiridion de fide, spe et caritate*, ed. E. Evans, SL 46, cap. 25, lines 1–3. Peter Lombard, *Sententiae in iv libris distinctae*, lib. 1, dist. 46, cap. 2, par. 2, line 7.

183. Augustine, *Contra Iulianum opus imperfectum*, CSEL 160, lib. 1, par. 141, line 63.

184. Augustine, *De diuersis quaestionibus ad Simplicianum*, ed. A. Mutzenbecher, SL 44, lib. 1, quaestio 2, cap. 15, lines 424–27.

185. See Peter Lombard, *In Epistolam ad Romanos*, PL 191, col. 1462A.; See Sedulius Scottus, *Collectaneum in Apostolum, In epist. ad Romanos*, PL 103, col. 90, line 18.

186. Peter Lombard, *Sententiae in iv libris distinctae*, lib. 3, dist. 31, cap. 1, par. 7, line 2–10.

CHAPTER 10

187. Ambrosiaster, *In Epistolam ad Romanos*, PL 17, col. 142D.

188. Augustine, *Contra mendacium*, ed. J. Zycha, CSEL 41, cap. 6, par. 13, p. 485, line 17: "cur ergo lacrimis diluit, quod ore negauerat, si saluti sufficiebat, quod corde credebat?" Translation here follows Augustine rather than Gloss, which has: "*Cum* enim lacrimis diluit, etc."

189. Vulgate follows LXX: "και ο πιστευων επ αυτω ου μη καταισχυνθη."

CHAPTER 11

190. Not found in Ambrose. William of Saint-Thierry, *Expositio super epistulam ad Romanos*, CCCM 86, lib. 6, line 620.

191. See Peter Lombard, *In Epistolam ad Romanos*, PL 191, col. 1489D.

192. Text reads: "without [repentance from] sin" ("sine peccato").

193. Augustine, *De spiritu et littera*, CSEL 60, cap. 36, par. 66, p. 228, line 20; p. 229, line 3.

194. Hervé de Bourge-Dieu , *In Epistolam ad Romanos*, PL 181, col. 764C.

195. "Sicut sapientia et scientia eius sunt incomprehensibiles, sic et iudicia pro quibus cepit de sa. et sci."

196. Isa. 9:6. Vetus Latina according to the LXX: "magni consilii angelus" ("μεγαλης βουλης αγγελος").

197. Peter Lombard, *Sententiae in iv libris distincta*, lib. 1, dist. 37, cap. 4, par. 1, line 13.

198. Augustine, *De trinitate*, SL 50, lib. 6, cap. 10, lines 45–54, 60. Augustine, *Contra Maximinum*, PL 42, lib. 2, col. 800, lines 7–14. See Peter Lombard, *Sententiae in iv libris distinctae*, lib. 1, dist. 3, cap. 1, par. 7, lines 3ff.; and lib. 1, dist. 36, cap. 4, lines 1ff., where he paraphrases Augustine.

CHAPTER 12

199. See Peter Lombard, *In Epistolam ad Romanos*, PL 191, col. 1496C.

200. Augustine, *De ciuitate Dei*, ed. B. Dombart and A. Kalb, SL 47, lib. 10, cap. 6, line 18. William of Saint-Thierry, *Expositio super epistulam ad Romanos*, ed. P. Verdeyen, CCCM 86, lib. 7, line 13.

201. Augustine, *De perfectione iustitiae hominis*, ed. C. F. Vrba and J. Zycha, CSEL 42, cap. 5, par. 11, p. 10, lines 15–22.

202. Augustine, *De trinitate*, SL 50A, lib. 14, cap. 16, line 1.

203. Augustine, *Enchiridion de fide, spe et caritate*, ed. E. Evans, SL 46, cap. 24, line 28.

204. Strasbourg 1480 omits "without being harmful to anyone" ("et nulli obsit").

205. "Patimini et sanctis passis vestra communia facite."

CHAPTER 13

206. Augustine, *Enarrationes in Psalmos*, SL 38, psalmus 32, enarratio 2, sermo 2, par. 12.

207. Peter Lombard, *Sententiae in iv libris distinctae*, lib. 2, dist. 44, cap. 1, par. 3, lines 8ff.

208. The second phrase only in Vetus Latina: "tyranni per me tenent terram."

209. Augustine, *De natura boni*, ed. J. Zycha, CSEL 25, par. 32, p. 870, lines 18–24.

210. Gregory the Great, *Moralia in Iob*, ed. M. Adriaen, SL 143B, lib. 26, par. 26, lines 157ff.

211. Augustine, *Sermones*, PL 38, sermo 62, col. 421, lines 1ff.

212. Augustine, *Epistulae*, ed. A. Goldbacher, CSEL 57, epist. 192, par. 1, p. 166, lines 4ff.

213. Augustine, *In Iohannis euangelium tractatus*, ed. R. Willems, SL 36, tract. 65, par. 2, lines 1ff. Peter Lombard, *Sententiae in iv libris distinctae*, lib. 3, dist. 27, cap. 7, lines 1ff.

214. Augustine, *De trinitate*, SL 50, lib. 8, cap. 6, lines 134ff. Peter Lombard, *Sententiae in iv libris distinctae*, lib. 3, dist. 27, cap. 5, par. 1, lines 9ff.

215. The glossator must be reading *proprior* (more our own) for *propior* (nearer) here.

CHAPTER 14

216. Augustine, *De agone christiano*, ed. J. Zycha, CSEL 41, cap. 27, par. 29, p. 130, line 4.

217. Augustine, *Enchiridion de fide, spe et caritate*, ed. E. Evans, SL 46, cap. 31, line 63.

218. Basel 1498 has *reddet* rather than *reddat*.

219. "Quia debes confirmare non sancta scandalisare."

220. Augustine, *Quaestiones euangeliorum*, ed. A. Mutzenbecher, SL 44B, lib. 2, quaestio 11, line 25. William of Saint-Thierry, *Expositio super epistulam ad Romanos*, CCCM 86, lib. 7, line 523.

221. William of Saint-Thierry, *Expositio super epistulam ad Romanos*, CCCM 86, lib. 7, line 741.

222. Prosper of Aquitaine, *Liber sententiarum*, ed. M. Gastaldo, SL 68A, cap. 106, lines 1–2. William of Saint-Thierry, *Expositio super epistulam ad Romanos*, CCCM 86, lib. 7, line 769–79. Peter Lombard, *Sententiae in iv libris distinctae*, lib. 2, dist. 41, cap. 1, par. 3, lines 3–4.

223. Augustine, *Enarrationes in Psalmos*, SL 38, psalmus 31, enarratio 2, par. 4, lines 3–4. Peter Lombard, *Sententiae in iv libris distinctae*, lib. 2, dist. 40, cap. 1, par. 2, lines 6–7.

Chapter 15

224. Strasbourg 1480: "qua possitis"; Basel 1498: "qua possitis cognoscere."

225. "Si enim illud facerem hoc inde contingeret, i.e., ne predicarem iam per alios conversis, non quod hoc non faceret si contigisset." He seems to mean that Paul's intention was to evangelize new places, not to avoid places evangelized by others.

226. Strasbourg 1480: *sciens*; Basel 1498: scio.

Chapter 16

227. Greek has *Junias* (Ἰουνιας).

228. See Peter Lombard, *In Epistolam ad Romanos*, PL 191, col. 1528C.

229. Strasbourg 1480: *dilectum*; Basel 1498: *dilectissimum*.

230. *Conterat*. Standard Vulgate has the future *conteret* following the Greek συντρίψει.

231. Standard Vulgate omits *frater et*.

232. Peter Abelard, *Commentaria in epistulam Pauli ad Romanos*, ed. E. M. Buytaert, CM 11, lib. 4, cap. 16, line 238.

233. Actually it is more likely derived from *arca* (chest or safe).

234. Strasburg 1480 has *and* (et) the obedience of faith.

235. Augustine, *Contra Maximinum*, PL 42, lib. 2, col. 770, lines 19ff. William of St. Thierry, *Expositio super epistulam ad Romanos*, CM 86, lib. 7, lines 1138ff.

✒ TEAMS COMMENTARY SERIES

Haimo of Auxerre, *Commentary on the Book of Jonah*, translated with an introduction and notes by Deborah Everhart (1993)

Medieval Exegesis in Translation: Commentaries on the Book of Ruth, translated with an introduction and notes by Lesley Smith (1996)

Nicholas of Lyra's Apocalypse Commentary, translated with an introduction and notes by Philip D. W. Krey (1997)

Rabbi Ezra Ben Solomon of Gerona, *Commentary on the Song of Songs and Other Kabbalistic Commentaries*, selected, translated, and annotated by Seth Brody (1999)

Second Thessalonians: Two Early Medieval Apocalyptic Commentaries, introduced and translated by Steven R. Cartwright and Kevin L. Hughes (2001)

John Wyclif, *On the Truth of Holy Scripture*, translated with an introduction and notes by Ian Christopher Levy (2001)

The "Glossa Ordinaria" on the Song of Songs, translated with an introduction and notes by Mary Dove (2004)

The Seven Seals of the Apocalypse: Medieval Texts in Translation, translated with an introduction and notes by Francis X. Gumerlock (2009)

✒ TO ORDER PLEASE CONTACT:

Medieval Institute Publications
Western Michigan University
Kalamazoo, MI 49008-5432
Phone (269) 387-8755
FAX (269) 387-8750
http://www.wmich.edu/medieval/mip/index.html

Typeset in 10/12 Adobe Caslon Pro
Designed by Linda K. Judy
Composed by Linda K. Judy
Manufactured by Cushing-Malloy, Inc.

Medieval Institute Publications
College of Arts and Sciences
Western Michigan University
1903 W. Michigan Avenue
Kalamazoo, MI 49008-5432
http://www.wmich.edu/medieval/mip

WESTERN MICHIGAN UNIVERSITY